China's Trojan Horses:

Red Chinese Soldiers, Sailors, Students, Scientists and Spies Openly Occupy America's Homeland

*With special Prologue and Postscript:
After September 11, 2001*

By Dr. Roger B. Canfield

China's Trojan Horses
Published by Military Magazine, 2002

2120 28th Street, Sacramento, CA 95818
Copyright© 2002 by Roger Canfield and Military Magazine
$15.00
ISBN 0-9705206-1-1

Other books by Roger Canfield:

- *China Doll: Clinton, Gore and the Selling of the U.S. Presidency* — 705,000 in print. (co-authored with Richard A. Delgaudio)

- *China Traders: Assessing the Legacy of Clinton-Gore's Appeasement Policy...*

- *Stealth Invasion: Red-Chinese Operations in North America* — over 600,000 in print.

- *What Red China Got For Its money — Why Did the People's Republic of China Invest in the 1996 Reelection Campaign of President Bill Clinton?* (co-authored with Richard A. Delgaudio)

- *Black Ghetto Riots and Campus Disorders*

I dedicate this book to the memory of

My father

Chief Petty Officer Roger "Red" Canfield, USN (Ret), who led a boarding party that put out a fire on a British oil tanker in the Atlantic, rebuilt boilers with "speed, dash and accuracy" after Pearl Harbor, served in every naval theatre in WWII and occupied a defeated Japan with respect and honor.

My mother

Ilene Mae Spradlin Canfield who, from Pearl Harbor until 1945, kept news clips of WWII in a USS Saratoga (CV-3) scrapbook for her infant son so that he might someday understand that the world is a dangerous place. She was killed at the age of 25, a wise but unheralded woman.

and my friend

Lieutenant Colonel Michael Mark, USA (Ret), Combat Infantry Badge, Bronze Star, Valor, Viet-Nam and editor of Military magazine, 1988-2000.

Dr. Roger Canfield
Executive Director
U.S. Intelligence Council
P.O. Box 919
Frederick, MD 21705

Dear Dr. Canfield:

I have recently learned that you are collecting signatures for a petition to the U.S. Congress, concerning the so-called "stealth invasion" by "Red China." After reading the letter shown by my friend, I cannot refrain from writing you this letter to express my displeasure and clarify on certain issues.

Your charges on Cosco and China as a whole are totally false and groundless. Even in your letter I have not seen any hard evidence of your accusation. I really doubt if anybody would believe in this absurd story. I do not know why you perceive China as an enemy to the United States, but I would like to take this opportunity to express some of my views on Sino-U.S. relations.

The relations between China and the United States have developed remarkably since the establishment of diplomatic ties in the late 1970s. President Bush's upcoming visit to China this year will give a further boost to our relations. Since the September 11 event last year, China has become an important partner of the United States in fighting against terrorism and safeguarding world peace. On the economic front, the United States is China's second-largest trading partner and our economic cooperation will be expanded and strengthened after China's accession to the WTO last year. The economies of our two countries are highly complementary. Trade with China has benefited American customers with low-price daily commodities and provided job opportunities for tens of thousands of American workers, I think most Americans will not view the expanded trade relations with China, in which the China Ocean Shipping Company has taken its due part, as a threat to the United States.

Your accusation of Chinese spying reminds me of the "Wen-ho Lee" case, which has proved to be a farce. Some people in the United States always want to raise, or even create some issues against China, out of misunderstanding, or evil intentions. But a lie, even repeated a thousand times, will not become truth. I am sure most American people will have a clear mind on this issue and support the sound and healthy development of Sino-U.S. relations, which is in the mutual interests of our two countries and the world as a whole.

Sincerely yours,

Wang Yunxiang
Consul General

copy of a letter sent to Dr. Canfield, postmarked January 22, 2002

Seek truth from facts

*— Michael Pillsbury via
Deng Xiaoping and Mao Zedong*

Table of contents

Acknowledgements

The research on this book took six years reviewing open public sources and leaked Chinese and American documents reported in daily newspapers, newswires and other publications. While the analyses — intelligence estimates — are my own, I have relied heavily upon others for basic facts and realist perspectives: Bill Rood, Bill Gertz, Richard Fisher, Gary Milhollin, Kenneth Timmerman, Al Santoli, Michael Pillsbury, Steven Mosher, Jasper Becker, Edward Timperlake, William Triplett, Joe Farah, Charles Smith, Jon Dougherty, Sally Foster, Gordon Chang, Philip Yang, Willy Lam, Chris Cox, Tom Tancredo, Bob Barr, Duncan Hunter, James Inhofe, Jesse Helms, Dana Rohrabacher, Paul Sperry, Mike Waller, Ken Puckett and many others who are credited in the text.

This work was completed with the encouragement and financial assistance of thousands of small contributors to the United States Intelligence Council (USIC) and Armond Noble, the publisher of this book and *Military* magazine. I thank the Chairman of USIC, Richard A. Delgaudio, for allowing me to serve as Executive Director of the USIC and for co-authoring the report *What Red China Got For Its Money* and our book *China Doll*. Richard also edited *Stealth Invasion* published by the USIC. In part, *China's Trojan Horses* expands upon and updates the themes contained in those publications and in my book *China Traders* as well as adding depth and detail to them. Finally, the USIC financed lobbying on China issues in Washington, D.C., and presentations before conservative conferences and meetings in Washington, Los Angeles, Miami and Panama.

Armond Noble, in addition to publishing this book, has also provided me the opportunity to publish several articles in *Military* about China's presence in Panama and across the globe. Moreover, Armond, our late friend and *Military's* editor Michael Mark, and I shared many days, particularly the Fourth of July, discussing America's future in a dangerous world. Debi Shank, Military's graphic designer, saw more versions of the text than she wished or was reasonable! I also thank her and my daughter for their work on the maps. And, finally, thanks to Cathy and Matthew Joyce for the cover design.

I thank my friends and professional colleagues — hardboiled reporters on the mean streets of Chicago, Baltimore, Managua and Saigon — for their eagle-eyed editing skills, informed cynicism and gracious tolerance of my strong views. This band of brothers among the starving writers class include Armond, Pat Joyce and others. They are to be forgiven for the company they keep.

I thank the taxpayers of California for providing me with a day job from time to time.

To my family — my wife Noel and our children Blaine, Carlton and Alicia — I apologize for my grievous neglect of their needs as well as my years of scattering piles of paper around several houses from coast to coast.

— *Roger Canfield*

Prologue – China's Trojan Horses

I wrote *China's Trojan Horses* (under earlier titles) from 1999-2001, before the terrorist attacks upon the World Trade Center and the Pentagon. Prior to September 11, 2001, the U.S. Intelligence Council (USIC) mailed over 300,000 copies of the publisher's proof of *Stealth Invasion,* in which I wrote, "Millions of Americans are today in harm's way on their own soil." I wrote about the "high vulnerability of U.S. seaports to espionage and terrorism." I noted that "sloppy security" had already led to the "blood of sailors and the tears of families" in the terrorist attack upon the USS *Cole* in Yemen. I concluded, as had others, that our seaport security at home was very bad indeed.

On boat tours of the Port of Long Beach in June of 2000 and June of 2001, I pointed out this vulnerability to attendees of the Western Conservative Conference — just as ABC's Dateline did in Norfolk, New York, and Groton, Connecticut in September and October 2000.

In the chapters that follow you will read where, prior to September 11, 2001, I tried to specify other persons, places, and things besides seaports, which might also bear careful watching because of a China threat.

Today I would argue that the China threat is far greater than the wildest hallucinations of the madmen running the terror network.

While terrorists infiltrated America with several score agents, the Red Chinese may very well have placed thousands of potential agents in American universities, research centers, nuclear labs, silicon valleys, defense industries, and military bases. Already Red Chinese agents, government officials, workers, students, and visitors have gained intimate knowledge of our technologies and our most critical infrastructures.

Furthermore, I would argue that Chinese knowledge of our technologies is far deeper and broader than the basic flying and primitive engineering skills of the few third world criminals who murdered 3,000 innocent Americans on September 11th. The Chinese pose clear and present dangers to our technologies, military facilities, and critical infrastructures (communications, computers, bridges, dams, power plants, transmission lines, etc.).

A Red Chinese merchant marine fleet of 100 ships serves all major U.S. seaports. It carries millions of cargo containers into the ports and towns of America every year. Easily smuggled within these 20-foot containers might be not only drugs or illegal immigrants, but also guns, bombs, missiles or nuclear, biological, or chemical weapons.

Each ship might ram or explode next to a U.S. Naval vessel, just like the USS *Cole*, or ram or explode near a bridge, oil refinery or nuclear power plant. (**Editor**: a barge rammed and destroyed a bridge over the Arkansas River on critical Interstate 40 in late May 2002.)

Container ships too large to pass through the Panama Canal could be scuttled to block a critical harbor choke point or breach a breakwater protecting vital U.S. seaport facilities from the angry sea. A Brookings Institute report estimates a $1 trillion loss from an attack upon our shipping industry.

I now hope that the distribution of *China's Trojan Horses* and like works will save American blood, treasure and tears in years to come. Americans may have to confront not only terrorists and their host states (Iraq, Iran, Syria, Libya, Sudan and North Korea) but also one of their major arms suppliers — the People's Liberation Army (PLA) of People's Republic of China, PRC. The PRC has already provided components and the secret technologies of weapons of mass destruction to the state sponsors of terrorism. Chinese violations of nonproliferation treaties likely continue to this day and remain a clear and present danger.

Indeed, on September 11, 2001 the PRC forged new relations with the Taliban in Afghanistan at the same time it was pledging support for the U.S. war against terrorism. Thereafter the Taliban used a wealth of Chinese arms and men against American forces in Afghanistan.

May God keep you and yours vigilant and free and give our leaders the wisdom to institute security measures that inconvenience us without loss of our fundamental liberties. Careful watching includes measures that do not undermine our liberties.

Roger Canfield
Fair Oaks, California
September 18, 2001
(Revised May 27, 2002)

Kandahar, Afghanistan, February 20, 2002 —A Navy Explosive Ordnace Disposal (EOD) technician in Afghanistan observes captured ordnace for destruction. The ordnace includes Chinese 82mm Type 65 recoilless rifle rounds and 82mm High Explosive Anti-Tank (HEAT) recoilless rifle rounds. — U.S. Navy photo

LOOSE LIPS SINK SHIPS:
Life After Slothful Security

In broad daylight and with no audible objections, Red China has forward deployed elements of its intelligence and military assets onto the U.S. homeland. Its sailors roam strategic U.S. seaports. Its soldiers observe U.S. military facilities and exercises. Its scientists visit and work in U.S. factories, research labs and universities. Its officials take notes and photos of the technical and structural vulnerabilities of critical infrastructures — water, power and communications. Its hundreds of potential front companies conduct business in major U.S. cities.

Yes, Red China's sleeper spies are placed throughout the U.S. economy and society. Its agents of influence, espionage and terrorism are well-placed to cause the loss of American blood and treasure upon U.S. soil.

The point is not that the "Chinese are coming." It is that they are already here. They come and go pretty much as they please without anyone bothering to notice or to care. In sight... out of mind.

Not since before Pearl Harbor *(and September 11, 2001)* has such a plain threat so apparent been so little noticed. And one aspect of our nation's reactions to Pearl Harbor — treatment of ethnic Japanese — is still very poorly understood. Indeed, in 2001 *MAGIC* written by David Lowman, a career officer of the National Security Agency (NSA), revealed "systematic recruitment of Japanese residents, citizens and noncitizens into networks designed to provide information to Japan both before and after the outbreak of [World War II]."

This writer discovered three messages of particular interest. In no less than three intercepted and decoded messages to Tokyo, Japanese agents reported movements of the USS *Saratoga* (CV 3) into and out of the ports of San Diego and Seattle. The *Saratoga* was my father's ship prior to Pearl Harbor. Hit later by torpedos and kamikazis.

Lowman's book contains declassified reports from three U.S. intelligence organizations showing the Japanese attempting to use "U.S.-based Japanese businesses, societies, churches, language schools, clubs, fishing boats, labor unions and individuals in the Japanese war effort." By contemporary accounts the vast majority of Japanese in America were believed to be loyal, but a minority of 3% to 20% just might not have been. No one knew until Pearl Harbor, no one had asked. There was a war and the nation defended itself at great cost to the civil liberties of some of its ethnic Japanese citizens.

At the present time only a few stalwart investigative journalists and a handful of brave souls in Congress have been among a cranky few sounding the alarm that Red China may endanger our nation's security. In prior publications of the United States Intelligence Council the author detailed the China threat: the China traders sellout of our national security in *China Traders* in August 2000; Red Chinese

Members of the local Chinese community gather to wish the crew of the destroyer Qingdao (DDG 113) of the People's Republic of China North Sea Fleet, a safe voyage departing Pearl Harbor. — *U.S. Navy photo*

espionage in *China Doll* (co-authored with Richard A. Delgaudio) in June 2000, and the Chinese political contributions and military technology transfers in *What Red China Got For Its Money* (co-authored with Richard A. Delgaudio) in April 1997, and its *Afterword* in February 2000.

This book, *China's Trojan Horses*, provides an overview of Red Chinese proxies — their soldiers, sailors, students, scientists and spies — who pose possible threats on American soil. While long silenced by Clinton-Gore appeasement of China, U.S. government intelligence agencies have frequently confirmed that it is prudent, not hysterical, to raise national security issues about Red China.

President George W. Bush's Administration has approached China with caution and occasional firmness, particularly with respect to Taiwan and the rights of U.S. citizens held against their will in China. Yet Bush has yet to explicitly identify China as a serious security threat to the United States. We hope that behind such diplomatic foreplay,

U.S. military planners and intelligence officers are already preparing for the worst — for that is their solemn Constitutional obligation.

Tragically, Americans must receive a shocking reminder every decade or so that the world is a dangerous place. U.S. citizens may die horribly when its elected officials violate their Constitutional duties by neglecting military preparedness, readiness, security and intelligence.

It was only after a terrorist attack in broad daylight in Aden, Yemen, on October 12, 2000, upon the USS *Cole* killed 17 and injured 39 American sailors, that the U.S. placed its military forces in the Middle East and the Arabian Peninsula on their highest alert, Delta.

That "high" alert merely required that U.S. bases perform routine security precautions in a hostile region of the world. They were only asked to limit access to suspicious visitors and suspicious vehicles. These are merely the routine measures of police officers and minimum wage security guards, not an alert military.

It took nearly two months for the U.S. Navy bureaucracy to approve additional sailors and Coast Guardsmen to "bolster port security" in the United States.[1]

Most telling was the retreat of American naval forces from seaports in the Middle East in late 2000 and early 2001. The U.S. put all ships out to sea. The U.S. Navy stopped all passages of U.S. warships through the Suez Canal. "Although no specific threats have been made against American Navy vessels passing through the [Suez] canal, U.S. Defense Department officials said that no U.S. warships have traveled through it since the Oct. 12 attack. The defense officials... said the Navy has been avoiding the Suez because of security concerns." The U.S. uses the Suez Canal to avoid taking the long sail around the whole of Africa. According to the AP, "Three to four U.S navy ships pass through the 101-mile canal every month" Defense spokesman Kenneth Bacon said that "no official decision was made to stop using the Suez Canal, linking the Mediterranean and Red seas. U.S. military commanders were reported to believe it is prudent to avoid it."[2]

The author, Stratfor, a Texas foreign policy think tank, and others had previously reported that China proxies — the China Ocean Shipping Company (COSCO), and Hutchison Whampoa — operate at both ends of the Suez Canal. Yet, the Pentagon did not use that reason for the withdrawal of the U.S. Navy from Suez.

By mid-December 2000, the U.S. Navy had still to call on a Middle Eastern port. In Naples a U.S. aircraft carrier, the USS *Harry S. Truman,* canceled its call at this friendly port due to a terrorist threat.

Doubtless, the U.S. Navy is not confident of the security of its

---

[1] *UPI*, December 5, 2000
[2] *AP*, November 1, 2000

forces against either rubber dinghies or Russia flyovers of U.S. aircraft carriers off Japan in 2001. The China threat is far, far greater.

The State Department was pathetically oblivious to reality. Days after terror aboard the USS *Cole*, Secretary of State Madeleine Albright was "unable to state with certainty that this was a terrorist act" and it took a week before State urged a "worldwide caution."[3]

One old satire describes the U.S. State Department as making a crucial decision — only after someone read a six-week old issue of *Newsweek* Magazine.

Early in the Bush Administration the Chinese sought to demonstrate their sovereignty over the South China Sea by forcing down a U.S. Navy reconnaissance aircraft (in international waters) and taking its crew hostage on Hainan Island. President Bush held firm against those urging a fawning apology and brought the hostages home.

In August 2001, the "American navy stage[d] big show of force in South China Sea."[4] Bush sent two U.S. aircraft carrier battle groups,

Hainan Island, China — Lockheed Martin Aeronautics Co. recover team members steady the the U.S. Navy EP-3E "Aries II" tail cone while disassembing the aircraft at Lingshui Airfield before its return to the U.S. The Fleet Reconnassaince Squadron One (VQ-1) aircraft collided with a Chinese F-8 fighter/interceptor on April 1, 2001, and made an emergency landing on Hainan Island. — photo courtesy of Lockheed Martin

---

[3] *Reuters*, October 24, 2000
[4] *Agence France-Presse*

led by USS *Carl Vinson* and the USS *Constellation*, to exercise jointly in the South China Sea. "...The meeting of the two aircraft carrier battle groups... demonstrates a commitment to providing peace and cooperation... while preserving the right to freedom of navigation," said a U.S. Navy website. "[T]he rare [and long overdue] U.S. show of force was a pointed message to Beijing as the People's Liberation Army conducts large war games on the southern coast facing Taiwan." China was preparing "its largest-ever military exercises" simulating an invasion of Taiwan, according to the Beijing-backed Hong Kong newspaper, *Wen Wei Po*.

In the shadow of the bloody light of the *Cole* tragedy and the Red Chinese forcing down of an American reconnaissance plane and holding American crewmen hostage, this book, *China's Trojan Horses* — like the author's book, *Stealth Invasion* (USIC, 2002) — focuses in greater, perhaps dull, detail on unappreciated espionage and terrorist threats. These threats to life, liberty and property of Americans are seen not just in the Middle East and not just in the South China Sea, but in our own homeland.

The FBI admits that U.S. vulnerability, specifically at seaports, is high. The National Intelligence Council of the CIA warns of "asymmetrical" attacks upon the U.S. homeland. The threat is Red China. China's potential agents are PRC citizens, overseas Chinese and others with easy access to our open and free society. These agents are China's soldiers, sailors, students, scientists and spies. Every day they enjoy unchallenged access to America's most vital military, industrial and infrastructure facilities.

We will emphasize one stunning vulnerability: the dangerous presence of the China Ocean Shipping Company (COSCO) with 100 container vessels in the USA calling on some major U.S. seaport every day.

Recently Geostrategy-direct.com reported, "The PLA [People's Liberation Army] conducted exercises on converting commercial [container] ships to join the war effort. The People's Liberation Army demonstrated for the first time in public how it can convert commercial freighters into warships."

The internet site of an official Chinese Communist Party newspaper said, "To meet the demand of future wars and give play to the formidable power of heavy guns, on 10 August, a certain PLA unit in Xuzhou under the Nanjing Military Region successfully conducted for the first time an exercise with live ammunition on a certain sea area of Huang Hai located in the northern part of Jiangsu province by deploying heavy-caliber guns on a container [ship] formerly used in ocean-going coastal marine transport. ...During the exercise, the traditional gun position was moved from the land to the deck of a large container [ship]." COSCO, the merchant marine of the PLA, has 600 container ships alone.

COSCO's CEO Wei Jiafu, dismisses claims of a military mission. He says he is not "an admiral" and his only "marching orders" are to make profits.[5]

Red Chinese sources and methods of intelligence

In 1991 Huo Zhonggwen and Wang Zongxiao of the China National Defense Science and Technology Information Center (DSTIC) in Beijing wrote *Sources and Methods [or Techniques] of Obtaining National Defense Science and Technology*. Openly distributed in China for nearly 10 years, the untranslated report was first published in English in the *Far Eastern Economic Review* in 2000. Western intelligence sources called it "incredible" and "astonishing" as late as 2000 despite a several thousand year history of intelligence as a common instrument of statecraft. The book details "how agents should obtain military technology, especially from America, by accessing open and secret sources."[6] Indeed, more than 80% of all Chinese spying focuses on open-source material obtained from government and business publications.

The Chinese report states, "It is also necessary to stress that there is still 20% or less of our intelligence that must come through the collection of information using special means, such as reconnaissance satellites, electronic eavesdropping and the activities of special agents purchasing or stealing, etc." Among this 20%, not available from open sources, the Chinese found "person-to-person exchange" to be very useful such as "...eliciting information from scientists at meetings, through documents supplied by agents...."[7]

Perhaps with less astonishment, recently the National Counterintelligence Center (NCIC) of the CIA warned federal agencies and private firms to beware of Red Chinese attempts to steal technology by recruiting their scientists. The vice-president of the Chinese Academy of Science has said China is seeking scientists "of Chinese nationality... willing to abandon their... citizenship." Red Chinese opportunities for recruiting agents abound in the U.S.

Red China targets Chinese citizens studying or working in the U.S. as well as Chinese Americans. Red China is "interested obsessively in people of Chinese-American ancestry to the exclusion of [other] people..." says a former director of the FBI's Chinese counterintelligence, Paul D. Moore. Many Chinese Americans may freely provide information in absolute and complete innocence.

As engineers, scientists and mathematicians proud of their knowledge and achievements, some may feel especially privileged to share their achievements with others of like interests and ethnic background.

---

[5] *Washington Times*, June 2, 2001
[6] Jasper Becker, *The Chinese*, December 2000
[7] Bill Gertz, *The China Threat*, p. 133-136

Everywhere Americans of all ethnic backgrounds greet visitors from Red China with the effusive friendliness born only in the USA. Like their brothers at Los Alamos, U.S. technical experts routinely show everything to visitors from China about critical infrastructures without a passing thought about security. Chinese visitors, lumped in with Australians, Egyptians, Vietnamese and Koreans, are shown the engineering details and the locations of California's most critical water, communications and energy infrastructures. Why? To the naive and well meaning to not do so would be unfriendly.

Security is little understood and poorly implemented, even after the evidence appears indisputable. From April 25 through May 11, 2001, Chinese hackers routed through China Telecom, breached the security on the computer system at the California Independent System Operator (ISO) in Folsom, CA. The ISO controls California's vulnerable electricity grid. "Very close to a catastrophic breach," a source told Dan Morain of the *Los Angeles Times*.[8] During one of the cyberattacks on May 7-8, some 400,000 households lost their electricity. Yet "Cal-ISO officials said... there was no connection between the hacking and the outages..." We'll have to take their word for it. The attack revealed grievous security lapses. There were no firewalls, tripwires or logs to frustrate hackers or to record the security breach. Dozens of computer ports were wide open to easy access.

During May 2001, hundreds of other computer attacks upon the USA originated in China. During the attacks, some suggested to state officials that the attacks might indicate a Chinese interest in the vulnerability of other critical infrastructures such as the dams and aqueducts that provide water to tens of millions of Californians. Indeed, Chinese visitors to California's State Water Project operations centers, dams, pumps and power plants outnumber those of any other nation. State officials believed their systems were secure and that the policy was that the State of California remained "open to the public." Chinese attacks on computers controlling California's electric grid did not warrant heightened security in other infrastructures. Though there are widespread security lapses, California officials, far from the nation's centers of defense and intelligence, ought not to be singled out. They do not believe national security is a primary function of state government and do not perceive major security threats.

Security lapses, like rotting fish, start from the head. I.C. Smith, a retired FBI agent who specialized in Chinese spying, said the FBI cut back counterintelligence against the Chinese during the Clinton Administration. "Their shortsighted view of the PRC, a view held by those with little intellectual capacity for counterintelligence, is that China doesn't pose a threat," Mr. Smith said.[9] "After all, they aren't

---

[8] June 9, 2001
[9] Gertz, December 26, 2000

out there making dead drops, communicating via short wave radio... as... expected... the spy business," said Smith. Similarly, "The Chinese do not spy as God intended it," said Paul Moore, a former FBI intelligence analyst. China uses students, business people, scientists or visitors abroad as collectors, not just intelligence officers.

Clinton-Gore actively cooperated with Chinese spy methods. The USA granted temporary visas for 315,536 Chinese in 2000. There were 200,000 illegals from Red China in the U.S. according to the 2000 Census. These numbers are very large — really incredible but true. Each year 50,000 students are issued visas from China. In 1998 alone, 25,000 foreign scientists visited three nuclear labs possessing all of America's nuclear secrets.[10]

By 1998 — though hidden from the American people — internal investigations had revealed Red China's espionage successes in acquiring nuclear and missile secrets were spectacularly obvious to all but the willfully blind.

China was "very adept" at gathering scientific and technological information using people such as scientists, academics and businessmen. This according to a late 1998 U.S. intelligence report titled "Foreign Collection Against the Department of Energy: The Threat to U.S. Weapons and Technology" quoted extensively by *Washington Times* reporter Bill Gertz in his *China Threat*.

Presumably backward, China is among many nations "known to intercept U.S. satellite communications and, in many cases... [had] extensive capabilities to intercept other communications," the report said. Official Chinese military literature pronounces its capacity to defeat the USA through weapons and strategic modernization despite its "asymmetrical" power imbalance with the USA.[11]

FBI Director Louis Freeh on January 28, 1998, testified to the Senate Select Committee on Intelligence. In part he said, "Press reports of recent espionage cases involving... China [missles, sattlelites, nuclear warheads] are just the tip of a large and dangerous intelligence iceberg. In addition to... covert intelligence operations run by intelligence officers... the FBI... encounter covert activity on the part of... visiting scientists or foreign businessmen... [W]hat some pundits have called the 'end of history' is definitely not the end of dangerous intelligence attacks against the United States."

Released in mid-1999 after months of delays and Clinton leaks and media spin, the Cox Report underlined Freeh's testimony. "The FBI has inadequate resources in light of the *extensive number of* PRC visitors, students, diplomats, business representatives and others who

---

[10] Canfield and Delguadio, *China Doll;* Gertz, *China Threat;* and *Washington Times*, December 26, 2000

[11] Michael Pillsbury, *China Debates the Future Security Environment*, National Defense University, 2000

may be involved in intelligence and military-related technology transfer operations in the United States." [emphasis added]

Red Chinese attempts to influence U.S. elections and to buy or steal America's most precious nuclear and missile secrets ought to have been a wakeup call. Yet, America slept through the Thompson Report on Red Chinese corruption of our electoral process. Americans yawned at the revelations of the Cox Report that U.S. nuclear and missile secrets were in Red Chinese hands. As Americans rubbed the sleep from their eyes, the media blamed the accusers and investigators for the sorry lot of prime suspect Wen Ho Lee. Just like prior cases of Soviet espionage agents: Alger Hiss and the Rosenbergs, Lee was the victim!

•

As the Clinton-Gore Administration made preparations for the transition, there were signs that the Clinton-Gore security guards just might be awakening before the change of the watch. At least at the end they wanted to appear alert at their posts.

In mid-December 2000 the National Intelligence Council, a body of advisors to the CIA presented a report, Global Trends 2015, describing attacks like those on the USS *Cole* as "asymmetric warfare" threatening U.S. interests at home as well as abroad. Enemies facing a militarily stronger U.S., rather than hitting it head-on, will target a weak point — an Achilles' heel — in cyberspace or by using chemical, nuclear or biological weapons. "Such asymmetric approaches — whether undertaken by states or nonstate actors — will become the dominant characteristic of most threats to the U.S. homeland," the NIC report said.

The report recognized missile attacks — biological, chemical and nuclear — as possible risks. (Chinese strategy believes that "asymmetric warfare" is the means by which it can defeat a stronger USA.) "The goal of the adversary would be to move the weapon within striking distance by using short and medium-range **missiles deployed on surface ships or covert missions using military special operations forces** or state intelligence services," said the NIC report [**bold** added].

In 2000 the CIA finally got around to begin translating the remaining 12,000 pages of Chinese language documents it had received from a Red Chinese missile expert in 1995. Voilà, the Cox Committee had received only 76 pages about the Chinese successes in nuclear espionage. Lacking the full translations, the Cox Report had likely understated U.S. losses of its nuclear and other technologies.

The Pentagon announced the hiring of 450 counterintelligence experts to track down missile technology losses — now admitted to be greater than the nuclear secrets lost at Los Alamos — to Wen Ho Lee and others.

Clinton's bumbling Attorney General Janet Reno and FBI Director Louis Freeh stood firm against President Clinton. Though the government plea bargained down to minor counts, they said they had the right man in charging Wen Ho Lee. They thought Lee was guilty of serious security violations that lost or gave away American nuclear secrets to Red China.

Slothful U.S. security dribbling down is deadly

The 2000-2001 Delta military alert and "worldwide caution" for American citizens came after terrorists in a slow putt-putting fiberglass skiff conducted a suicide bombing attack on the docked destroyer USS *Cole* at 11:18 a.m. on October 12 in Aden, Yemen. A shaped C-4 explosive tore a 40-foot by 40-foot hole in the side of the technologically advanced guided-missile destroyer killing 17 sailors and wounding 39. Moments before, armed sailors (without ammunition) waved back to two smiling occupants of the fiberglass skiff. The boat had sailed around the bow of the *Cole* and leisurely traversed it lengthwise until reaching amidships and exploding.

Several reports suggested that the ship's captain had not kept his crew at a sufficient level of alert. That may have been true, but it was also true that the Clinton-Gore Administration was seeking to improve relations in the region. It wanted to avoid offending the natives by "standing off" approaching craft by threats of violence or armed patrols. Retired Navy Chief Kenneth Baker, responding to the attack on the USS *Cole* said, "To see our sailors placed in a high-threat terrorist environment for the sake of showing the flag [in Yemen] sickens me. The new Secretary of Defense must do a clean sweep of the Pentagon. The Clinton virus has infected the top brass."[12] Indeed.

While terrorist attacks are always difficult to detect, the assault on the USS *Cole* dramatized the bloody consequences of lax security. Despite a number of warnings and an Embassy at full alert, the ship's captain was not alerted and his crew failed either to order the unidentified vessel to stand off or to fire warning shots from fire hoses at the ready had the terrorists failed to withdraw.

Five days after the attack on the *Cole*, Russian aircraft buzzed the U.S. aircraft carrier *Kitty Hawk* unmolested. On one of three passes U.S. jets took 40 minutes to scramble in response. The Russians e-mailed their photos to the *Kitty Hawk*.[13] Clearly, U.S. security remained scandalously slothful even after *Cole*. Doubtless, the hapless sailors and aircrews of the *Kitty Hawk* were occupied chipping paint and saluting their superiors — the usual preparedness activities of the peacetime U.S. Navy before every war.

Such bad security practices and attitudes in the Naval command and on board the *Cole* may have dribbled right on down from the Com-

---

[12] Colonel David Hackworth
[13] Scarborough, *Washington Times*, December 7, 2000

mander-in-Chief to U.S. Naval forces in the region and to the ship's crew itself.

Widespread inattention to security has put thousands of American sailors, soldiers and airmen in harm's way in far more ways than a single rubber dinghy loaded with C-4.

Negligent security part of the Clinton culture

The Clinton-Gore Administration willfully neglected and ridiculed even the most rudimentary and prudent security measures. They did not believe in background checks, security clearances, document control, secured sources and methods, registration of foreign agents and export controls. They did not sanction Red Chinese for treaty violations. They did not vigorously conduct civil and criminal prosecutions for espionage.

In December 2000 a Pentagon commission reported to Secretary William Cohen poor military security in the Middle East prior to the bombing of the destroyer *Cole* in Yemen. "...We've done a lot... to improve force protection, but it is still not deeply rooted in our culture," said a senior defense official to *The New York Times*.

From the White House to the Departments of State, Commerce, Defense and Energy — everywhere — national security was neglected and dismissed as a useless nuisance.

From the very beginning of the Clinton-Gore Administration, according to FBI agent Gary Aldrich, the office of the Commander-in-Chief dismissed routine FBI background and security checks of White House employees. Throughout the U.S. government the Clinton Administration declassified millions of files willy-nilly including thousands of pages of old, but still secret, nuclear weapons files.

Benefitting Clinton-Gore contributors both domestic and foreign, Secretaries of Commerce — Ron Brown and William Daley — waived long-standing national security limits on exports. They facilitated the out-right sale and give-aways of militarily valuable technologies — missile guidance, super computers, telecommunications, navigation — to Red China. Commerce employees John Huang, Ira Sockowitz, William Ginsberg and others carried classified documents on trade policies (involving China) and military technologies (satellite encryptions and surveillance, remote sensing, intelligence personnel and capabilities) out of the Department of Commerce and never accounted for their disposition.[14] Congress appropriated funds to improve security at Commerce, but Secretary William Daly used the money for employee retreats and seminars. Congress ordered a listing of Red Chinese front companies but never got it and is still waiting for it.

Director of the CIA, John Deutsch, loaded his laptop computer

---

[14] Paul Sperry, *WorldNetDaily*, October 17, 2000

COSCO containers behind locked gates at the Port of Long Beach in December 1999. — photo by Roger Canfield

with classified reports and secrets and took them home.

The CIA sat for five years on 13,000 pages of Chinese language documents — left slothfully untranslated — showing Chinese espionage on ballistic missiles and reentry vehicles that just might be more extensive than the theft of nuclear warhead designs highlighted in the Cox Report.[15] Chinese use of nuclear weapons is perhaps unthinkable to most people. Yet so too is a communist regime which has murdered tens of millions of its own citizens in the past. To this day the regime uses child, slave and prison labor in its state-owned enterprises. Today it still executes political opponents as well as minor criminals and sells the body parts to rich Asians and Americans who want transplants. Such people should not have effective weapons of mass destruction.

In January 2000, an Inspector General's report said that State Department security officers did not sweep 140 rooms for bugs and frequently failed to account for the most highly classified intelligence documents called "sensitive compartmented information" (SCI). Over three months of 1998, some 239 of 1,890 SCI reports distributed by National Security Agency's Cryptological Support Group were never returned to it. One State Department pouch was returned empty. Private business employees guilty of such bungling would be fired or sent to jail.

Of 1,673 instances of mishandling of classified documents, the report said, only 218 employees were cited — AFTER each had vio-

---

[15] *Washington Post*, October 19, 2000

lated security four times — a singularly lackadaisical standard for discipline. And none were dismissed.

Another 350 contractors, e.g. janitors, worked inside State headquarters without security clearances. Perhaps thousands of foreign government officials were given unescorted access. During only two days in September 1998, the Inspector General found 1,726 visitors, including 326 foreign officials, most moving "about the building unescorted." Disneyland has better security.

During 1998, a tweed-coated man wandered into the outer office of Secretary of State Madeleine Albright and walked off with documents in full view of secretaries — one of whom was actually honored the following year as a "secretary of the year!" In another instance, a bug was placed in a conference room on the seventh floor of the State Department itself. A Russian diplomat, Stanislav Borisovich Gusev, was caught listening. A laptop that held classified information on proliferation issues was taken from under a chair outside a secure conference room being redecorated.

The State Department gave multiple winks and nods to Chinese violations of 14 nonproliferation commitments not to transfer nuclear, chemical and biological and missile technology to other states.

According to Senator Jesse Helms, the Communist leadership of the People's Republic of China "has given terrorist regimes deadly chemical capabilities, nuclear technology to vaporize cities and missiles capable of raining terror on innocent people from above."[16]

Breaking its promises and easily placating Clinton-Gore, Red China transferred such technologies to "sponsors of state terrorism" just like that visited upon the USS *Cole* — to Iran, Syria, Libya and North Korea. One of these rogue nations may have aided, abetted or sponsored the killing of members of the crew of the USS *Cole*. In late November 2000, Clinton Administration officials, NSC's Gary Samore and Assistant Secretary of State Robert Einhorn — doubtless in midnight meetings — quietly dropped all sanctions against China for proliferation of missile technology. They cleared away all roadblocks to American company satellite launches in China.

All Clinton-Gore contributors again appeared to be getting their payoffs. In the midst of the disputed Presidential election of 2000 no one noticed. China was aiding state sponsors of terror with the active complicity of the Clinton Administration.

The Department of Defense cordially extended invitations to Chinese intelligence and military officers to participate in U.S. war games, simulations and training operations. Congress ordered an end to visits involving simulations of war fighting tactics, but the Administration renamed the visits and actually expanded them.

Secretary of Energy Hazel O'Leary, with no security background

---

[16] Jesse Helms, September 11, 2000, floor of U.S. Senate

and on her own volition, crossed "SECRET" off the top of a design drawing of a nuclear warhead and handed it over to a magazine reporter.

Old documents containing nuclear secrets were declassified.

Classified documents were sent out in 27 separate mailings to unauthorized addressees.

Unidentified persons from China and Russia accessed nuclear weapons designs floating on the Internet and on unsecured lab computers.

From 1993-1998, "more than 250 known or suspected intelligence officers from 27 countries visited or were assigned to various Energy Department facilities."[17] The Energy Department's nuclear weapons laboratories were operated like university campuses. They were open to unescorted foreign visitors. By neglect employees were allowed to casually mishandle nuclear secrets.

With recognized Constitutional limits in the post-Clinton era, the United States must deploy the full measure of its intelligence resources, not only to determine the espionage and intelligence activities of Red China around the world (such as the presence of its proxies and agents at critical choke points at the Panama Canal, Suez Canal, Straits of Taiwan and Straits of Malacca), but at home as well.

---

[17] Reuters review; Gertz, *China Threat*

WELCOME TO THE USA: Red China's Soldiers, Sailors... Spies

Congress and the Bush Administration must thoroughly investigate the national security implications of the ubiquitous presence on U.S. soil of potential agents of Red China. We call them soldiers, sailors, students, scientists — and spies. Our elected representatives need to review existing security measures for preventing visiting military officers, sailors, scientists and students from stealing America's military secrets from U.S. agencies and defense contractors.

This book focuses upon the vulnerability of specifically identified U.S. ports to smuggling and espionage via the China Ocean Shipping Company (COSCO). The book also sketches out another set of largely uninvestigated potential dangers — Chinese businessmen, students, scientists and military visitors who may pose dangers to our national security.

For seven years, the Clinton-Gore Administration appeased a bellicose Beijing with free trade, free technology, military and scientific exchanges and free access to nuclear facilities, military bases and the White House. Clinton-Gore did their work too well and now is the time for President Bush to fix the damage.

Soldiers in military exchanges, intelligence on the cheap

In late October 2000, the Pentagon hosted a Red Chinese military delegation headed by People's Liberation Army (PLA) General Yu Yongbo, leader of the PLA's Political Department — propaganda minister for the PLA. The Clintonistas compared General Yu's entourage to U.S. chaplains. The Communist ideologues visited West Point, the U.S. Pacific Command and bases in Washington, South Carolina and Florida. It would "build mutual confidence and trust," said a Pentagon press release and it would accelerate "cooperation in... humanitarian relief," reported *Reuters*. Defense Secretary Cohen reportedly expressed displeasure with the Chinese delivering missile and arms technologies to states sponsoring terrorism. Yet, within a month, Clinton-Gore inked a deal. It forgave Chinese weapons proliferation and dropped U.S. export limits on missile guidance technologies given to the Chinese.

One official told Bill Gertz of the *Washington Times* that the real

Secretary of Defense William S. Cohen (right) escorts Gen. Yu Yongbo, of the People's Republic of China Central Military Commission, into the Pentagon on October 31, 2000. — photo Department of Defense

mission of General Yu was to gather intelligence on how U.S. morale might be dashed — e.g. a surprise, massive attack on Taiwan. The visit continued hot tub and Chardonnay diplomacy by those Col. David Hackworth calls the "perfumed princes" of the U.S. military. Congressional limitations on military exchanges were ignored and Red Chinese military intelligence officers were welcomed to the USA.

Since 1997, Harvard's Kennedy School has hosted American national security officials and military officers. The school invited Americans knowing all the nation's secrets to break little pieces of bread and sip dainty wine glasses with colonels and generals of the People's Liberation Army of the People's Republic of China. The very same people who have threatened to "shed blood" over Taiwan and to "incinerate Los Angeles with nuclear weapons."

Sailors in open ports

To improve port facilities, in large measure for the China trade, the vast majority of the business and political leaders of America's major port cities are investing billions of dollars. They are using both tax revenues and private funds to build new port structures and to convert former U.S. military bases to container ports for the Chinese and others. Whether it is Los Angeles, Long Beach, Oakland, Portland, Seattle, New Orleans, Houston, Miami, Savannah, Charleston, Norfolk, New York or Boston the port investment story is almost always the same and the Chinese are always welcome.

Surely, wise investments in the infrastructure of world trade will increase the wealth of the nation. Is this wealth gained at the expense of national security and freedom? Unfortunately, there is no evidence that locally-run seaports take much interest in national security. What is inside millions of 20-foot cargo containers? What are the risks of Chinese ships commingling with U.S. warships in every major U.S. seaport and waterway? Nobody asks. Nobody knows. This, despite the terrorist attack on the USS *Cole*. This, despite a *Washington Times* story about a secret July 2000 CIA report on "Russian merchant ship intelligence collection efforts against U.S. nuclear submarine bases" in the "Strait of Juan de Fuca, above Washington state's Puget Sound." If the Russians, why not the Chinese?

The Bush Administration has initially shown only a vague inkling of possible dangers. In testimony before Congress in early May 2001, Treasury Secretary Paul H. O'Neill called the Customs Service the nation's "first line of border defense." The thought makes any informed person shiver or laugh out loud. O'Neill let stand a claim by Sen. Ernest F. Hollings (D-SC) that Customs inspects only 10% of containers unloaded daily in U.S. ports in New Jersey. "One of the stunning things to me, when you sit and think about the compact nature of some weapons that can be transported fairly easily and concealed fairly easily [in containers], is how enormous this job is for people who are on the front line," O'Neill said.

The true number of containers inspected is 2% — 98% are not inspected! Security is surely not "job one" for the U.S. Customs Service. Similarly, Coast Guard resources expanded to defend U.S. ports is about 2% of its budget.

Students and scientists — open laboratories and classrooms — secrets out the door?

The Silicon Valley and America's finest universities lust for the world-class talents of skilled Chinese (and other foreign) scientists and engineers who can do the tough work in math, engineering and science necessary for the new economy. Indeed the student products of a criminally negligent U.S. public school system have been woefully incompetent in math and the sciences for two decades and more.

Desperate for competent workers and giving no consideration to national security, Congress recently extended H-1B visas and work permits, renewable up to six years, for 600,000 foreign high-tech workers and scientists — 200,000 a year for three years. Indeed, foreign students, among them Red Chinese nationals, have dominated taxpayer-subsidized classrooms in American graduate schools of math, science and engineering for several decades.

Yet, among the bountiful blessings of this American "brain drain" from the rest of the world — fresh testimony of America's beacon of liberty — may be agents of foreign powers, such as Red China, who do not wish us well. The Communist government of China approves, and the U.S. government concurs on, each and every Mainland Chinese student — 50,000 a year — who sets foot on American soil. The Communist elite send their own sons and daughters.

Our national security demands that we take a careful look before we grant visas and that we keep track of visa holders. Once assured of their intentions, or that they are kept out of activities vital to national security, we ought to thank them publicly and frequently for the miracles they have helped create in our silicon valleys. As Ronald Reagan said about the Soviets, "trust, but verify."

Front companies —

The Cox Report said, "... The PRC uses commercial and political contacts to advance its efforts to obtain U.S. military, as well as commercial, technology. The PRC has adopted policies... [to] increase access to U.S. military, as well as commercial, technology. To this end, the PRC has used access to its markets to induce U.S. business interests to provide military-related technology. The PRC also uses access to its markets to induce U.S. businesses to lobby in behalf of common goals, such as liberalized export standards and practices. Agents tied to the PRC's military industries who have illegally provided political contributions may have used these contributions to gain access to U.S. military and commercial technology."

In a semiannual CIA report to Congress covering July-December 2000, Bill Gertz reports, "China supplied missile technology and related goods to Pakistan, Iran, North Korea and Libya..." The CIA said, "...firms in China have provided dual-use missile-related items, raw materials and/or assistance to several other countries of proliferation concern such as Iran, North Korea, and Libya. ...[T]he [Bush] Administration is seeking to address these questions with appropriate Chinese authorities... Release of the [CIA] report comes a week after the Bush Administration slapped economic sanctions on China and Pakistan for violating U.S. laws aimed at halting the spread of missile technology..."[1] All the nations cited as receiving assistance from Red China also have been identified as state sponsors of terrorism.

China trade: empty promises — empty containers

"Between 1992 and 1999, the United States ran a cumulative trade deficit with the People's Republic of $391 billion — more by

---

[1] Gertz, *Washington Times*, September 8, 2001

a third than the entire U.S. defense budget... The PRC has used this wealth transfer to buy advanced weapons systems..."[2]

In 2000, despite opposition from 79% of the public, Congress voted 237-197 in the House and 83-15 in the Senate to grant China Permanent Normal Trading Relations (PNTR) — perhaps encouraged by an average contribution of $47,000 per Republican and $37,000 per Democrat by the pro-China members of the Business Roundtable. Boeing, a heavy promoter of PNTR, laid off 23,000 employees while Chinese workers were building components for 3,100 Boeing aircraft.[3]

By April 2001, U.S. manufacturers had laid off 638,000 workers since June 1998 and, according to some Democrats in the House 60% (about 380,000 jobs lost), could be attributed to the trade deficit with China.

By the end of 2000 the annual U.S. trade deficit with China was $83.8 billion. That is, the U.S. imported $100 billion from China in 2000, but in exchange the PRC allowed entry to only $16 billion in U.S. export goods to China. This is a negative balance of 6:1.

Phyllis Schlafly writes, "Every month, China collects up to $6 billion in U.S. cash by selling its slave-labor products to Americans, but only buys $1 billion worth of U.S. goods. The Chinese pocket $5 billion every month and use it to build their military-industrial complex."

Clearly, all the trade was one way — the wrong way. U.S. trade deficits of $80 billion annually provide excess cash subsidizing the modernization of Chinese military forces, perhaps 17¢ per every import dollar.[4]

Still U.S. business remains mesmerized by the illusion of the future profitability of an imaginary 1.3 billion new customers. The illusion compares to investing in a high-tech, low-profit dotcom whose current annual income might equal the value of its stock in 1,000 years. (Price earning ratios of 1,000 to 1.)

The trade deficits favoring China are dramatically observable every day at most U.S. ports:

"...One of the larger export categories... these days are empty shipping containers being sent back to Asia for reloading with imports," reported the *Business Journal* of Portland, Oregon.[5] In 1998 and 1999 the Port of Oakland shipped out 353,945 and 353,700 empty TEUs (Twenty-foot Equivalent Units). In fiscal 1998 and 1999 the Port of Long Beach exported 1,068,103 empty containers and 1,090,338 empty containers. The story is similar in every port.

---

[2] Don Feder, February 20, 2001
[3] Sheila Cherry, *Washington Times*
[4] *Military* magazine, December 2000
[5] November 2, 1998

"ONE OF THE LARGER EXPORT CATEGORIES... ARE EMPTY SHIPPING CONTAINERS BEING SENT BACK... FOR RELOADING WITH IMPORTS."

The major U.S. export to China is empty containers — next to nothing — only one out of every six containers carries any American goods to China. Such a deal.

The U.S imports Chinese toys, games, sporting goods, apparel, computers and computer components. The U.S. exports its high technology to the Chinese military. And it exports its jobs to China — much as slave, child and prison labor.

Emptier than the containers and the ballast-laden ships returning to China is the claim that China will liberalize its regime with increased trade. *The New York Times* noticed that China was moving to "stamp out all remnants of political opposition" by jailing the last free leaders of the China Democracy Party — Wang Zechen and Wang Wenjiang for four- to six-year sentences. They joined 30 others imprisoned as the China traders lied about liberalization. Thousands of an "evil cult," the Fulan Gong, which meditated and exercised in public without permission, were imprisoned. In April 2001 the emboldened Chinese held 24 U.S. servicemen (from an aircraft forced down by a military aircraft in international waters) hostage and prosecuted three American civilians on phony charges of spying.

Meanwhile, the United States is open sesame to foreign visitors for virtually any purpose whatsoever. Incredibly, the U.S government admits granting temporary visitor visas for business or pleasure to 3,567,578 persons in 2000, of which Red China accounted for 315,536. That's 864 Chinese nationals a day every day of the year — roughly half the size of the city of San Francisco.

In the next chapter we focus upon two classes of visitors that have the greatest potential to endanger national security — military officers and technical (students, scientists and industrial) workers.

Red Soldiers Play War Games in the USA

In 1989 General Kui Fulin directed tank assaults upon unarmed citizens in Tiananmen Square grinding bloody human flesh under tank treads — massacring untold thousands of peaceful pro-democracy protesters. By 1993, according to documents acquired by Charles Smith of *WorldNetDaily* from the Federal Aviation Administration, the very same PLA General Kui Fulin, accompanied by Lt. General Li Yongtai and 13 others, visited the U.S. as a civilian interested in "air traffic control." The Chinese military officers were briefed on sophisticated electronic systems. In 2000, Undersecretary of Defense Walter Slocombe characterized these briefings on electronics systems as neither military, tactical nor navigational. Either nothing was shown or the Chinese were blindfolded!

From 1993 through 2000, the Clinton-Gore ties to the Chinese military officers were long and continuous.

In November 1993, Clinton aide Charles Freeman met General Xu Huizi, Deputy Chief of Staff of the PLA. In August 1994, Defense Secretary William Perry met Foreign Minister Qian Qichen, Defense Minister Chi Haotian, Generals Lui Huaquing and Ding Henggao.

In 1995 General Huai Guomo and others toured the Department of Energy under Commerce Department sponsorship. They were invited to join a joint nuclear project on nuclear fusion and fission R&D.

American businesses sought contact persons for 49 objects desired by the Chinese generals and their agencies. General Ding gave the list of Chinese PLA-owned defense industry contacts to the Department of Commerce.

In October 1996, General Chi Haotian met President Clinton and toured American military and research facilities for several days. In May 1997, Chairman of the Joint Chiefs of Staff, General John Shalikashvili visited China. In October 1997, General Fu Quanyou visited the U.S. The Clinton Administration gave China fine satellite images of Siberia, South Korea and Okinawa. Hughes Aircraft provided China with "world class remote sensing" equipment.

In November 1997, Clinton and President Jiang Zemin agreed to a "strategic partnership" that expanded military-to-military contacts. In December Adm. Joseph Prueher, Commander in the Pacific, visited China and General Xiong Guangkai visited the U.S. Defense Sec. Cohen signed a Military Maritime Consultative Agreement and formed "working groups" on issues of mutual concern. The Chinese denied Cohen access to two military facilities, including China's military command center.

Secretary of Defense William J. Perry (right) presents a model of a B-24 Liberator bomber to People's Republic of China General Chi Haotian at the Pentagon on December 9, 1996. — *Department of Defense photo*

Congress enacted Smith/DeLay to restrict U.S.-PRC military to military visits and specifically prohibited PRC exposure to U.S. war fighting experiments,[1] but Clinton continued the exchanges anyway.

In 1998 the Air Force provided briefings of a simulated F-16 bombing northwest of Prescott, Arizona. Responding to Congressional criticism, Undersecretary of Defense Walter Slocombe claimed it was "imaginary training." Also during 1998, the U.S. Air Force invited an entire war college class of the Chinese PLA Air Force (PLAAF) to COPE THUNDER, U.S. war games and exercises in Alaska.[2] The Chinese military was invited back in 1999.

According to documents acquired by Charles Smith of *WorldNet-Daily*, in May 1999 the U.S. Air Force and the Defense Department instructed three Chinese colonels in "combat readiness" — bombing and strafing — at Edwards Air Force Base. Ever the master prevaricator or just a hapless "public information" officer, Slocombe claimed the Chinese were air traffic controllers on a civilian "safety" mission — at a U.S. Air Force base, practicing simulated bombings.

Meanwhile returning favors, during 1999, the Chinese denied the U.S. Fleet long-standing ports of call to a previously free Hong Kong.

---

[1] Gertz, *Washington Times*, August 24, 2000
[2] Charles Smith, *WND*, May 18, 1999

Defense Secretary Cohen had to plead for a reopening of calls at Hong Kong.

By September 14-17, 2000, a Chinese guided-missile destroyer, *Qingdao*, flagship of Rear Adm. Lu Fangqui, chief of North Sea fleet, called upon the U.S. Naval Station at Everett, Washington, home port to destroyers and one aircraft carrier after a visit to Pearl Harbor. The Chinese made a "goodwill" visit upon the nuclear carrier USS *Carl Vinson*. They also visited Boeing and the Bremerton Naval Station and played soccer.

Naval Station Everett, Washington *— The People's Liberation Army (Navy) destroyer Qingsao (DDG 13) (middle) pulls into port during the People's Republic of China Goodwill Cruise 2000.* — *U.S. Navy photo*

William Triplett, author of *Year of the Rat* and *Red Dragon Rising*, said, "The Chinese army is coming... to learn how we fight." Russia is selling China weapons like the SS-N-22 Moskit missile... [which] has one purpose — killing American carriers and Aegis warships."

In Pearl Harbor 1,000 Chinese were invited aboard to "see the inside" of the Aegis guided-missile cruiser USS *Chancellorsville*.

In early September 2000, columnist Don Feder, following upon the relentless vigilance of Charles Smith of *WorldNetDaily*, wrote an article, "Chinese colonels at Harvard — only in Clinton's America." Feder noted that "the People's Republic of China is engaged in a vast program of military expansion, has looted our nuclear secrets, sees America as its principal adversary, threatens war with Taiwan... and promises to launch a nuclear strike against us if we intervene."

And yet, "what are 24 senior colonels of the People's Liberation Army doing at Harvard's John F. Kennedy School... being lectured by current and former national security officials on how the United States would respond militarily to a crisis over Taiwan?"

People's Republic of China Rear Admiral Fu Quanyou visits the USS Arizona Memorial at Pearl Harbor. — *U.S. Navy photo*

It was the third group of Chinese colonels invited to Harvard since 1997. Joseph Nye, a globalist advocate of worldwide integration of nations, a former Clinton defense official and a former Soviet and now China "soft-liner" set up the military exchanges in 1997. Marshall Goldman, for decades a recognized Harvard expert on Soviet Communist strategy and tactics, says, "Almost all the Chinese are intelligence people."

The lectures at Harvard fly in the face of an amendment to 1999 defense appropriations limiting military exchanges with the PLA. Chinese officers observing the training of Navy fighter pilots at Top Gun angered Congress. (The author trained electronic technicians there.)

Feder describes military exchanges as, "a Wal-Mart for intelligence gatherers."

In January 2000, the Administration "rolled out the red carpet" for Gen. Xiong Guangkai, the PLA's Deputy Chief of Staff, who had threatened to incinerate Los Angeles over a 1996 Taiwan crisis and had also test-fired missiles over airspace close to Taiwan. Clinton threatened to veto the House-passed Taiwan Security Enhancement Act if it reached his desk from the Senate. Moreover, the Clinton State Department discouraged diplomatic exchanges with America's ally forcing Taiwan's democratically-elected president, Chen Shui-bian, to refuse a meeting with a group of Congressmen on a stopover in California in August.

Al Gore said, China is an "extremely important partner." He said he opposes "isolating and demonizing" China and wanted to "build a bridge." Feder asks, "[a bridge] to Tiananmen Square?" In Red China in 1997 Gore said, "We seek real progress on human rights, not confrontation."

Feder points out that on March 6, 2000, Beijing announced a military budget increase of 12.7% in 2000 after eight straight years of double-digit growth. The *Liberation Army Daily* warned that U.S. help to Taiwan would do "serious damage to U.S. interests." The PLA organ observed its "capacity of launching a long-distance strike."[3]

The *Washington Times* and Charles Smith in August 2000 reported extraordinary military-to-military exchanges. Norfolk, Virginia, houses the Joint Forces Command where "the U.S. military is developing its most advanced war-fighting techniques and doctrine — information known to be a target of Chinese military spying."

In late August 2000, the Clinton Pentagon escorted three PLA generals, China's own strategic military planners, from China's Academy of Military Sciences to the Norfolk facility. The Chinese Academy, the "most secretive and least visited" institute in China is developing RMA, a Revolution in Military Affairs. RMA is the use of high technology such as nuclear weapons, magnetic pulse and cyberwar to enable a weak, "asymmetrical," China to defeat a stronger foe: the USA. Much as Trojan horses, crossbows, catapults, gunpowder, fire and repeating rifles altered the military balance in history. So, too, might the RMA.

Incredibly, in August 2000, at the Kennedy School two U.S. generals and two admirals actually lectured 25 senior Chinese military (and intelligence) officers on American lessons of recent wars and its future concepts of fighting wars. They told the Chinese how to defeat the United States!

Outraged, Congress enacted the Smith/DeLay amendments to restrict U.S.-PRC military-to-military exchanges and to specifically prohibit PRC exposure to U.S. war fighting experiments.[4] In August 2000, Rep. Tom DeLay objected to "tour guides for People's Liberation Army officials visiting sensitive American military [installations] when only last week it stopped members of Congress [Christopher Cox] from meeting with the democratically-elected leader of Taiwan when he was visiting Los Angeles."[5]

According to Charles Smith in *WND*, during 2000 national security sources claimed American military attachés in Beijing and other military intelligence operations were closed down inside China. Poking out its own eyes and ears in China, the Clinton-Gore Administration was depending upon military exchanges — Red Chinese generals visiting the USA — to reveal Chinese military strategies and tactics.

Of course, according to Jasper Becker, a journalist living in China

---

[3] Don Feder, September 6, 2000
[4, 5] Gertz, *Washington Times*, August 24, 2000

and reporting on it for 20 years, "foreigners are rarely taken to military installations or allowed to see PLA forces taking part in exercises."

Just before the November 2000 election, Chairman of the Joint Chiefs of Staff, General Henry Shelton visited Beijing to meet with General Fu Quanyou, Defense Minister Chi Haotian, Foreign Minister Tang Jiaxuan and Central Military Commission Vice Chairman Zang Wannian. They discussed "mutual concern, mutual interest and also our military-to-military relationship," General Shelton said. "I also will be discussing… peace, prosperity and security…"[6] Peace in our time?

Shelton's appeasement was met with Chinese threats. They warned that U.S. missile defense for Taiwan would "by no means [be] accepted…" according to spokesman Zhu Bangzao. Defense Minister Chi Haotian *who has called a long war with the U.S. "inevitable"* demanded that the U.S. end all arms sales to Taiwan immediately. Shelton counterpart Fu Quanyou told Shelton that China would "never commit to giving up the use of force" over Taiwan. Chinese Premier Zhu Rongji, joined by a visiting Russian delegation, condemned U.S. missile defenses for Taiwan.[7] Perhaps for emphasis during Shelton's visit the Chinese completed their second test of their DF-31, a road

Minister of National Defense General Chi Haotian (left) escorts Secretary of Defense William S. Cohen at the Ministry of National Defense Headquarters in Beijing, China, on July 12, 2000, where they signed an agreement on the environment. — Department of Defense photo

---

6, 7 *Agence France-Presse*, November 3, 2000

mobile intercontinental ballistic missile many believe was configured to carry the W-88 miniature missile the Chinese likely stole from Los Alamos, very probably using Wen Ho Lee.

Accompanied by the verbal warnings, Shelton was promised he could view "live-fire Chinese military exercises." If so, he would be the first U.S. military officer to do so in the eight-year "reciprocal" relationship.

By December 2000, the lame duck Clinton-Gore Administration inked agreements with General Chi Hoatian and General Xiong Guangkai to expand military exchanges with China. Walter Slocombe said that war-promising Chinese military documents were merely "unhelpful." On December 15 yet another Red Chinese pledge to stop proliferating weapons of mass destruction "brightened the atmosphere." No pun intended, we presume. In the final weeks of Clinton's term, his holdover Slocombe pushed through a new 2001 military exchange program.

Clinton and Gore were beneficiaries of over $1 million in illegal foreign Chinese contributions and shamelessly appeased even those who are making plans for war with the United States. A photo of Al Gore amiably reviewing armed PLA troops at attention perhaps best shows the Clinton-Gore destruction of U.S. Intelligence capabilities against China. [cover, revised, *The Year of the Rat*] "Relations" could hardly be better.

In a provision of the fiscal 2001 defense-authorization act Congress required the President to present his exchange plan by March 31, 2001. As the Bush ascendance became certain on December 22, General Shelton suddenly discovered for the first time that China was a future threat. His term as Chairman of the Joint Chiefs would thankfully run out in September 2001 under the Bush Administration.

Many urged the Bush Administration to approve each and every military exchange *de novo*. The early Bush Administration seemed to waffle on military exchanges — in its initial review it decided at first to eliminate prior Clinton commitments after May 2001, then to eliminate them entirely, then on a case-by-case approach.[8]

In March 2001, Adm. Dennis Blair, chief of the Pacific Command, scheduled the first of 30 planned exchanges by U.S. and Chinese high-level military officers. "We seek to include China, not exclude China, from participation in multilateral activities common to the interests of all nations," said a Pentagon spokesman. During the Hainan incident contacts were reduced. After the release of American hostages in April, Lt. Cmdr. Don Jewell, the "action officer" for military exchanges said they were "on track... We're going ahead with it."[9]

---

[8] *Washington Times,* March 14, 2001; *UPI,* March 15, 2001; *NewsMax.com Wires,* March 15, 2001

[9] *NewsMax.com,* April 20, 2001

Finally, the Bush Administration withdrew invitations to Chinese officers to seminars at the Asia-Pacific Center for Security in Honolulu. It also instructed American officers to "minimize contact" with their Chinese counterparts and to reduce port calls in Hong Kong. In addition, a trip by Vice Admiral Paul Gaffney of U.S. National Defense University was canceled, visits by NDU scholars were canceled and a planned visit to the United States by a senior Chinese army officer, General Gu Bo Xiong was halted.[10]

Then, on May 3, 2001, President Bush told Beijing that he wanted "a positive relationship for both countries." Military contacts would have to be approved in advance, but not eliminated outright. "We're going to review all opportunities to interface with the Chinese," Bush said. "If it's a useless exercise and it doesn't make the relationship any better, then we won't do that. ...But what the Chinese must understand is that we'll be firm in our philosophy..." Meanwhile, "We are trying to calibrate our response to this incident in a very, very careful way to make sure we don't cut off our nose to spite our face, and I think we have done rather well," Colin Powell said.[11] On May 3, China, which regularly denied access to its facilities, stressed the importance of military ties with the United States: "Military to military exchanges have always been two-way and based on equality and consultation," a foreign ministry official told *Reuters*.

After the Chinese agreed to return the P-3 aircraft, on June 6, 2001, U.S. Defense Secretary Donald Rumsfeld said that limited military links with China would resume. "I have been approving things as we have gone along," he said. "Now, some (exchanges) are down the road."

While the Bush Administration has diminished military exchanges with China it has done so as a diplomatic tool, not as a security measure. That could very well be a mistake.

---

[10] *Reuters*
[11] *Chicago Tribune*, May 4, 2001

STEALTH INVASION:
Red Chinese Operations in North America

It is less noticed than Red Chinese generals sipping wine and eating tiny sandwiches in military exchanges at public events at Harvard and in the Clinton White House. Though occurring in broad daylight and in morning fog every day of the year, it is a "stealth invasion" of America's shores at every major American seaport on the West, Gulf and East Coasts. The invasion force is a fleet of Red Chinese ships, the merchant marine of Red China's People's Liberation Army (PLA), delivering millions of cargo containers of unknown content into the strategic waters of the U.S. and Canada every year.

The sloppy security that killed 17 and wounded 39 sailors on board the USS *Cole* is worse in U.S. homeports. Similarly, the number of U.S. forces exposed in Seattle and Norfolk are considerably greater

The author observed a COSCO vessel entering the Port of Long Beach. — photo by Ron Wilcox, June 2001

than the single reconnaissance plane forced down after an encounter in the South China Sea in international waters in April 2001. Millions of Americans and some of their armed forces are today in harm's way on U.S. soil.

Everyday Chinese vessels call unnoticed and uninspected. Usually the China Ocean Shipping Company (COSCO), and its shadow, the Orient Overseas Container Line (OOCL), follow the rules and fill out the paperwork. Reported instances of smuggling guns, drugs, technology, prostitutes and labor are rare. Indeed COSCO officials are publicly courted for their business at every port in North America. Billions in taxpayer's money are offered as inducements.

School children were once told the story of the Trojan horse used to smuggle soldiers inside the walls of Troy. Today no one talks of the millions of sealed containers aboard Red Chinese ships, let alone their cross-continental distribution by railcar and truck trailer to every town in America. Only 2% are physically checked for contents. An occasional story of drugs or human cargo makes the news. The high vulnerability of U.S. seaports to espionage and terrorism is seldom suspected and virtually never investigated.

Discerning the COSCO threat

While opposing the COSCO takeover of the Long Beach Naval Station and after a daylight inspection of Pier J in Long Beach in December 1999, the author decided to investigate the security of all U.S. seaports and home ported U.S. Naval forces. The successful terror attack upon the USS *Cole* renewed security concerns of others. Unfortunately this renewed interest was purchased by the blood of sailors and by the tears of families. The open Chinese attack upon an American reconnaissance plane and the holding of the U.S. crew hostage at Hainan Island was still another object lesson of a possible clear and present danger from China.

In 1997 Senator John McCain was concerned about the national security implications of awarding a taxpayer-subsidized contract for $157 million between COSCO and a Mobile, Alabama, shipbuilder. Yet the CIA, the Coast Guard and the Customs Service all told Congressmen Steve Horn and David Dreier that, "COSCO represents no threat to our national security."[1] Harold J. Creel, Maritime Commission Chairman, denied any COSCO threat but he testified that COSCO engaged in bribes, kickbacks and predatory pricing. "They are not profit-driven... They want to have their flag... on their ships," said Creel. Since COSCO is not driven by profits and is interested in flying the Red Chinese flag, it is clearly advertising its master, the People's Liberation Army, and it is an everyday available instrument of the

---

[1] *Washington Times*, April 4, 1997

military objectives of the People's Republic of China (PRC). Indeed, the PLA has forward-deployed about 100 of its COSCO fleet into the waters of the USA. [See Appendix A]

One of COSCO's potential threats is its vessels commingling with U.S. Navy ships within the waterways and chokepoints of strategic U.S. seaports. COSCO ships in Seattle and Tacoma in Puget Sound lie just off the Straits of Georgia and Juan de Fuca. There COSCO ships sail amidst many of the U.S. warships in its Pacific fleet. Similarly, COSCO also now sits in the middle of the U.S. Navy's Atlantic Fleet at Norfolk past Hampton Roads, the waterway entrance to Chesapeake Bay.

Since men and women of the USS *Cole* are dead and wounded because of a mere rubber dinghy, it is prudent to watch the PLA deployment of COSCO's worldwide fleet of 600 vessels. It is rational and reasonable to improve security measures for vessels, facilities and citizens at American seaports where COSCO calls.

Soon after the *Cole* disaster, WABC *Dateline* found it easy to move vessels amidst U.S. warships in Norfolk and New York. Later too did KFWB in Los Angeles.

Beijing-friendly families – Tung and Li

In addition to COSCO, U.S. intelligence and law enforcement agencies ought to add the Beijing-dependent, Tung family-owned Orient Overseas Container Line (OOCL) to its watch list.

It is long past mentioning that authorities should be aware of the presence of Beijing-tied Li Ka-Shing enterprises in the waterways of Vancouver (B.C.)-Seattle-Tacoma where the U.S. Navy home ports major submarine and destroyer forces and, currently, one aircraft carrier. Heightened security is desirable in those ports where Chinese commercial vessels, both COSCO and OOCL, commingle with the naval forces of the U.S. Navy, particularly in Seattle-Tacoma, Charleston, Norfolk and Long Island Sound. The problem with commingling is that one day a Chinese freighter may blow up a U.S. warship like the *Cole* or block chokepoints in key naval ports. Measures are needed to protect national security from COSCO and other PRC front companies such as Orient Overseas and Hutchison Whampoa.

Open secrets – commission reports "poor to fair" seaport security

The little-advertised, but long-named federal commission — the Interagency Commission on Crime and Security at U.S. Seaports — in the fall of 2000 completed an obtuse report that ploddingly revealed shocking evidence of rampant crime, corruption and slothful security at major American seaports.[2]

---

[2] Report... Fall 2000

The Interagency Commission made on-site surveys of 12 seaports of which seven — Charleston, Long Beach, Los Angeles, Miami, New Orleans, New York/New Jersey and Tacoma — are of interest because of COSCOs presence. In addition to these, this book also covers seaports in Portland, Seattle, Vancouver, New Orleans, Houston, Savannah, Norfolk and Halifax where COSCO and, often, OOCL, offer shipping services.

The Commission reported that indeed only 2% of all trade cargo is physically inspected despite widespread evidence of inaccurate or misleading paperwork. The FBI said U.S. ports are "highly vulnerable" to attack. The Interagency Commission said port security is "poor to fair."

There is no excuse for this terrible lack of even the most rudimentary security precautions at the seaports and in waterways of the United States. This is a matter of great import to our nation's security and economic interests. The failures of local and federal governments to have basic security safeguards in place are appallingly negligent.

Readiness for military mobilization lacking

Poor or fair security is unwarranted given the importance of seaports to our national security and economy.

- The U.S. Navy, Marine Corps, Army or Air Force have vital facilities within five of the 12 ports surveyed by the Interagency Commission on Crime and Security at U.S. Seaports.

- Thirteen other seaports have additional obligations to be ready for a national military mobilization in a war or a crisis. The Interagency Commission studied four and found them all wanting in adequate security for a mobilization, lacking readiness exercises, and having incomplete vulnerability/threat assessments.

- Nine of 12 ports had "no waterside security measures" to protect from foreign vessels (let alone rubber dinghys).

- Nine of 12 ports could be blocked at as few as one to three geographic chokepoints.

- "...U.S. seaports have become critical chokepoints for future military mobilizations... [for overseas operations]."

Rampant crime on our waterfronts

While concerns for espionage or terrorism at seaports go unaddressed, knowledge of crime waves on America's waterfronts have been known for perhaps a century. Massive underreported crime is known, but runs rampart on U.S. waterfronts.

Organized crime has little difficulty stealing cargoes or smuggling drugs or human beings. The Interagency Commission reported that organized crime is concealing drugs in cargoes at nine of the 12 ports it investigated. The Commission found that only three of 12 ports use modern technology to identify contraband or to verify shipments — in a few suspicious cases only.

Criminally-organized alien smuggling is common on the West Coast. Alien stowaways were found in 10 of 12 ports. "Immigration has no way of knowing whether manifested crews actually leave on the ship they arrive on... or remain illegally in the United States."

The CIA reported that 50,000 women and children enter the U.S. illegally each year to serve as virtual slaves and prostitutes, according to the *New York Times*. Some arrive in COSCO containers.

These vulnerabilities to crime are well known. Their implications for organized espionage and terrorism ought to be transparent. The Canadian Mounties, in their government-suppressed "Sidewinder" report, reveal intimate ties between the Chinese Triads (gangs) and the Communist PRC. Clearly, American ports are open to theft of technology and destruction of human life and property. So too are vital water, power and communications infrastructures closeby.

In contrast to these street crimes, there is near total silence and little apparent action to explore vulnerability to espionage — export of militarily valuable technology — or to terrorism.

Terrorism in closed containers?

Prior to the loss of 17 lives aboard a poorly-secured USS *Cole*, the FBI told the Interagency Commission that the vulnerability of U.S. seaports to terrorist attacks was high, but said the terrorist threat was low.

In other words, attacks upon U.S. ports were entirely in the hands of America's enemies who could choose the time and place of their attacks as long as our ports did nothing about their high vulnerability.

Eleven of 12 ports are located in urban areas where millions of innocent lives are in harm's way and where vital infrastructures (ports, roads, rail, telecommunications, water, electricity) are vulnerable to attack.

Nuclear, biological or chemical weapons, with or without missiles, might be secreted among the millions of cargo containers delivered to American ports on Red Chinese ships.

Typically, ports lack basic intelligence information about terrorist threats provided to others. The Commission said, "Increasing awareness of security-related threats among port facilities... and expanding the availability of threat information... would do much to alleviate this problem... The federal government should establish baseline vulnerability and threat assessment for terrorism at U.S. seaports."

The Interagency Commission said none of the dozen ports met "the minimum port security criteria." Only a third had barriers to halt or slow down a terrorist driving through fences. Half had "nonsecure" communications. With the exception of lighting and gates in most ports, persons and vehicles had easy physical access to most ports. Foreign sailors and domestic workers roam freely. Except for paper forms, foreign cargo is handled no differently than cargo from Kansas. It is inspected alongside domestic cargo in every port.

Smuggling U.S. technologies

Seaports are undefended against those who might acquire weapons, munitions and critical technology that affect national security." Federal inspectors working in remote locations spend more time behind computer terminals than on the docks. "The [Customs and Commerce] inspection and criminal investigation personnel... devoted to export transactions are only a small fraction of those devoted to imports..."[3] Shipper's Export Documents (SEDs), delivered as late as four days after a ship leaves port typically contain inaccurate, vague, misleading or false information. No wonder that over two years (1996-98) in the 12 ports, the Commission reported only 296 offenses, 26 arrests and 323 seizures valued at $33 million. "...[F]ederal agencies are probably detecting only a small portion of the controlled commodities that are being exported illegally," said the Commission. Surprisingly, there is no criminal punishment under law for illegal exports.

The unstated policy of local ports is perhaps "don't ask," and the policy of U.S. intelligence agencies is "don't tell." Our seaports are unaware of most security threats. The FBI, CIA, Customs, Coast Guard, local police and sheriffs tell port officials little or nothing about possible security threats. Our seaports are not ready for prime time, not prepared for attacks like that on the USS *Cole*.

Nobody is looking. The President, the Congress and other government agencies must do their jobs defending national security. "Don't know and don't tell" is a dangerous policy of willful blindness. Our highly-vulnerable seaports are open to Red Chinese vessels every day in every port.

U.S. Customs asleep on the docks?

The U.S. Customs Service is responsible for border enforcement, having authority to search any shipment that crosses the U.S. border.

---

[3] Interagency Commission on Crime and Security in U.S. Seaports, Fall 2000

One essential duty of the Customs Service is to cooperate with the State Department's Office of Defense Trade Controls in conducting end-use checks of exports. Who gets the product? What is it used for? The State Department sets criteria, but Customs carries them out.

As astonishing as it seems, despite the Cox Report and other intelligence agency evidence, during the entire Clinton-Gore Administration U.S. Customs Service indicted only one PRC entity for violating U.S. export laws. The China Aero Technology Import and Export Corporation (CATIC) was indicted for using U.S. B-1 and missile machine tools from McDonnell Douglas to manufacture military aircraft and silkworm missiles in Nanchang.[4] Meanwhile, Customs devoted considerable resources to interdicting imports of drugs, child pornography, counterfeit clothing and software and forced labor goods.

Customs "discrepancy" statistics show China very faithfully following Custom's rules and regulations for processing paperwork. COSCO is virtually always below the radar screen. COSCO virtually never appears in U.S. daily newspapers, seldom in business journals and infrequently in U.S. port websites. This stealth company quietly dominates container cargo ports throughout the U.S. COSCO does not draw attention to itself in its routine commerce in the U.S.

Though China (plus Hong Kong) was far and away the world's worst violator of slave labor, Customs reports in 1999 and 2000 shockingly said, "this [slave produced] merchandise... does not appear to be a large violation of the law." Only 250 people were prosecuted despite the CIA reporting a slave trade of 50,000 persons. Many local ports contined to catch handfuls of this wretched human cargo in COSCO containers on their docks. COSCO was seldom, if ever, mentioned as the carrier — sometimes with photos proving COSCO's complicity.

As its annual report shows, Customs did vigorously move to halt the import of Chinese artificial flowers, tea and other products through 20 detention orders and four findings in 1999. Yet, Customs appeared to give scant resources and made no mention on its website of preventing the export to China of U.S. nuclear, missile, stealth, fiberoptic and other technologies vital to our nation's defense. Custom's website shows only one Chinese company and three foreign nationals indicted for export violations.

U.S. Custom's automated export system flags all military goods destined for China as "error 853" and does not allow China a low value exemption from reporting detailed shipping information. Yet, in fiscal 1999, Customs apparently found hardly any instances of violations that it considered prosecutable except for the indictment of three foreign nationals (fiberoptic, stealth and antimissile technologies).[5]

Indeed, Customs has granted COSCO — the nearly exclusive

---

[4] *U.S. Customs Today,* January 2000
[5] *U.S. Customs, FY 1999 Accountability Report*

shipper to China and a PLA-PRC-owned entity — special processing of its cargoes usually accorded to private and to free world shippers. For COSCO these privileges include automated filings from remote locations and exemptions (since early 1997) from submitting cargo declarations with manifests and from presenting copies to Customs for review.

Are paperwork efficiencies worth the national security risks of potentially dangerous cargoes or exports of militarily valuable technologies escaping inspection?

Another vulnerability is Red Chinese-controlled freight forwarders, which often control the manifests, the paper trail on the contents of ships and containers. Freight forwarding is a legal business. The problem is the loyalties of Red Chinese company owners.

Kenneth Timmerman writing in the October 1997 issue of the *American Spectator* lists Red Chinese-controlled freight forwarders such as Pan Ocean Lines, North China Cargo, CU Transport, Inc. (a creature of the China National Foreign Trade Transportation Corporation) located in Alhambra, Rosemead and Monterey Park, California. In Compton, the China Interocean Transport, Inc. (China National Foreign Trade Transportation Corp.); in West Covina, CCIC North America, Inc. (China National Import and Export Commodities Inspection Corp.), and in El Segundo, Morrison Express.

The whole Clinton-Gore response to Chinese espionage was bizarre, as described by Johnny Chung of *WND*, "This White House Administration not only delivered Permanent Normal Trade Relations (PNTR), but it also called Taiwan an intelligence threat to the U.S. and listed the country as a terrorist threat along with Russia, China, North Korea, Serbian-controlled Bosnia, Vietnam, Syria, Iraq, Iran, Libya and Sudan."

Under Clinton-Gore the espionage threat of China inside the United States was undiscussed and unexplored. Under Bush there is heightened emphasis on the vulnerability of critical infrastructures, but the Clinton holdovers are focused almost entirely upon long-recognized threats to computer systems to the neglect of infrastructures such as telecommunications, electric, water, transport and seaports.

Kenneth Juster, Bush appointee to the Department of Commerce, told a conference on Information Security Assurance in May 2001 that he recognized the stakes — viability of our nation's infrastructures to continue delivering critical services essential to our defense, economy and way of life. What was needed was an appreciation of a need to establish and maintain security measures.

There is some hope. "…[W]e must confront the threats that come in a shipping container or in a suitcase." President George W. Bush, February 13, 2001, to U.S. Naval personnel in Norfolk, VA.

We will concentrate most of our attention upon Red Chinese presence in U.S. seaports.

A Red Chinese Sailor in Every U.S. Seaport

T he Red Chinese government owns the 600-ship China Ocean Shipping Company (COSCO), one of the world's largest container shipping companies. It operates as the merchant marine of the People's Liberation Army (PLA) and as such, has been caught transporting AK-47 rifles to street gangs, components of weapons of mass destruction to Iran, Iraq, Libya and North Korea. Yet COSCO has few critics and many friends.

The many American friends of COSCO

Old salts like the author's father, a career Navy man, remembered the days when signs saying "dogs and sailors keep off the grass" littered the lawns of American beach towns when U.S. sailors "hit the beach." Those days are gone. There are far fewer American sailors now and Red Chinese sailors are welcomed everywhere. In Long Beach, Boston and Seattle locals ooze with affection for foreign sailors — in particular those from COSCO.

With help from the Clinton White House, the City of Long Beach tried mightily to give the former U.S. Naval Station to COSCO and their local officials have actively aided COSCO's quest for a larger (secure) facility in the region. For nearly three years, the United States Intelligence Council (USIC) and its more than 350,000 petition signers implored leaders to reconsider their short-sighted interest in trade. Finally, only acts of Congress nixed a 20-year lease of the Long Beach Naval Station to China and also nudged the Port of Los Angeles out of a Pier 400 deal with COSCO.

COSCO CEO Wei Jiafu said, "All the big liners have terminals on the West Coast. We would still very much like to have one as well."[1] Maybe it does have its own terminal in Long Beach. Outwardly spurned, COSCO quietly stretched out and doubled its prior shared space at new berths at Pier J in Long Beach when an Israeli company vacated contiguous space and a Danish company planned to do the same, providing even more contiguous space to COSCO.

In the Los Angeles region proponents of increasing trade with China have largely silenced debate about the strategic importance of the Ports of Long Beach and Los Angeles to the nation's security.

COSCO's Beijing website happily exclaims — misspellings and all: "On May 8, [2000] the Long Beach Port Authority held a ceremony at the Hyatt Hotel for President Chen Zhongbiao of COSCO Group, in which President Chen got the honorary Long Beach Pilot Award. During the ceremony, Madam O'neill [sic], the mayor of Long Beach, expressed her sincere thanks for President Chen's support for the establishment of friendly cooperation between COSCO and Long Beach, especially under the complicated situation two years ago. The Chairman of Long Beach Port Committee song [sic] high praise for President Chen's superior working style and his devotion to the development of shipping industry of China and the U.S., and even the whole world. After the speech, he awarded President Chen the honorary Long Beach Pilot Award on behalf of Long Beach Port Authority."[2]

The city and port of Seattle actually surpass the Long Beach kowtow. Seattle genuflected with uniforms and music provided by a hopefully reluctant U.S. Navy. One suspects the U.S. Navy was keelhauled, dragooned and impressed against its will.

Commemorating the 20th anniversary of the China trade with Seattle in April 1999 a "...fireboat fired towering columns of water... [And].... a 13th [U.S.] Naval District band broke into 'It's a Small World.' The red and gold flag of the People's Republic of China and the Stars and Stripes were raised and snapped together...

"There is a larger meaning... connections with... one of the leading countries of the world in the next century," said Port of Seattle

---

[1] *Washington Times*, June 2, 2001
[2] COSCO website

Commission President Patricia Davis. "[The]... arrival of each Cosco ship... [is]... vital for world stability and security and prosperity..."[3]

So what is COSCO? What's the problem with thousands of jobs and billions of dollars of trade with China?

COSCO worldwide — Scale

COSCO is "one of the world's largest shipping lines, with more than 600 vessels, several hundred [300] subsidiary companies and [has] 80,000 employees handling trade in 150 countries," said Seattle-based COSCO spokesman Mike Foley in the April 19, 1999, issue of the *Seattle Post-Intelligencer*. According to its website "COSCO Group ships visit more than 1,200 ports."

Of COSCO's fleet of 600 vessels, close to 100 ships call on U.S. ports and about 300 use the Panama Canal. Its larger container vessels have a capacity of 5,250 TEU (Twenty-foot Equivalent Units).

In 1997, the volume of cargo carried by COSCO's world container fleet was 3.4 million TEUs over 653.4 billion ton-miles. Headquartered in Beijing, COSCO Group has major offices in Hong Kong, Japan, Singapore, USA, Europe, South Africa and Australia, etc. China Ocean Shipping Company Americas, Inc., has more than 85 subsidiaries and offices throughout the American continent with more than

COSCO vessel at Panama Canal. — *photo by Susan Blake*

---

[3] *Seattle Post-Intelligencer,* April 19, 1999

700 employees. COSCO Americas, Inc. is headquartered in Secaucus, New Jersey, upriver from the Port of New York.

COSCO is listed as a "red chip," a PRC-owned company, on the Hong Kong Stock exchange[4] and is seeking a co-listing on New York exchanges. Five subsidiaries have listings on the world's stock exchanges. COSCO floats loans in American markets. COSCO Group, Ltd. appointed BankBoston NA to arrange a $50 million loan to refinance debt.[5]

COSCO has an increasingly routine presence in America's ports. COSCO ships sail in and out of American ports every day — Charleston, Houston, New York, New Orleans, Norfolk, Oakland, Port Elizabeth (NJ), Portland (OR), Seattle and Tacoma. Others, like Boston and Newport, beg for their business.

In Washington, D.C., thanks to the adept leadership of Rep. Christopher Cox (R-CA), COSCO has received some unwanted notice. Congress issued the highly revealing report of Red Chinese theft of U.S. nuclear secrets and U.S. missile guidance technology. "The China Ocean Shipping Company (COSCO), the PRC's state-owned shipping company... operates under the direction of the Ministry of Foreign Trade and Economic Cooperation and answers to the PRC State Council..." The Clinton-Gore Administration suppressed further information within the full-classified Cox Report.

Perhaps the Bush Administration will see fit to reveal more about COSCO than did Clinton-Gore. In another House report: "Although presented as a commercial entity," according to the House Task Force on Terrorism and Unconventional Warfare, "COSCO is actually an arm of the Chinese military establishment."

The PLA's merchant marine

The China Ocean Shipping Company (COSCO) is quite simply the merchant marine of the People's Liberation Army of the People's Republic of China (PRC). The PRC refers to "COSCO ships as 'zhanjian' or warships and boasts that COSCO workers are and will be 'ready for battle into the next century'," according to *Year of the Rat*.

The Thompson Report and the Canadian Mounties have described COSCO as the merchant marine of the Chinese military. The Red Chinese government flat owns it. COSCO's Beijing website carries quotations from top Communist party officials. COSCO is intimately linked to the China International Trust and Investment Corp. (CITIC), a key fundraiser for the Chinese government and a technology-acquiring source for China's military. COSCO serves its master.

The *New American* in November 10, 1997, described COSCO as

---

[4] *Reuters*, May 15, 2000
[5] *Bloomberg News*, May 9, 2000

"hardly a typical state-owned shipping company. COSCO ships have been used to: ferry tanks to the Marxist regime in Burma, ship North Korean rocket fuel to Pakistan, smuggle heroin into Canada, ship AK-47s bound for California street gangs, technology smuggling to China." COSCO, the "shipping" company, purchased a Russian K-3 submarine from Finland.

"*The Clinton Administration has determined that additional information concerning COSCO that appears in the Select Committee's classified Final Report cannot be made public...*" [Cox Report]

Espionage and the clandestine

COSCO ships have been caught and cited for carrying components of weapons of mass destruction such as Chinese missile-technology and nuclear, chemical and biological weapons components, materials and fuels into North Korea, Pakistan, Syria, Iraq and Iran, according to U.S. intelligence and international authorities. COSCO has been repeatedly cited over many years including 1999, 2000, 2001.

Ominously, COSCO is "known to be associated with Chinese intelligence operations," according to Edward Timperlake and William Tripplet in their book *Year of the Rat*. Like Soviet trawlers before them, COSCO ships sail in the waterways and dock at strategic locations all across the globe and in every major American port. These locations enable them to intercept electronic communications everywhere.

COSCO Senior Advisor and owner of Hutchison Whampoa, operators of ports worldwide, "Li Ka-Shing is to the Chinese army intelligence HQ what Howard Hughes was for the CIA," says William Triplett, co-author of *Red Dragon Rising*.

Recently, the Chinese were caught monitoring Japanese radio signals and mapping undersea approaches to Japan for their submarines. In July 2000 a secret CIA report described Russian merchant ships gathering intelligence signals north of Puget Sound and the ports of Seattle and Tacoma. It is prudent to presume that, like the Russians, the Chinese are gathering intelligence in the USA with their forward-deployed assets — COSCO ships and agents.

Before a U.S. Senate Armed Services Committee hearing chaired by John Warner, Richard Delgaudio testified that Li Ka-Shing is "China's Red Billionaire." Delgaudio's testimony and his book *Perils in Panama* amply document China's threats to the Panama Canal and to the U.S. from missiles smuggled into Li's ports there.

The *New American* calls COSCO "a PLA-connected container shipping fleet that specializes in drug and weapon smuggling." In 1996 COSCO smuggled 2,000 AK-47 assault rifles into the Port of Oakland bound for Los Angeles gangs — the largest seizure of smuggled automatic weapons in U.S. history. Smuggled aboard the COSCO vessel *Empress Phoenix*, the weapons were "destined for Asian street gangs founded by illegal immigrants who were once members of the PLA's elite Red Guard," according to the *New American*.

Added Canada's *Globe and Mail* in a May 4, 1996, story: "Top officials of the two Beijing-based companies Norinco and Poly Technologies that make weapons for the Chinese military participated in the smuggling [of rifles into the United States]."

In February 1996, President Clinton met with Poly Technologies Chairman Wang Jun after taking a donation from Charlie Trie. A Rand report says, "Wang Jun is both director of China International Trust and Investment Corporation (CITIC) and Chairman of Poly Group, the arms trading company of the General Staff Department."

Wang Jun's employer of record is COSCO, according to the *New American*. "Wang Jun, chairman of the Poly Group, is a business partner with Ng Lap Seng, described by the *New American* as a "Macau mobster," who, in turn, is a business partner with Macau casino king Stanley Ho and through Charlie Trie, a conduit of other Chinese money to Clinton-Gore.

"Poly's U.S. subsidiaries were abruptly closed in August 1996," states a Rand Corporation report. "Allegedly, Poly's representative, Robert Ma, conspired with China North Industries Corporation's (NORINCO) representative, Richard Chen, and a number of businessmen in California to illegally import 2,000 AK-47s into the United States." Their customers were undercover U.S. Customs and Bureau of Alcohol, Tobacco and Firearms (BATF) agents.

COSCO has become a dominant force in modern container shipping in the world while the U.S. retreats from maritime activities vital to its own defense.

SURRENDERING THE HIGH SEAS
America's retreat from maritime responsibilities

In contrast to COSCO's massive merchant marine fleet of 600 vessels, the U.S. Navy Military Sealift Command operates only 110 ships across the globe. While these ships are identified as "USNS" (United States Naval Ships) they are not commissioned ships of the U.S. Navy.

Civilians man U.S. sealift ships, not military personnel.[6] In contrast, COSCO is large and under the absolute control of the People's Liberation Army.

Most U.S. sealift vessels are in reserve and require time to activate. Historically, the National Defense Reserve Fleet (NDRF) has activated up to 600 ships to meet sealift needs during the Korean War, Berlin Crisis, Suez Crisis, Vietnam War and to ship coal to Europe and grain to India. These historically proven needs aside, "Currently, the NDRF consists of [only] 258 vessels... However, 85 are no longer militarily useful and are slated for scrapping. In addition... another 51 ships are held... on a reimbursable basis. Forty-one of these are naval vessels awaiting disposal. These vessels are maintained at Benicia (Suisun Bay), California; Beaumont (Neches River), Texas, and Fort Eustis (James River), Virginia, and at designated outported berths."[7]

Thus, America's available defense reserve fleet, its NDRF ships, now consist of 143 ships — far less than the 600 found necessary several times since WWII and about equal to the 100 ships of COSCO's fleet servicing U.S. seaports alone.

In addition, American capacity to draw upon private U.S. shippers is quite limited. "U.S.-flag oceangoing vessels play a small role in carrying the nation's international commerce. ...[T]the United States ranks 26th in the number of [U.S. flagged] ships and 11th in total DWT (Dead Weight Tons). ...The United States ranks 13th in the number of tankers, 9th in tanker DWT, 8th in containerships and 6th in containership DWT." While, "approximately 45% of the world fleet by deadweight capacity calls at U.S. ports,[8] most is carried in foreign — increasingly Red Chinese — bottoms.

China leads the container revolution

Enclosed 20- and 40-foot-long metal containers are increasingly the standard of efficiency. Most containers are truck trailer sized bodies easily moved from truck to railcar to ship. Containers ease storage, retrieval and transfers of bulk cargo among ship, railcar or truck, but they are major security problems. Drugs, weapons and human beings are easily hidden from view and closed containers are difficult to inspect.

The latest container ships have a capacity of 5,200 20-foot equivalent container units (TEUs) or more. The ships require drafts of 40 to 46 feet when fully loaded.

---

[6] U.S. Navy website

[7] U.S. Department of Transportation, Bureau of Transportation Statistics, Maritime Administration, U.S. Coast Guard Maritime Trade and Transportation 1999, BTS99-02, Washington, D.C., 1999

[8] *U.S. Industry and Trade Outlook 1998*

COSCO vessel at the Panama Canal. — photo by Susan Blake

To accommodate megaships at U.S. ports, ship channels and berth depths must be at least 50 feet. Only five of the top 15 U.S. container ports — Baltimore, Tacoma, Hampton Roads [Norfolk], Long Beach and Seattle — have sufficient channel depths. Only the West Coast has adequate depths at dockside berths.

Ports need to improve terminal infrastructure — cranes, storage yards, and information systems — to handle the increased volumes of cargo from container ships. And on the land side there are higher volumes of rail and truck traffic. "Many ports have initiated expansion projects to accommodate these ships."[9]

Local port expansion projects of over a billion dollars are common as U.S. ports compete for new container traffic — much of it by Beijing-owned COSCO and the Beijing-friendly Orient Overseas Container Line (OOCL). While using taxpayer funds is common, the use or swapping of former military port facilities is well hidden by land swaps among shipping companies and by new Chinese holding companies in the transactions. As we shall see below, elements of such slick deals are found in Long Beach, Oakland, Charleston, New York and Newport.

The world's containership fleet increased 15% per year between 1993 and 1997 as the larger ships handling over 4,000 20-foot equivalent container units came into service.

Who is building ships? Japan and South Korea alone build a third

---

[9] *U.S. DOT MARAD 1998, 49–51*

of all new ships. China may be a distant third, but the U.S. ranks 14th, accounting for an anemic 1% of gross tonnage of ships built. In late September 2000 the *Washington Times* discovered a Clinton Pentagon proposal to build American auxiliary military ships overseas. After protests from Congress, Rear Adm. Craig Quigley claimed that Clinton's Defense Secretary William Cohen had "emphatically not" supported the idea.

The only remaining support ship builders in the U.S. are National Steel in San Diego and Avondale Industries in New Orleans. American shipbuilders shrunk from 21 firms in the 1980s to six defense shipyards in 2000.

Foreign flagged, built and manned vessels are landing on U.S. coasts — 42% of the value of U.S. waterborne trade hit the West Coast, 38% the East and 18% Gulf in 1997.[10] COSCO leads this foreign armada.

The ports of Long Beach and Los Angeles dominate West Coast trade, but waterways contiguous to the ports of Vancouver, B.C., Seattle and Tacoma are strategic assets for U.S. Navy submarine and aircraft carrier operations on the Pacific Rim. The port of New York/ New Jersey leads the East Coast in both value ($68 billion) and in containers (1.7 million TEUs) handled in 1997, but Charleston and Norfolk also are major container ports. The Gulf ports of Houston and New Orleans handle bulk commodities and crude petroleum making them the top two U.S. ports by gross tonnage.

COSCO's role in Red China's naval strategy

There is much evidence suggesting that COSCO performs duties above and beyond its role in commerce. It may be the hidden "naval arm" of the People's Liberation Army of the People's Republic of China. As indicated above, the Red Chinese government refers to "COSCO ships as 'zhanjian' or warships and boasts that COSCO workers are and will be 'ready for battle into the next century'," according to authors of the *Year of the Rat*. "There is a consensus among military specialists that China is prioritizing two areas of military growth: its missile program and its navy. COSCO is essential to its naval program."

China seems to be preparing to contest with the U.S. Navy, Taiwan, Korea and Japan not only in its own region in the East China Sea and the South China Sea, but it is also beginning to project its power far beyond to the Philippines, Indonesia and the Marshall Islands in the deep blue Pacific. Six hundred COSCO merchant vessels do not yet appear as major combatants anywhere. They perform other functions of naval strategy — COSCO is China's forward-deployed naval force across the globe.

---

[10] *U.S. DOT Census 1997, table 1069; U.S. DOT MARAD 1998*

China's naval strategy for COSCO might be described as follows: Some vessels might conceivably serve as platforms for guns, cruise missiles or theater ballistic missiles as well as containers for hiding and transporting nuclear, biological and chemical weapons into the homelands of its enemies. They might serve as mobile bases for the cyberwar much discussed as part of China's RMA (Revolution in Military Affairs).

Properly equipped COSCO ships can provide signals intelligence from every important U.S. seaport.

Richard Delgaudio, in *Perils in Panama,* citing Admiral Thomas Moorer shows how COSCO can secretly deploy an intermediate-range nuclear missile at Li Ka-Shing's Panama ports to threaten 100 or more U.S. cities.

COSCO might conceivably serve as an expeditionary force forward-deployed exercising power far from China with or without guns or missiles mounted on its decks.

The U.S. Navy describes naval forces as "sea-based, self-contained and self-sustaining... relatively unconstrained by regional infrastructure requirements or restrictions. Further, naval forces can exploit the freedom of maneuver afforded by the seas... [further the U.S. Navy continues]

Mobility and adaptability

"Naval forces can operate anywhere on the oceans, free of diplomatic restraint. As such, they have an unmatched ability to operate forward continuously, react to contingencies... and act as the enabling force for follow-on Army and Air Force power...

Presence and visibility

"Ships can be purposely conspicuous or exceptionally difficult to detect. In peacetime... visibility... signal[s] interest, readiness and ability to act if a crisis brews. The same ships, stationed close in, on the horizon, just over it, or in unlocatable places and circumstances, can be used as needed in crisis or conflict. With the ability to cumulate forces, naval power can be adjusted or scaled at will, increasing or decreasing pressure... as... leadership chooses to raise or lower... commitment, and engage or disengage much more easily than land-based forces... the enduring attractiveness of naval power is the flexibility that stems from these inherent characteristics and attributes. Investments in the Navy and Marine Corps are like money in the bank. We do not need to know precisely how and where we will use this resource in order to see its value — indeed our value is greater because we are useful virtually anywhere and anytime. Our expeditionary character, mobility, adaptability, variable visibility and cooperative and independent capabilities...

an especially relevant and useful force. Entering this new century, the technology, information, strike and telecommunications revolutions are rapidly undoing... bounds on naval power. ...Communications capacities... have increased by several orders of magnitude. Information processing capabilities have expanded concomitantly. Sensor and surveillance systems provide ship-based forces with information about and insights into the land environment that can equal that of land-based forces."[11]

The China Ocean Shipping Company has a vast fleet capable of the classic uses of sea power. It also has additional naval assets in the hands of influential allies in the ports and shipping business. These include Li Ka-Shing and Tung family of Orient Overseas Container Line (OOCL).

COSCO's reserve forces: other friends in the Navy business

The China Ocean Shipping Company does not work alone. Some surprising friends supplement its worldwide web — a Chinese billionaire operating ports across the globe, former U.S. Secretaries of State and a "shadow" container company bailed out by the Chinese Mafia and probably the Chinese Communist Party itself.

The "Red Billionaire" — Li Ka-Shing

In *Perils in Panama* and in testimony before the U.S. Senate, USIC chairman Richard Delgaudio has detailed the career and activities of Li Ka-Shing.

A plastic flower king at 30, Li met Y.K. Pao, a Hong Kong banker, who introduced him to banker Michael Sandberg. Sandberg was looking for a Chinese person with the best *guanxi* (influence) to the Beijing leadership. Li was just the right man. Sandberg helped Li get a bargain price for his bank's 22% stake in a British-owned *hong* (company) — Hutchison Whampoa. Today Li Ka-Shing's worldwide interests in ports, water, energy, telecommunications have made him one of the world's richest men. As the head of Hutchison Whampoa, Li owns and operates strategically located port facilities at both ends of the Panama Canal.

By late 1999, a secret "Intelligence Assessment" by the U.S. Army's Southern Command Joint Intelligence Center said, "Li Ka-Shing, Hutchison Whampoa's owner, has extensive business ties in Beijing and has compelling financial reasons to maintain a good relationship with Beijing. ...Hutchison's containerized shipping facilities

---

[11] U.S. Navy, *Posture Statement 2000*

in the Panama Canal, as well as the Bahamas, could provide a conduit for illegal shipments of technology or prohibited items from the West to the PRC, or facilitate the movement of arms and other prohibited items into the Americas."

Li Ka-Shing has a longstanding relationship with Red China's bloody communist dictatorship, dating back to the 1970s with Deng Xioaping. *Nikkei Weekly* reports that Li Ka-Shing "converted to the pro-China camp in the late 1980s" and "started establishing close relations with the family of Deng Xiaoping by helping Chinese companies affiliated with the PLA..." Li Ka-Shing publicly mourned the death of Deng the day after he died.[12] At the same time, a "small group of demonstrators staged a demonstration against Deng Xiaoping." One demonstrator asked "why do people mourn him today, and not remember" that Deng ordered the troops to massacre the peaceful protesters at Tiananmen Square.[13]

In his biography, *Li Ka-Shing: Hong Kong's Elusive Billionaire,* Anthony B. Chan describes many of the intimate ties between Li and Red China. On April 28, 1992, Li received an honorary degree from Red China's Beijing University. Granting the honors upon Li was none other than Jiang Zemin, the current dictator of Red China. Mr. Chan said, it was "making public what in private any China-watcher had long known — that even Beijing was capable of loving the most revered capitalist in Hong Kong." (*Li Ka-Shing*, p.1) *The Financial Times* reported (March 13, 1998): Li Ka-Shing has a picture of Communist China's leader, Jiang Zemin, in his office.

The communists could always count on Li because in 1989, "He never showed distress over [the massacre at] Tiananmen... or castigated Beijing for its actions. As Li later explained: 'I was of course saddened [by the Tiananmen massacre]. But as a Chinese, China is my motherland. No matter what happened, I am still willing to work for the future of my country.'" (*Li Ka-Shing*, p.5) Similarly, visitors to Shantou University see a video of Li Ka-Shing, "My only true purpose is to contribute what I can to my... motherland. It is my life purpose."[14]

Li has also "been a close friend of General Ji Shengde, former military intelligence director of the PLA... and is still close to General Xiong Guangkai... General Ji's superior," according to journalist Peter Zhang. Li Ka-Shing is honored as a citizen of Red China in Shantou, Guangzhou, Shenzhen, Nanhai, Foshan, Jiangmen and Chaozhou.

Li Ka-Shing's vast global shipping empire also requires watching because of his intimate connection to COSCO as its Honorary Senior Advisor. COSCO's Beijing website says: "Mr. Li is one of Hong Kong's most prominent businessmen; as Chairman & Managing Director of Cheung Kong Holdings and Hutchison Whampoa, Ltd., Hong Kong he requires no further [sic] introduction."

12, 13 *Agence France-Presse,* February 20-21, 1997
14 Jasper Becker, *The Chinese,* preprint 2000

"MR. LI IS ONE OF HONG KONG'S MOST PROMINENT BUSINESSMEN; AS CHAIRMAN & MANAGING DIRECTOR OF CHEUNG KONG HOLDINGS AND HUTCHISON WHAMPOA, LTD., HONG KONG HE REQUIRES NO FORTHER [SIC] INTRODUCTION."

China military specialist William Triplett, co-author of *Red Dragon Rising* describes Ka-Shing as "the banker" for the Chinese army. The Rand Corporation, the U.S. Bureau of Export Affairs and the U.S. Embassy in Beijing, all report that Li Ka-Shing and his companies serve the Chinese military as financiers and acquirers of high technology for the PLA.[15]

Li Ka-Shing is a major investor in the China International Trust and Investment Corporation (CITIC). Both the White House in 1994 and the Rand Corporation in 1997 revealed Li Ka-Shing's role in CITIC. As Charles Smith reports for *WorldNetDaily* "According to the 1994 White House dossier, Li Ka-Shing is a 'member of the board of directors of the China International Trust and Investment Corporation (CITIC).' The CITIC bank is also more than it seems. The Rand report said, "CITIC does enter into business partnerships with, and provide logistical assistance to, PLA and defense-industrial companies like Poly (Technologies)." Poly Technologies, Ltd. is the primary commercial arm of the PLA General Staff Department's Equipment Sub-Department. CITIC, according to the Rand Corporation, "became identified with the PLA as a result of the scandal surrounding (Poly Technologies chairman) Wang Jun and his visit to the White House on 6 February 1996."

Li Ka-Shing's strategic investments

According to the 1994 dossier provided to participants in a trade mission, Li has "significant economic and political ties to China" including investments in a "power station, a highway construction project and a large contribution to Shantou University."[16]

In 1997, the Rand Corporation's secret report on the "Chinese defense industry" revealed, according to Charles Smith, Li Ka-Shing's direct connections to the Chinese military. "Hutchison Whampoa of

---

[15, 16] Charles Smith, *WorldNetDaily*

Hong Kong, controlled by Hong Kong billionaire Li Ka-Shing, is also negotiating for PLA wireless system contracts, which would build upon his equity interest in (Chinese army) Poly-owned Yangpu Land Development Company."

"Li is no ordinary investor. Just as British imperialism followed trade, Chinese military intelligence always follows Li," wrote Australian journalist Peter Zhang.[17]

The author's search of recent financial and stock market news reveals Li Ka-Shing, his family and his companies are heavily invested in infrastructure investments worldwide — Internet, telecommunications, telephones, cable, electricity, water, port operations, oil, power plants and apparently whatever else his friends in Beijing want. As one example, Li is a major partner in Global Crossing, a company laying fiberoptic cable across the Pacific linking Hong Kong and the U.S. "The largest pipes the world has seen."[18] Li has hands on infrastructures critical to the survival of modern world.

China's new military doctrines — a Revolution in Military Affairs (RMA), — advocate cyberwar against the Internet and disruptions of telecommunications. This doctrine taken with the Chinese appreciation of the vulnerability of infrastructures is disturbing — given its possible use of agents to exploit Li Ka-Shing in strategic industries and locations around the world. Prudent intelligence services must keep a close watch.

COSCO senior advisory board member, Li Ka-Shing, has his own shipping empire mostly concentrated in port facilities used by COSCO outside of the USA. Li's principal property holding company Cheung Kong owns a maritime arm, Hutchison Port Holdings Ltd. (HPH). HPH has 18 major ports around the world (four in the U.K. alone) and eight other affiliates. Li's companies recently handled 10% of the world's global shipments. Li could shut down big pieces of the world's economy with an order from Beijing.

Hong Kong International Holdings (HIT) operates at Container Terminals 4, 6 and 7 in Hong Kong and, through its joint venture with COSCO, at Terminal 8 East. In 1996, HIT was offered the right to develop and operate two berths in Container Terminal 9 (CT9). HPH owns three other incomplete container terminals in Hong Kong.

HPH is purchasing port facilities at the Suez Canal, owns Frazer docks in Vancouver, and has interests in other shipping container companies.

Li Ka-Shing's globe-spanning container facilities include: Freeport Container Port, Bahamas; Panama Ports Company, Balboa and Christobal; Port of Felixstowe, Harwich International Port and Thamesport in the U.K.; Europe Combined Terminals, Rotterdam; Port Said,

---

[17] March 2000
[18] Asian internet source, TechBuddha

Eygpt; Jakarta International Container Terminals, Jakarta's Koja Container Terminal; Myanmar International Terminals (Burma); Thilawa, Yangon.

Indeed, Li's Hutchison Whampoa is the only company that Red China trusts to run its own ports, most of south China's seaborne trade. Li Ka-Shing operates port facilities in Shanghai, Yantian, Shenzhen, Nanhai, Jiangmen, Zhuhai (Jiuzhou), Shantou, Xiamen, Zhuhai (Gaolan), Hong Kong and Nigbo.

Joe Studwell wrote in *Journal of Commerce* of Hutchison Whampoa's "cozy relationship" with Red China, "close as lips and teeth."

A former Secretary of State — Alexander Haig

Li serves with retired General Alexander M. Haig, Jr. as a COSCO advisor, according to the COSCO Beijing website in the first week of June 2000. Alexander Haig, former NATO Commander, Secretary of State, Presidential Chief of Staff, has been a paid "domestic and overseas senior honorary advisor" to COSCO. Haig lobbied to obtain the Naval Station in Long Beach for the Chinese.

Haig, owner of Worldwide Associates, advises United Technologies, a manufacturer of jet engines, air conditioners and elevators. The company has made billions in 17 joint ventures in China. It is reminiscent of Armand Hammer's exclusive franchises in the Soviet Union for pencils, asbestos, chemicals, artwork, banking, medicines and oil. Hammer was a secret agent of the Soviet Union. How deep have the Red Chinese penetrated into the life of Alexander Haig who announced "I am in charge" after the attemped assassination of Ronald Reagan?

As we shall see below, Haig is just one of six, yes six, former Secretaries of State (Henry Kissinger, George Shultz, Warren Christopher, Lawrence Eagleburger and Cyrus Vance) who publicly support Permanent Normal Trade Relations (PNTR) with Red China — whatever its record on hostage taking, nuclear espionage, human rights or weapons sales. Bernstein and Munro mince no words: "Kissinger and Haig are the two most conspicuous practitioners of this corrupt trade, and also the most slavishly devoted to the Beijing party line."

The quiet little company in COSCO's "shadow"

According to the Royal Canadian Mounted Police, Li Ka-Shing is very connected to Tung Chee-Hwa, the Beijing-appointed Chief Executive of Hong Kong, and shares many ventures with the Tung family company Orient Overseas Container Line (OOCL).

Orient Overseas (International) Ltd. (OOIL) has a 23% stake in $1.8 billion Oriental Plaza in Beijing. The OOCL Tungs are backed by Richard Li (Pacific Century) and Li Ka-Shing (Hutchison).

The brothers Tung of Hong Kong have a successful family business and profitable political relations with Beijing. Younger brother C.C. Tung, chairman of the OOCL since 1996 is a member of advisory boards for both COSCO and the Panama Canal. Rescued from bankruptcy by Beijing and Li Ka-Shing, C.C.'s older brother Tung Chee-Hwa was CEO of Orient Overseas until he was chosen by Beijing to run Hong Kong as its chief executive after the Communist takeover in July 1997.

Despite Tung's high position, a man named Henry Fok may really be "the puppet master in Hong Kong." In 1986 when Tung Chee-Hwa's OOCL shipping business was on the brink of bankruptcy owing some $2.7 billion to its creditors, Red Chinese interests came up with the $120 million he needed to stay in business. They restructured $1.6 billion in debt and declared $1 billion of it as equity. Pretty fancy bookkeeping. The Justice Department identified Fok as member of the Chinese Mafia triad and a Hong Kong businessman with extensive ties to the Red Chinese. It is widely believed that Henry Fok brokered bridge loans from Li Ka-Shing and PLA-owned COSCO to keep Orient Overseas afloat. Fok was a decades-long Communist Party activist who assisted the PRC during the Korean War.[19] "Further support for Tung in Peking came from Li Ka-Shing, who also helped rescue Orient Overseas."[20]

According to the *Far Eastern Economic Review*, Fok and his Red partners invested still again two years after the bailout, "giving them a key role in the restructuring of the Tung empire." Though having a financial stake in Orient Overseas International, they allowed Tung to recover equity very quickly. In 1987 Tung's wealth was "peanuts." A vehicle called Tung Holdings Trust (THT) held 65% of the company that controlled 74.6% of Orient. Fok acquired 27.48% of THT in 1989. In 1991 Tung borrowed to buy back 23% from Fok. In 1992 debts were converted to Tung shares of Orient Overseas. By 1996 Tung had recovered 57.6% of a now very profitable company. The Tung brothers are presumably very grateful to such generous friends.

One well-placed source (nameless when discussing Fok) says: "Henry Fok could become the next leader of Hong Kong just by asking the Chinese for it. But Fok seems to have concluded that he can exercise all the power he wants through his man, Tung Chee-Hwa, while maintaining the very low profile he [Fok] craves."[21]

His financial future secure and his loyalty certain, Beijing appointed Tung Chee-Hwa to become Hong Kong's executive officer and his brother C.C. Tung took over OOCL in October 1996.[22]

---

[19] Chapter 8, *The Year of the Rat*
[20] Dr.Karl-Heinz Ludwig, Ursulastr. 5 D-80802, Münich, Germany
[21] *Forbes Today*, November 18, 1996
[22] *Henry Who: A Friend Indeed*, by Simon Fluendy; *Far Eastern Economic Review*, January 9, 1997; *Fortune*, April 1, 1996

In late June 2000 the *South China Morning Post* reported that Chinese leaders in Beijing "told a group of visiting Hong Kong tycoons they should support Hong Kong Chief Executive Tung Chee-Hwa for a second term in exchange for favorable business treatment." The paper's largest shareholder, Robert Kuok, complained that the reporter, Willy Lam, didn't appreciate "manifestations of patriotism to the mother."[23] Chinese President Jiang Zemin "lashed out at journalists [Lam] for asking whether Tung was the 'emperor's choice' to serve for another five-year term," reported *Reuters* on November 11, 2000. Demoted as China editor Lam resigned.[24]

A Beijing revitalized OOCL is back as "one of the world's largest international integrated containerised businesses" according to its website. In 2000 OOCL had 13 offices and very extensive business activities in the People's Republic of China and 160 offices in 50 other countries. With 21 branches in China, OOCL "covers virtually every province and major trade center." OOCL calls at 13 Chinese ports — Dalian, Fuqing, Fuzhou, Huangpu, Ningbo, Qingdao, Shanghai, Shantou, Shekou, Taiping, Xiamen, Xingang and Yantian. Li Ka-Shing operates many of these ports including where the Tung's OOCL also calls — Shanghai, Yantian, Shantou, Xiamen and Nigbo.

In the United States OOCL operates in many of the same ports as COSCO. OOCL in the U.S. is headquartered in Pleasanton, CA, in the San Francisco Bay area. OOCL has service offices in the coastal cities of Boston, Charleston, Houston, Long Beach, New York, Seattle and Vancouver, B.C. as well as Panama. In addition to services in cities with OOCL offices, OOCL ships also deliver cargoes to Savannah, Norfolk, Miami, Los Angeles and Oakland.

OOCL owns Long Beach Container Terminal at berths 6-10 of Pier F in Long Beach, Global Terminal in New Jersey, Howland Hook on Staten Island, New York, and Deltaport and Vanterm vessel berths on Stewart St. and Roberts Bank in Vancouver, B.C.

OOCL claims its business in Vancouver and New York-New Jersey was particularly profitable in 2000. Its Long Beach terminal was twice cited as the "Best Container Terminal Operator in North America." Given Orient Overseas' intimate ties to Beijing, U.S. intelligence agencies ought to keep close watch on OOCL.

A clear and present danger

Every American port competes for ships and sells itself as "having quick turnaround times and efficient operating systems." Indeed, "the contest to have the most efficient and modern facilities is not new... Shipping lines are undergoing a lot of consolidation — and the competition... [can]... get even more intense... [a] bidding war between

---

[23, 24] *Reuters*, November 4, 2000

East Coast ports erupted [in 1998]... when Maersk Sealand... owned by the Danish industrial group A.P. Moller, threatened to move its hub out of New York," said Ken Cottrill, logistics and maritime editor at *Traffic World*.

"EVERYONE WAS FALLING ALL OVER THEMSELVES TO OFFER THEM TAX BREAKS AND THE BEST POSSIBLE FACILITIES."

— ATLANTA BUSINESS CHRONICLE, AUGUST 7, 2000

Competition for business among America's ports is a national phenomenon that has pushed considerations of national security entirely outside the scope of local thinking. Persons favoring free markets and competition argue that local efforts to aid COSCO and OOCL are critical to successful trade with China. Yet commerce may come at a high cost — our nation's defense.

The Beijing-owned COSCO security problem is not confined to Long Beach/Los Angeles, which first gave rise to public concerns about the loss of a naval base. It is nationwide. COSCO ships sail in and out of American ports every day — Charleston, Houston, New York, New Orleans, Norfolk, Oakland, Port Elizabeth (NJ), Portland (OR), Seattle, Tacoma and contiguous Vancouver, B.C., and, of course, OCCL services Boston, Charleston, Houston, Long Beach, Los Angeles, New York, Norfolk, Miami, Oakland, Savannah, Seattle, Vancouver, B.C., and Panama.

As the Interagency Commission revealed most American seaports have "fair to poor" security, rampant crime, corruption and high vulnerability to terrorist attacks. It is in this context that it is prudent to alert the public and port authorities to the potential security risks presented by Beijing-owned COSCO and perhaps Beijing-intimate OOCL.

More CIA and NSC resources must be devoted to preventing the export of U.S. military secrets to China. Moreover, Congress and the Bush Administration must budget additional funds to the CIA, NSC, NSA, Customs, FBI and other agencies to halt such exports dangerous to our nation's survival.

The Bush Administration and Congress ought to provide Customs with the resources necessary to perform its export control duties. For example, Custom's Automated Export System (AES) can account for only 39% of all U.S. exports and its Automated Commercial System is near meltdown. A new Automated Commercial Environment (ACE), system needs funding of $130 million.

At the very least COSCO's ubiquitous presence on U.S. soil must be considered a possible instrument of espionage for Red China as well as the major conveyance of revenue in the trade deficit financing China's military modernization. In the worst case, COSCO may comprise the forward-deployed forces of an enemy who has already achieved a "stealth invasion" on our home shores.

Free from the scrutiny of U.S. authorities, COSCO and other front companies and other agents of the PRC may conduct any clandestine activities they choose: intelligence gathering, theft and transport of U.S. high technology to the PRC, and smuggling of arms, slave labor, prostitution, drugs — or weapons of mass destruction — onto our shores.

COSCO was caught smuggling 2,000 AK-47 assault rifles bound for Los Angeles street gangs in 1996 — the largest seizure of smuggled automatic weapons in U.S. history. What is to stop it from smuggling nuclear, biological or chemical weapons into a major U.S. seaport? Virtually nothing.

A hundred COSCO ships and millions of unopened and uninspected containers are a clear and present danger — perhaps recognizable by President Bush who has said, "With shared intelligence and enforcement, we must confront the threats that come in a shipping container or in a suitcase." — *President George W. Bush, February 13, 2001, to U.S. Naval personnel in Norfolk, VA.*

We now detail the specifics of COSCO's presence in particular U.S. seaports and later turn to front companies and to military exchanges.

COSCO in Pacific Coast Ports
Long Beach, Los Angeles, Portland-Vancouver, Seattle-Tacoma and Vancouver, B.C.

Ports of Long Beach and Los Angeles —
strategic gateway to the USA

Once grudging host to thousands of sailors storming its rough and tumble bars, hotels, and renowned Pike roller coaster theme park, Long Beach is now a gentrified beach town. Long Beach welcomed the *Queen Mary* as it was throwing the U.S. Navy out. In 2000 the U.S. Navy homeported no combat ships in Long Beach. None. Zero. The ships have gone — to mothballs, to Seattle and to San Diego, every one.

The city fathers of Long Beach, with the able assistance of the Clinton White House, tried mightily (and failed) to give the shuttered, and then demolished U.S. Naval Station to Red China's COSCO. Unwelcome, the U.S. Navy also closed the Long Beach Naval Shipyard and with it, shipbuilding, conversions and repairs. Down the road it closed the Marine Corps Air Station in El Toro and the Marine Corps Air Station in Tustin.

In contrast, the welcome wagon has come out for COSCO's operations in America's economically most strategic seaport complexes.

The man-made ports of Long Beach and Los Angeles in San Pedro Bay are by far the highest volume ports in the nation. The Port of Los Angeles accounts for 259,000 jobs and $1.4 billion in state and local tax revenue. Statewide, the port industry accounts for 1.2 million jobs and $21.8 billion in personal income. With ready access to Southern California's expansive rail and road network, the ports of Long Beach and Los Angeles are America's principal trade gateway to the world, to the 17 million people in the region and — by truck and rail — to commerce all across the continental United States.

With 3,000 acres spread across six square miles — Long Beach is the busiest cargo container port in the United States. It has a deep dredged channel of 76 feet. The equivalent of 4.8 million 20-foot cargo containers (TEUs) crossed Long Beach's seven container terminals in 1999-2000 with a value of $89 billion.

Similarly, the contiguous Port of Los Angeles is the second busiest port in the United States (eighth busiest in the world). Its 28 terminals on 28 miles of waterfront sprawl across 11¾ square miles. All shipping channels are 45 feet. It had 3.5 million TEUs crossing its piers in 1999 and a cargo value of $79.3 billion in 1998.

China trade requires port expansions

China is Los Angeles' number-two customer at $18.9 billion, closely behind Japan at $20.9 billion. (Taiwan, $6.2 billion; South Korea, $2.4 billion.) In anticipation of a doubling or tripling of cargoes in 15 to 20 years — much of it from China — the ports of Long Beach and Los Angeles are constructing new piers (S and 400). The massive landfill to construct Pier S in Long Beach used 700 trucks a day and four million tons of dirt from 30 locations. The fill goes to a depth of 15 feet on 150 acres at a cost of $33 million dollars. It's valuable real estate.

In the contiguous Port of Los Angeles the Pier 400 container terminal covers 484 acres — about 366 football fields. Pier 400 will be the world's largest privately-owned container terminal. The Port will invest $500 million in improvements. In late 2000 Congress set aside $750,000 to begin engineering to deepen the main channel at the Port of Los Angeles.

On August 23, 2000, the Port of Long Beach docked the largest ship to ever berth in U.S. West Coast, the *Stena Commerce* at 300,144 dwt., 1,108 feet long and 190 feet wide. When Long Beach completes dredging its Queens Gate opening in the breakwater to 76 feet it will regularly dock larger ships.

Rapid growth and rail gridlock have pressed port authorities to make major port expansions and to support the Alameda Corridor project. Rail mergers, cargo volume and labor shortages have exacerbated congestion at the California ports.[1]

Alameda Corridor

Pier 400 will also be the southern end of the Alameda Corridor transportation project. Alameda Corridor will radically alter railroad and highway access to the ports of Long Beach and Los Angeles. The Alameda Corridor reshapes 90 miles of rail with 200 at-grade roadway crossings into new 20-mile-long, high-capacity and fully grade-separated railways linking the ports with national railroads. It also widens the truck routes paralleling the railway. Current truck and train traffic adds to the region's legendary gridlock. The project will relieve congestion.

---

[1] *Business Journal,* Portland, OR, November 3, 1997

COSCO objectives in the Los Angeles region

Home of the first and second largest ports in the USA and gateway to both the Pacific Rim and to the American Heartland, the ports of Los Angeles and Long Beach have immeasurable strategic value to Red China and to the United States.

The danger is of COSCO gaining a secure "West Coast... naval base on U.S. soil... to transfer secret high-tech equipment back to the People's Liberation Army, or PLA, in sealed [un-inspected] containers aboard huge COSCO ships."[2]

During December 1999, the author conducted daylight roadside observations of COSCO security at its shared facility at Pier J in Long Beach. In June 2000 he led a boat tour of the harbor to observe COSCO's activities from the water.

COSCO does <u>not</u> now operate, control or protect its own exclusive port facilities and that is why COSCO originally wanted the U.S. Naval Station so badly.

COSCO's current operations are open to public view (close to the *Queen Mary*, a scenic drive, sailing and fishing); are shared with five other companies at berths 232-234 (including Taiwan); and easy for U.S. security agencies — if they chose — to conduct unannounced inspections.

On any day anyone can drive down the public road entering Pier J. One can see COSCO containers at berths 232 through 234, cranes loading COSCO containers, an unguarded security gate, COSCO company truck tractors entering International Transport Services (ITS) terminal and ITS's terminal open to its public parking lot. An ITS sign shows COSCO sharing the ITS terminal with Taiwan's Yang Ming Marine, K-Line, Mexican Line, and Great Western SS Co. on a cramped 123 acres.

Meanwhile, Oriental Overseas Container Line, whose CEO, C.C. Tung, sits on the COSCO and Panama Canal advisory boards, owns Long Beach Container Terminal at berths 6-10 of Pier F in Long Beach. Its Long Beach Terminal has twice been cited as the "Best Container Operator in North America."

Once operating greatly depreciated facilities, OOCL owes its survival and subsequent success to Red Chinese loans. Its former CEO, older brother Tung Chee-Hwa, was chosen by Beijing to run Hong Kong.

Long Beach Naval Station

Before the AK-47 incident, after the active intervention of the Clinton Administration[3] COSCO had obtained a 20-year lease of the

---

[2] *Insight*
[3] *WorldNetDaily, Insight and New York Times*, March 13 and May 9, 1997

THE PORT OF LONG BEACH — SAN PEDRO BAY, SOUTHERN CALIFORNIA

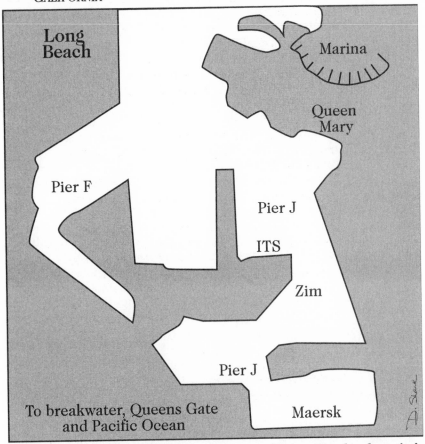

Long Beach

Marina

Queen Mary

Pier F

Pier J

ITS

Zim

Pier J

To breakwater, Queens Gate and Pacific Ocean

Maersk

COSCO is located at Pier J in the Port of Long Beach where it is expected to expand over 300 acres as other shippers, Zim and Maersk Sealand, vacate space by moving elsewhere. In addition, the Beijing-friendly Tung family owns OOCL, which owns and operates Long Beach Container Terminal at Pier F in Long Beach.

former Long Beach Naval Station in 1996. Through Johnny Chung, President Clinton allowed Hongye Zheng of the COSCO to attend one of his Saturday morning radio broadcasts. Just days afterwards Dorothy Robyn, member of a Presidential economic advisory group, called City of Long Beach (CA) officials offering a Chinese deal to lease the Long Beach Naval Station. (Chung admits to much, but denies *any* role in helping COSCO.) COSCO "...attempted to lease port space that was being vacated by the U.S. Navy in Long Beach, California. The lease proposal led to a heated debate between Congress, which wanted to prevent the lease based on national security concerns, and President Clinton, who supported the lease. Legislation passed by both houses of Congress in 1997 barred the lease and voided the President's authority to grant a waiver."[4]

COSCO has not given up. For awhile COSCO was suspected of using a front company to take over where it left off. Astoria Metals Corp., trying to operate a ship repair facility at the same site, denied any COSCO affiliation. Two closed public hearings of the Long Beach Port Authority on November 8 and 15, 1999, followed the AMC denial. Instead of COSCO, Hanjin Shipping Co., of free South Korea signed a 25-year lease for a 375-acre project at the former naval station and former naval shipyard worth $1 billion on October 27, 2000. Clinton-Gore's first choice, COSCO — the merchant marine of the People's Liberation Army — lost out to opposition in Congress and local grass roots opposition. Yet this was not a defeat for COSCO.

Investigations of public source materials reveal that COSCO is far from discouraged. While COSCO has been denied access to the former U.S. Naval Station at Long Beach, the ports of Long Beach and Los Angeles continue to fall all over themselves to give COSCO improved facilities.

Pier J — Currently COSCO shares cramped access of Pier J, berths 232-234 with Taiwan's Yang Ming Marine, K-Line, Great Western SS Co. and Mexican Line. International Transport Service controls and operates these facilities, not COSCO. In April 1999 Zim-American Israeli Shipping Company — operating six container ships between Long Beach and China — vacated contiguous Pier J facilities (243-244) and thus provided COSCO with 110 acres — space nearly equal to that sought at the naval station. The Port of Long Beach swapped real estate with other tenants (Zim and Maersk) so COSCO will have "some needed room to grow," at Pier J according to port insiders. In June 2000 the author's boat tour revealed COSCO containers fully occupying Pier J space once shared with Zim. Will this new space be sufficient for COSCO — the merchant marine of the People's Liberation Army of Red China? COSCO can expand to still other locations nearby. As early as 2002 when Phase I — 318 acres of container facilities — at Pier 400 is completed in the Port of LA, Maersk Sealand will vacate Berths 266-270 at Pier J, and Sea-Land Services will vacate at Pier G. Finally, there is newly landfilled-space at Pier S. These three alternatives at Piers G, J and S give COSCO options galore.

The Port of Los Angeles has tried to offer COSCO a better deal.

COSCO — Los Angeles, Pier 400

In November 1997, the *New York Times* reported that the Port

---

[4] Cox Report

of Los Angeles hoped to woo COSCO to the new Pier 400.[5] The *Long Beach Press Telegram* and *Insight* magazine reported in 1999 that the Port of Los Angeles was seeking COSCO. Perhaps the COSCO brouhaha over the naval station, caused the Port of Los Angeles in late 1999 to quietly sign an "exclusive" agreement with Maersk Sealand for Pier 400 (once it is completed) thus ruling out a COSCO expansion at that particular location.

COSCO ships serving Long Beach and Los Angeles from samples of COSCO shipping schedules for American ports in 1999 and 2000 are:

Port of Long Beach

Using 11 vessels — *Seto Bridge, Lu He, Astoria Bridge, Akashi Bridge, Jin He, Ambassador Bridge, Mosel Bridge, Yue He, Tower Bridge, Chuan He* and *Wan He* — COSCO made twice-weekly calls at the Port of Long Beach from Hong Kong on two routes and once weekly from two different routes. These twice-weekly rotations were via Seattle and Vancouver and Oakland. The weekly calls were via Tacoma, Vancouver and Portland, and the fourth through Vancouver according to COSCO schedules for September 1999 through April 2000, August and September 2000.

Using nine vessels — *Manhattan Bridge, Rainbow Bridge, Mackinac Bridge, H. Hudson Bridge, George Washington, Ambassador Bridge, Bay Bridge, Golden Gate Bridge* and *Harbour Bridge* — COSCO made weekly calls at the Port of Long Beach and Oakland on an Asia Express (12-day voyage) from Hong Kong and other Asian ports, according to COSCO schedules for September 1999 through March 2000.

Using six vessels — *River Crystal, Maple River, Beauty River, Pretty River, Honor River* and *Dainty River* — COSCO made weekly calls at the Port of Long Beach after a call at Vancouver from northern China and Japan, according to COSCO schedules for in June through October 2000.

Using six vessels — *Gao He, Yu Gu He, Pu He, Dong He, Tai He* and *Min He* — COSCO made weekly calls from Southeast China and Japan to the Port of Long Beach followed by Oakland, according to COSCO schedules for March through July 2000.

Port of Los Angeles

Using six vessels — *M. Plenty, M. Pleasure, M. Propitious, M. Progress, M. Peace* and *M. Promotion* — COSCO made weekly calls at the Port of Los Angeles from Chinese and Japanese ports via Oak-

---

[5] *The New York Times*, November 1, 1997

land, according to COSCO schedules for April, August and September 2000.

OOCL ships also deliver cargoes to Los Angeles.

San Francisco Bay area — Port of Oakland

The San Francisco Bay area once provided the U.S. Navy with a wide range of facilities, but for many decades that liberal area has been very unfriendly to the U.S. Navy and even to civilian maritime commerce generally. In contrast, recently, local leaders did effusively welcome Mikhail Gorbachev to the U.S. Army's former facilities at the Presidio, which once guarded the entrance to the Bay.

Today the most prominent Naval activity is a floating armada of mothballed ghost ships, a Ready Reserve fleet, moored in the Carquinez Strait off Benicia, out of sight from the Golden Gate and the city.

Meanwhile the U.S. Navy has closed the Alameda Annex Fleet Industrial Supply Center (FISC), the Alameda Naval Air Station, Hunters Point Annex, Mare Island Naval Shipyard, Moffett Naval Air Station, Naval Medical Center, Oakland FISC, Pacific Grove NAVESCEN, San Francisco PWC and Treasure Island Naval Station. Properties at Mare Island and Moffett are up for sale and lease.

COSCO at U.S. military facilities in Oakland

In August 1993, Clinton signed special legislation allowing the transfer of closed Naval properties at the former Naval Air Station at Alameda to the Port of Oakland for nominal value. In August 1997, the Navy signed over all Alameda properties to the port.

The Oakland Base Reuse Authority is also preparing the closed Oakland Army Base for the City of Oakland, which plans to give over half of the 422 acres to the Port of Oakland.[6]

Both COSCO and OOCL are likely to benefit from use of these former U.S. military properties in Alameda and Oakland. A land swap such as those occurring in Long Beach and Charleston, is still another way of doing so without raising public awareness.

•

The U.S. Navy has no warships homeported in San Francisco Bay though it still has a San Francisco Navy Base. It also retains a weapons supply depot at nearby Concord, which was a favorite target of the Bay area's many Viet Cong sympathizers during the Vietnam War.

In contrast with the U.S. Navy, the PLA-owned COSCO has many very good friends in the Bay area. "American leaders have been pleading for COSCO's business ever since Nixon normalized relations in 1972. San Francisco mayors Feinstein, Agnos and Jordan have all

---

[6] *Army News Service*, October 20, 1999

paid homage to COSCO officials on visits to Beijing, hoping for more Chinese ships in San Francisco ports."[7]

Senator Dianne Feinstein (D-CA), began her friendly relationship with COSCO in the late 1970s. As mayor of San Francisco Feinstein pleaded with COSCO to dock at the Port of San Francisco. Later mayors, including Art Agnos and Frank Jordan, also met COSCO officials in trade missions to Beijing.

Such conviviality was set back in 1996 when a COSCO ship was seized across the Bay in Oakland with 2,000 contraband assault weapons allegedly headed for Los Angeles gangs. This upped the ante in the fight over the U.S. Naval Station in Long Beach. Senators Feinstein and Barbara Boxer (D-CA) sent a letter to Clinton's Secretary of Defense William Cohen in early March 1997 "asking him to explore whether there are any 'security reasons' to reject the city of Long Beach's plans to lease the port..."[8]

It was discovered that Richard Blum, Feinstein's wealthy husband, had a business partner, Peter Kwok. Blum and Kwok had a $100 million China investment venture, Newbridge Capitol. Kwok also served as a "consultant to a Hong Kong subsidiary of COSCO, known as COSCO Hong Kong Holdings," according to the March 27, 1997, *San Francisco Chronicle*. Blum's partner sat on the Board of COSCO's Hong Kong arm.[9] So today COSCO North America, Inc. has an office on Spear Street in San Francisco. But no ships!

Port of Oakland

Unlike San Francisco, working-class Oakland — headed by a number of black entrepreneurial mayors and the reborn former California governor, Jerry Brown — has welcomed not only commerce with COSCO's Communists, but with American capitalists as well.

The Port of Oakland lies off the Golden Gate and across the San Francisco Bay down two one-mile entrance channels dredged to 42 feet. Oakland was one of the first ports to adopt intermodal container operations in the U.S. Port facilities occupy 665 acres, providing 20 berths along 19 miles of waterfront. Handling 1.7 TEUs in 1999, the seaport ranked fourth in the nation and 20th in the world in container traffic. Good road and rail connections allow Oakland to serve as a gateway to America.

COSCO is one of 34 shipping lines which dock at the crowded Howard Terminal in Oakland. Orient Overseas Container Line (OOCL) is headquartered in an office on Hacienda Drive in Pleasanton and its ships call in Oakland.

---

[7] Marc Sandalow, *San Francisco Chronicle*, March 23, 1997
[8] *San Francisco Chronicle*, March 13, 1997
[9] *Wall Street Journal*, March 26, 1997

The Port of Oakland — east side of San Francisco Bay, on a harbor channel between mainland and Alameda Island

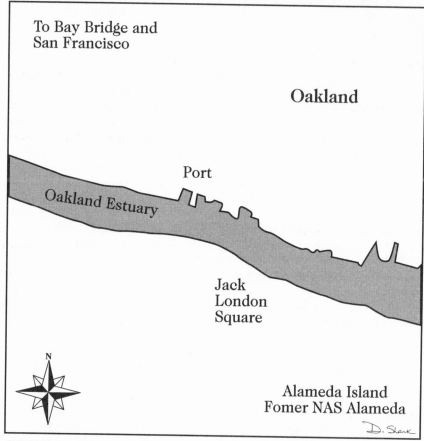

To Bay Bridge and
San Francisco

Oakland

Port

Oakland Estuary

Jack
London
Square

N

Alameda Island
Fomer NAS Alameda

D. Slark

COSCO operates out of Howard Terminal, which it shares with other shippers. The Port of Oakland has ambitious plans to expand and has many options including portions of the former U.S. Naval Air Station on Alameda Island.

Through 2006 Oakland has $1.7 billion in projects planned to construct new terminals, a Joint Intermodal Terminal and a dredging project to deepen the port's channels and berths from 42 to 50 feet. The Port of Oakland sold $400 million in port revenue bonds in March 2000. $560 million is being spent on Vision 2000 upgrading Berths 55-56, containerizing 150 acres at Berths 57-58, associated street realignment and access roads.

The port has purchased six of the world's largest and fastest container cranes, weighing 1,600 tons with a 65-meter-reach able to snatch a single container across 23 container widths. Delivered from

Shanghai, China, in late October 2000 the cranes cleared the bottom of the Bay Bridge to Oakland by only 24 inches. Oakland is dredging its middle harbor to a depth of 50 feet along 3,600 feet of continuous berths.

COSCO shipping service to Port of Oakland

Using 11 vessels — *Seto Bridge, Akashi Bridge, Concord Bridge, Elms Bridge, Victoria Bridge, M. Plenty, M. Pleasure, M. Propitious, M. Progress, M. Peace* and *M. Promotion* — COSCO made twice-weekly calls at the Port of Oakland from Hong Kong via either Long Beach or via Los Angeles, and Chinese and Japanese ports, according to COSCO schedules for September 1999 through April 2000.

Using another nine vessels — *Manhattan Bridge, Rainbow Bridge, Mackinac Bridge, H. Hudson Bridge, George Washington, Ambassador Bridge, Bay Bridge, Golden Gate Bridge* and *Harbour Bridge* — COSCO made weekly calls at the Port of Oakland after a call at Long Beach on an Asia Express (12-day voyage) from Hong Kong, according to COSCO schedules for September 1999 through March 2000.

Using another six vessels — *Gao He, Yu Gu He, Pu He, Dong He, Tai He* and *Min He* — COSCO made weekly calls from Southeast China and Japan to the Port of Oakland after a call in Long Beach according to COSCO schedules for March through July 2000.

THE COLUMBIA RIVER PORTS: PORTLAND, OREGON, AND VANCOUVER, WASHINGTON

Port of Portland

With growth problems in Los Angeles and Long Beach the Port of Portland aspires to fill the breach.

One hundred miles up the Columbia River from the Pacific Ocean, the modest river Port of Portland had revenues of only $60 million in 1998 and operated mostly in the red. It serviced 11 commercial carriers of which nine were container ship lines. The port claims to be the second largest on the West Coast for bulk export cargoes such as grain, minerals, wood chips and cattle hides. The port's ambitions are to expand its capacities.

Planned port expansions include a $200 million taxpayer-funded Columbia River channel-deepening project to improve the flow of traffic from the marine terminals at Rivergate. Deepening the Columbia River shipping channel by three feet will enable the port to remain competitive.

Portland also suffers from traffic congestion on Interstate 5 and Highway 26 for trucks making deliveries to warehouses and factories.

The proposed solution is a "fast corridor" on I-5 between Seattle and Tacoma costing from $350 million to $500 million.

At best port improvements will allow vessels that can carry less than 3,000 20-foot-equivalent units of containers (TEUs). These are about half the size of the deep draft ships dominating the industry."[10]

Modest as it is, COSCO makes weekly calls upon Portland. Using five vessels — *Tower Bridge, Astoria Bridge, Bay Bridge, Golden Gate Bridge* and *Harbour Bridge* — COSCO made weekly calls at the Port of Portland from Chinese and Japanese ports after calls at the northern and southern ends of Puget Sound — Vancouver, B.C., and Tacoma.[11]

Port of Vancouver in Washington

The Southwest Washington port. The Port of Vancouver extends along 3.5 miles of Columbia River waterfront opposite the Port of Portland. Vancouver, Washington, is smaller than Portland, but it operates in the black. Moreover, the port controls 1,000 acres of undeveloped land known as the Columbia Gateway. Plans are to build 1.5 miles of access to new marine terminals for a major break-bulk port, cargo loaded by pallets.[12]

COSCO vessels dutifully land at Vancouver, Washington, every week. They then steam north to the Seattle area, turn east and then south into Puget Sound past major U.S. Naval facilities and the Port of Seattle. COSCO also makes calls on the Port of Tacoma on the southwest end of Puget Sound.

PUGET SOUND PORTS — SEATTLE, WASHINGTON, AND VANCOUVER, B.C.

Port of Seattle

According to the April 19, 1999, issue of the *Seattle Post-Intelligencer*, "the red and gold flag of the People's Republic of China and the Stars and Stripes were raised and snapped together..." Celebrating 20 years of trade with China, a "...fireboat fired towering columns of water... as a tug assisted the 637-foot... M.V. *Liulinhai* to the Port of Seattle's Terminal 91..." And "...a 13th [United States] Naval District band broke into 'It's a Small World'."

Small world perhaps with COSCO and OOCL sailing the same cozy waters as the U.S. Navy. The U.S. Navy homeports nine nuclear

---

[10] Portland, OR, *Business Journal*, February 16, 1998, January 24, 2000 and March 13, 2000

[11] COSCO schedules for September 1999 through February 2000

[12] Portland, OR, *Business Journal,* June 12, 2000

Rear Admiral Lu Fangqui, Chief of Staff, North Sea Fleet, People's Liberation Army (Navy), accepts a gift from Paul Schell, the mayor of Seattle. — U.S. Navy photo

submarines at nearby Naval Submarine Base Bangor, the aircraft carrier *Carl Vinson* and six support vessels at the Puget Sound Naval Yard at Bremerton, and the aircraft carrier *Abraham Lincoln* and six support destroyers and frigates at Naval Station Everett.

The Navy is closing down the Puget Sound Naval Station (Sand Point) and the Naval Undersea Warfare Center, Keyport, Washington. On the other hand there is a bustling China business.

Many shipping lines out of Seattle have commercial intercourse with cargo to and from China. COSCO began using Seattle in 1979 and is currently one of Seattle's largest shipping customers. At Terminal 18, COSCO maintains a weekly service to Xiamen, Yantian and Hong Kong in the People's Republic of China, Kobe, Japan and Los Angeles. In addition, the China Shipping Container Lines, a subsidiary of China Shipping Group of Shanghai, uses six vessels to provide weekly service to the Port of Seattle.

Stevedoring Services of America and its terminal operations partner, Matson Navigation Co., operate Terminal 18, a facility that COSCO, OOCL and China Shipping Group must share with seven other steamship lines.

In addition, Beijing-dependent OOCL delivers cargoes to Seattle and owns major berths up Puget Sound in Vancouver, B.C.

China was Washington State's number three trading partner, after

More than 350 people welcome the People's Republic of China naval ships Taicang (AOR 575), above, and Qingdao (DDG 113), at Naval Station Everett, Washington. — U.S. Navy photo

Japan and Canada, in 1998 — $12 billion in two-way trade — $8 billion in imports and $4 billion in exports. Perhaps half or more of China's containers went back empty without exports to China. The Port of Seattle handled $6.6 billion worth of trade with China in 1998. China trade was only $723 million 10 years ago.

Expanded trade with Seattle provides China with modern technologies, some of them militarily useful. Trade deficits, represented by empty containers, provide cash to finance improvements in China's technology.

Technological giants Boeing and Microsoft were major supporters of expanded trade with China and also potential violators of trade laws limiting exports of militarily useful technology. Trade with China "...opens up vast new markets for U.S. goods and services, and I have supreme confidence that America's highly skilled and productive work force will win substantial new business in those markets in the years to come," said Boeing Chairman Phil Condit. "Congress now must act with dispatch to grant China the same Normal Trade status... so that the U.S. can reap the full benefits of this market-opening agreement," Condit said.

Since China's aircraft factories turn out such poor products, Boeing is surely supplying the PLA as well as the PLA-controlled civilian aircraft industry. Boeing has since moved its headquarters out of Seattle to Chicago. Boeing also contracted the Chinese to manufacture some aircraft parts in China rather than the U.S.

Microsoft Corp. has done business in China since 1992 and has sales, support and research offices in China according to Microsoft's Erin Brewer. "We have always supported granting Normal Trade Relations status and entry into the WTO (World Trade Organization) for China," Brewer said. "From our perspective — and from the technology industry's perspective — we feel it benefits both the United States and China and helps assure that China's information technology sector is healthy and robust."

Operating at capacity, the Port of Seattle is engaged in a $350 mil-

THE PORT OF SEATTLE IS LOCATED IN ELLIOTT BAY OFF PUGET SOUND; THE U.S. NAVY IS NEARBY IN BANGOR, BREMERTON AND EVERETT, WASHINGTON

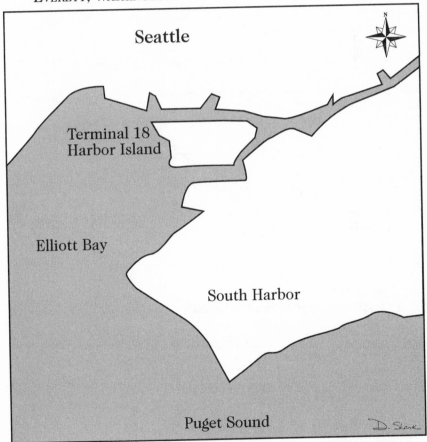

COSCO is at Terminal 18 shared with OOCL and China Shipping Group of Shanghai. The Port of Seattle plans to double container space at Terminal 18.

lion expansion of COSCO's berths — Terminal 18 container shipping facilities on Harbor Island. Terminal 18 will double from 106 acres to 200 acres as will its rail capacity.

The expanded container terminal will provide 1,300 jobs. By 2010, growth in container trade will create 60,000 jobs. The new Terminal 18 will generate up to $330 million annually in new business and nearly $15 million annually in tax revenue. Special facility bonds backed by lease revenues will finance the Terminal project.

The port also expanded the $270 million Terminal 5 in West Seattle. In a project with the U.S. Army Corps of Engineers, 3,000 feet of the East Waterway of the Duwamish River Waterway will be dredged to 50 feet making it accessible to the largest — read Chinese — container vessels.

Shipping news from the Marine Exchange of Puget Sound reveals five major COSCO vessels — *Chuanhe, Jinhe, Luhe, Wanhe* and *Yuehe* — docking at Seattle's Terminal 18 about twice a month throughout 1999 and 2000. Most vessels came from Long Beach and were bound north up Puget Sound to Vancouver, B.C., according to sampled COSCO schedules for February-July, August and September 2000.

In 1999 a Seattle harbor tax may have reduced COSCO's enthusiasm for Seattle. "Howard Finkel, vice president of commercial operations for China Ocean Shipping Co., or COSCO, in Secaucus, NJ, said his growing steamship line is concerned about the [Seattle] harbor tax."

In May 1999, COSCO initiated a Pacific service that would make the Port of Vancouver its first inbound port of call before heading to the Port of Long Beach. COSCO claimed to want to continue expanded use of the Port of Seattle. The [Seattle] harbor tax "wasn't the driving force in the decision (to make Vancouver the first port of call), but we are concerned about it," Howard Finkel said.[13]

Port of Vancouver, British Columbia, Canada

COSCO pulled-out of its efforts to obtain the U.S. Naval Station in Long Beach — and the Pier 400 option in Los Angeles — because of Congressional actions. COSCO relocated in part to Vancouver, B.C. In the summer of 1999, two years after the port police of Vancouver were disbanded, the Port of Vancouver signed a contract with COSCO.

Though Vancouver is a bit far north to be a gateway to North America, it has great strategic value — it is the only major port on the West Coast of North America without a police force and it occupies the same waterways as much of the U.S. Pacific Fleet.

The Port of Vancouver, B.C., shares waterways of the Pacific

---

[13] *Seattle Post-Intelligencer*, April 19, May 26, November 16, 20 and December 8, 1999

Ocean and generally surrounding Vancouver Island with the Port of Seattle and three critical U.S. Naval facilities: Naval Submarine Base in Bangor, Naval Station Everett and Naval Air Station Whidbey Island.

Vancouver Island is bounded on the north and west by the Strait of Georgia approaching Vancouver on the mainland and is bounded on the south and west by the Juan de Fuca Strait approaching Puget Sound which contains the cities of Seattle and Tacoma and critical U.S. Navy facilities.

THE PORT OF VANCOUVER, BRITISH COLUMBIA, IN BURRARD INLET, NORTH OF PUGET SOUND

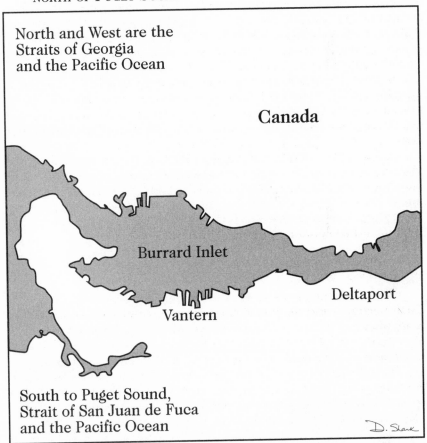

North and West are the Straits of Georgia and the Pacific Ocean

Canada

Burrard Inlet

Deltaport

Vantern

South to Puget Sound, Strait of San Juan de Fuca and the Pacific Ocean

D. Slark

COSCO is at Vantern Terminal operated by OOCL at the Port of Vancouver. OOCL also operates Deltaport and Li Ka-Shing owns Surrey Fraser docks in Vancouver.

The *Washington Times* has said that in July 2000 the CIA reported on "Russian merchant ship intelligence collection efforts against U.S. nuclear submarine bases" in the "Strait of Juan de Fuca, above Washington State's Puget Sound." On a separate occasion the Russians also were accused of firing a laser at a Canadian reconnaissance helicopter and blinding a Canadian officer.

COSCO is well located to conduct similar operations for China. Port of Vancouver officials deny any evidence of COSCO being directly involved in any illegal activity. Port officials even deny, <u>falsely</u>, ever having receiving warnings about COSCO from the Candian Mounties despite credible press reports to that effect.

COSCO is among several shipping lines operating facilities at both Vancouver and Seattle.

In Vancouver, COSCO has friendly company.

COSCO advisor C.C. Tung owns Orient Overseas Container Line (OOCL), which operates two container terminals — Deltaport and Vanterm vessel berths on Stewart St. and Roberts Bank in Vancouver. OOCL claims its business in Vancouver was particularly profitable in 2000.

Li Ka-Shing of Hutchison Whampoa owns the Surrey Fraser docks in Vancouver. Li and his son own "at least one-sixth to one-third of downtown Vancouver" according to Canadian sources.[14]

According to the May 28, 2000, issue of *The Province* of Vancouver, B.C., in 1997, "Vancouver ports police had assembled an intelligence file and issued a warning to the port [of Vancouver] about its negotiations with COSCO, a Chinese shipping company whose vessels had been linked to global weapons smuggling. COSCO has since moved into the port and the port's chief executive officer, Norman Stark, says he has no memory of the warning."

Meanwhile Ottawa disbanded the national port's police and all the files disappeared, according to *The Province*. "The investigations died with the force's controversial dismissal in 1997, *The Province* has learned."

"The Vancouver Port Authority ignored warnings about the Chinese business interests it was wooing in the 1990s — allowing a number of questionable business connections to take root in the port."

Indeed, "In the mid-'90s, as courting efforts aimed at Chinese shipping giant COSCO went into overdrive, intelligence officials — including local ports police — sounded alarm bells about the conglomerate's questionable connections."[15]

---

[14] *Post-Intelligencer*, August 12, 1999, and *Report* (a Canadian newsmagazine), November 6, 2000

[15] *The Province*, Vancouver, May 8, 29, 2000

COSCO service to Vancouver, B.C.

Using five vessels — *Lu He, Jin He, Yue He, Chuan He* and *Wan He* — COSCO made weekly calls at the Port of Vancouver, B.C., and Port of Seattle from Hong Kong, according to COSCO schedules for February-July and August and September 2000.

Using six vessels — *River Crystal, Maple River, Beauty River, Pretty River, Honor River* and *Dainty River* — COSCO made weekly calls at the Port of Vancouver and Long Beach from northern China and Japan, according to COSCO schedules for in June through October 2000.

COSCO IN GULF COAST PORTS
Houston and New Orleans

Port of Houston

Ships use the Gulf of Mexico as the entrance to America's heartland. In war it is the soft underbelly of America. The Port of Houston is 50 miles up the 40-foot Houston Channel from Galveston Bay in the Gulf of Mexico. Houston competes with New Orleans up the Mississippi River from the Gulf. More than half the container traffic in the Gulf of Mexico comes through the Port of Houston. Houston is the nation's ninth largest container port.

The Port of Houston generated $755 million in revenues in 1998, adding 200,000 jobs and $7.7 billion to the local economy by exporting grain, petroleum products and chemicals and importing crude oil, iron/steel, plastics and chemicals.

COSCO virtually never appears in the Houston press, but the People's Republic of China maintains a Houston office for a Consulate on Melrose Boulevard. COSCO's Barbours Cut facilities are over capacity. The draft at the Container Terminal is only 39 feet.[1]

Beijing-favorite OOCL also has a service office and delivers cargoes to Houston.

The Port of Houston proposes a massive project on the Bayport Channel. The ambitious project includes seven wharves covering 1,000 acres extending 7,000 feet — a mile and a half. The project would create a container terminal about three times larger than the current 250 acres at Barbours Cut. The project will cost $1.2 billion. The capacity of the new Bayport will handle 57 lengthy trains a week and 7,000 trucks a day.

The $1.2 billion will come in major part from public funds — federal and local funds, port revenues and $387 million in bond sales.[2] COSCO like other container carriers using Barbours Cut, will benefit from these expenditures from public treasuries.

Using five vessels — *M. Longevity, Gulf Bridge, C. Atlantic, Ming Ocean* and *Atlantic Bridge* — COSCO made weekly calls from Northern Europe (via Charleston, Miami and New Orleans) to the Port of Houston, according to COSCO schedules for April through August 1999.

---

[1] *Houston Press*, July 2, 1998
[2] *Houston Press*, July 2, 1998, September 30, 1999

THE PORT OF HOUSTON IS IN A SHIP CHANNEL NORTH OF GALVESTON BAY OFF THE GULF OF MEXICO.

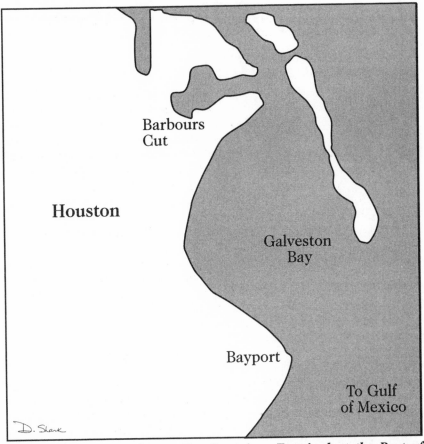

Barbours
Cut

Houston

Galveston
Bay

Bayport

To Gulf
of Mexico

D. Shark

COSCO uses the Barbours Cut Container Terminal at the Port of Houston, which is over capacity. The port plans to build at Bayport tripling the size of Barbours Cut.

Port of New Orleans

COSCO's usually low profile everywhere was broken in New Orleans briefly when a COSCO vessel, *Bright Field* (twice the length of a football field), heavily laden with corn, lost power from its poorly-maintained engine. Its Mississippi River pilot was unable to halt the ship's destructive plunge along a crowded boardwalk of dockside shops, restaurants, e.g. Café du Monde and a hotel, in mid-December 1996.

COSCO's presence along the Mississippi River at America's soft underbelly has otherwise gone unnoticed. COSCO advertises weekly docking at the Port of New Orleans carrying full container loads from

Northern Europe. Using five vessels — *M. Longevity, Gulf Bridge, C. Atlantic, Ming Ocean* and *Atlantic Bridge* — COSCO made weekly calls from Northern Europe (via Charleston and Miami) at the Port of New Orleans followed by a call to Houston, according to COSCO schedules for April through August 1999.

THE PORT OF NEW ORLEANS IS IN A SHALLOW SHIP CHANNEL OFF THE MISSISSIPPI RIVER OFF THE GULF OF MEXICO.

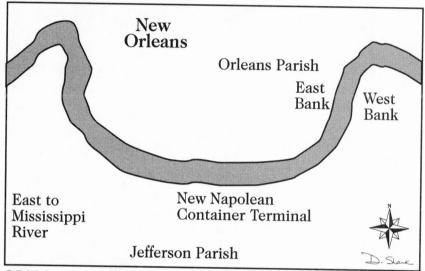

COSCO uses container facilities off Napolean Avenue in the Port of New Orleans. The port hopes to build a new Millennium Port on deeper channels of the Mississippi River.

The Port of New Orleans describes itself as "at the center of... World's Busiest Waterway" More than 6,000 ocean vessels annually move through New Orleans on the Mississippi River. Six major railroads and a nearly 15,000-mile inland waterway system feed the funnel.

Only a third of the $17.2 billion in products shipped from Louisiana's ports in 1999 were made in the state. Indeed Louisiana is the funnel for bulk cargoes barged down the Mississippi.[3]

New Orleans imports steel, natural rubber, plywood and coffee. Exports through New Orleans include chemicals, petroleum, coal, processed foods, agricultural commodities and paper products.

The port's container terminals on the Industrial Canal lie off the Mississippi River-Gulf Outlet which, at 36 feet deep, is 11 feet shallower than the Mississippi River's 45-foot draft. This limits the size of container ships and their cargoes.

[3] *New Orleans City Business*, July 10, 2000

Fully loaded container ships do not call at the port.[4] The Napoleon Avenue site is too small for a container yard. When Hurricane Georges shut down New Orleans, cargo fled to Charleston and Houston.

The Port of New Orleans has spent $500 million to modernize its existing breakbulk terminals and container terminals at Nashville Avenue Wharf A and Napoleon Wharf B on the east bank of the Mississippi River.

It is also constructing a new 64-acre container facility at its Napoleon Avenue complex consisting of a new 1,739-linear-foot wharf, a 44-acre marshalling yard and 4,453 linear feet of riverfront crane rail. The interim facility at Napoleon Avenue provides a quick response to the marketplace, but this will not be enough.

Ocean carriers and terminal operators want to move the container terminal to the Mississippi River, where there is a 45-foot-draft. A study recommends building a mega-container terminal on the Mississippi River, south of New Orleans called the Millennium Port, a container complex, in deeper water allowing larger ships to unload at existing docks. New docks on the Mississippi River would allow vessels to load up in New Orleans.[5]

The terminal will be privately financed, but public funds will pay for highway and rail improvements.

The Millennium Port would increase New Orleans' market share for container cargo including that from China and COSCO. Outbound shipments to China are the State of Louisiana's seventh largest export market. Exports to China are expected to increase if China actually cuts its tariffs and import license fees after joining the World Trade Organization.

[4, 5] *New Orleans City Business*, July 31, 2000

COSCO IN ATLANTIC COAST PORTS: Miami, Savannah, Charleston, Norfolk, New York, Halifax

Though modest — only 242,855 TEUs on the entire East Coast in 1998 — COSCO has been expanding its services to the East Coast. Local officials are just as anxious to help as they have been on the West and Gulf Coasts.

COSCO has been expanding its Panama Canal use, taking its cargoes directly to the East Coast thus bypassing some of the massive American truck and rail services from West Coast ports. On May 18, 2000, a COSCO vessel, the Mv *Yu Gu He*, passed through the Panama Canal starting a new container shipping service between Asia, the East Coast of the United States and Central America. The ship was outbound from Hong Kong bound for New York. COSCO's new line, AEX, included nine vessels with a capacity of 3,400 TEUs. The new service adds to the 300 of COSCO's 600 vessels already using the Panama Canal.

Port of Miami-Dade

The Port of Miami-Dade is best known as the world's busiest ocean cruise port attracting 1.5 million cruise passengers in 1999. Miami's seaport is only the 10th busiest cargo port in the country. The Port of Miami Terminal Operating Company (POMTOC) can only handle 1,400 20-foot cargo containers a day and has a backlog of nearly 8,000 containers stacked everywhere including parking lots.

The port is considering a number of capacity improvements including a tunnel to the port and dredging from 43 to 50 feet.

A review of new accounts about the port reveals that Miami Port officials complain about U.S. Customs inspections against cocaine smuggling. There are accounts of the Immigration and Naturalization Service (INS), breaking rings smuggling Chinese illegals from Cuba and the Caribbean to Miami and to New York.

The Coast Guard was heavily occupied in a major investigation of an oil spill that touched a 30-mile stretch of Broward County beaches. The Guard boarded nine tankers to take oil samples.

One hopes COSCO violations are no worse than oil spills. No one really knows because no one is looking. Unlike oil spills, which are bad for cruise ship tourism, COSCO security risks are on no one's radar. Indeed the radar is not turned on.[1] Using five vessels — *M. Longevity, Gulf Bridge, C. Atlantic, Ming Ocean* and *Atlantic Bridge* — COSCO made weekly calls from Northern Europe via Charleston to the Port of Miami followed by calls at New Orleans and Houston, according to COSCO schedules for April through August 1999. Beijing-friendly OOCL also ships cargoes into the Port of Miami.

Port of Charleston, South Carolina

Charleston was once a Navy town. No longer. With the Charleston Naval Station closed and the Naval Weapons Center scaled back, Charleston no longer relies on the U.S. Navy for high-paying civilian jobs.

Charleston Harbor lies 15 miles up a well-dredged 40- to 42-foot channel — 35 feet at low tide. The Wando Welch Terminal has rapidly made Charleston the nation's fourth-largest container port since opening its first berth in 1981. The Port of Charleston has four container terminals with 15 berths on 450 acres.

Charleston ships 1.5 million TEUs a year. In the South Atlantic area, in 2000 the Port of Charleston was No. 1 providing 85,000 jobs, growing 16% and increasing container traffic 21%.[2]

Charleston moves cargo through its terminal faster than any other port in North America, holding a record of 64 gross container moves per hour, per crane.

By dollar value of imports, China is Charleston's No. 2 trader behind Germany, but ahead of Japan and Britain.

In 1998 Port authorities happily reported: "The Port of Charleston landed several important carriers... The one that... had the most significant impact was the COSCO/K-Line/Yang Ming group... start[ing] a North Europe service last year including... Charleston." In October 1998, "COSCO added another weekly call on the Med service."

The Tung family's OOCL also delivers goods to Charleston.

Fast growing COSCO is a heavy user of Charleston's Columbus Street Terminal where a COSCO ship calls every other day.

Using five vessels — *M. Longevity, Gulf Bridge, C. Atlantic, Ming Ocean* and *Atlantic Bridge* — COSCO made weekly calls from Northern Europe at the Port of Charleston followed by calls at Miami, New Orleans, and Houston (April-August 1999). Using another eight vessels — *Chesapeake Bridge, Xi Bo He, Na Xi He, Yu Gu He, Ha Ni He, Rainbow Bridge, Ming Prominence* and *Jing Po He* — COSCO made

---

[1] *Miami Herald*, February 18 and 19, March 12, and August 10, 2000
[2] *Atlanta Business Chronicle*, August 7, 2000; *The Post and Courier*, April 6 and July 16, 2000

THE PORT OF CHARLESTON IS OFF THE COOPER RIVER IN CHARLESTON, SOUTH CAROLINA.

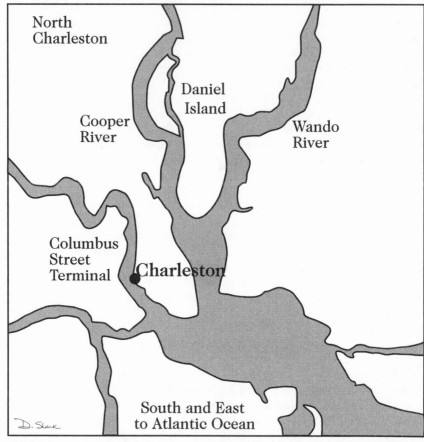

COSCO uses expanded space at the Columbus Street Terminal off the Cooper River. Swapping space with other shippers relocated to the former Charleston Naval Station created the new space. Navy munitions upriver from the Naval Weapons Station sail past COSCO berths on the Cooper River. The port plans to triple container capacity with a new facility on Daniels Island between the Cooper River and the Wando River.

weekly calls at the Port of Charleston and New York from Hong Kong (August-September 2000).

Like Long Beach, the South Carolina Ports Authority tried to place a container terminal on the former Charleston Naval Base. Yet the City of North Charleston zoned the property to prohibit this use. So, on August 12, 1999, South Carolina State Ports Authority (SPA) approved another lease of the former Naval Base at North Charleston.

By September "ten ships, including four breakbulk cargo vessels... [had]... docked at former Charleston Navy Base piers..."[3]

In effect, COSCO and other containerized business had pushed breakbulk cargo activities to the north end of the old Navy Base on the Cooper River. A land swap accomplished what a direct transaction could not achieve. COSCO had improved its space at Columbus Street Terminal by pushing breakbulk cargo off to the Charleston Naval Station.

The 17,000-acre Naval Weapons Station still operates its own wharf and piers shipping U.S. Navy ordnance and missiles 13 miles down the Cooper River — past COSCO ships berthed at the Columbus Street Terminal — to the Atlantic. These ammunition facilities are vulnerable just like Port Chicago near Concord, CA, which blew up during WWII and the Roseville rail yard (near Sacramento, CA) which blew up during the Vietnam War. The Naval Weapons Station also houses the Naval Nuclear Power Training Command and 8,000 sailors.

The Port of Charleston is spending millions aiding COSCO at its Columbus Street Terminal. State Ports Authority plans to use federal and state funding to allow the world's largest container ships — COSCO's — to use Charleston's docks. Charleston has spent $139 million to deepen its inner harbor from 40 to 45 feet and its channel entrance from 45 to 47 feet to accommodate bigger container ships.[4]

Deepening channels is only the beginning

By stages the port is moving to develop a $1.2 billion "Global Gateway" tripling current container capacities on an area the size of 636 football fields which it owns on the Wando River and Cooper River sides of Daniel Island.

The South Carolina State Ports Authority plans to build seven 1,000-foot berths on the Cooper River side. Its wharves will be 2½ miles long to handle megaships — 1,000-foot container vessels as big as aircraft carriers.

Cranes will tower hundreds of feet over a giant, 660-acre, parking lot for thousands of 20- to 40-foot containers.

More than three million cubic yards of mud, sand and silt will be dredged from the harbor, slightly less than the bulk of the Great Pyramid at Giza. The new Daniel Island Terminal and four existing terminals could attract 6,300 ships per year compared to 2,400 vessels in 1998.

---

[3] *The Post and Courier*
[4] *The Post and Courier*, October 13 and 22, 1999, August 3, 2000; *Atlanta Business Chronicle*, August 7, 2000

Port leaders do not yet know how they're going to pay for this massive undertaking, but believe they can sell it.

The SPA used $56 million in general revenue state bonds to build the Wando Welch Terminal in 1978. Recently, port revenues have covered new cranes and terminal improvements.

SPA officials are confident of acquiring state and federal funds. The first half of 200 acres is being filled with two million cubic yards of ocean sand and will berth three ships by 2007.[5]

The State Ports Authority is considering working with a private company. "We're actively investigating possibilities for private involvement with some international terminal operators," port officer William Bethea said. "We've had some discussions with shipping lines, and we expect to have some more."[6]

Of course, the world's largest "international terminal operator," is Li Ka-Shing's Hutchison Whampoa. On any list of shipping companies is also Beijing-friendly Orient Overseas (also a port operator) or COSCO itself.

Port of Savannah, Georgia

In the South Atlantic area, Savannah is No. 2 and grew by 13% in 2000. It is the nation's ninth-largest container port, shipping 850,000 TEUs a year. Savannah supports 80,100 jobs and generates $585 million in tax revenues a year.[7]

Savannah, having many rail connections, leads in shipments to Asia. Indeed, Savannah had 54% of the Asian business in the South Atlantic in 2000.

In June 2000, COSCO announced, "COSCO Container Lines and Zim Israeli Lines plan to [share]... container slots-leasing... on the Mediterranean-U.S. East Service. Once... implemented... COSCO will be able to use container slots from Zim Lines [in] Savannah, New York, Harifax [sic], Barcelona, Haifa, Piraeus, Leghorn..." OOCL also delivers cargoes to Savannah.

Savannah competes with the ports of Charleston, SC, and Jacksonville, FL, for container shipments. Savannah is deepening its harbor for large ships from 42 feet to 48 feet by 2004. Gov. Zell Miller also proposed spending $31 million to dredge the Savannah River's navigational channel and expand berths and storage facilities. Savannah is also building a new intermodal transfer facility to move containers from trucks to railcars.

Carlos Martel, deputy commissioner of the Georgia Department

---

[5] *Charleston Post and Courier*, October 22, 1999; *The Post and Courier*, November 29, December 26, 1999, January 14 and July 16, 2000

[6] *Charleston Post and Courier*, September 21 and October 22, 1999

[7] *Atlanta Business Chronicle*, August 7, 2000

of Industry, Trade and Tourism says, "Anything that provides a more expedient method of transportation in both directions — importing or exporting — would make the state an even stronger gateway in the Southeast."

The ports of Hampton Roads — Norfolk, Portsmouth and Newport News

As it does in Vancouver-Seattle on the Pacific, COSCO now sits in the middle of the U.S. Navy's Atlantic Fleet. Hampton Roads — the waterway entrance to Chesapeake Bay — is guarded on the north by Fort Monroe and on the south by the Norfolk Naval Station.

THE PORT OF NORFOLK IS OFF THE HAMPTON ROADS ENTRANCE TO CHESAPEAKE BAY.

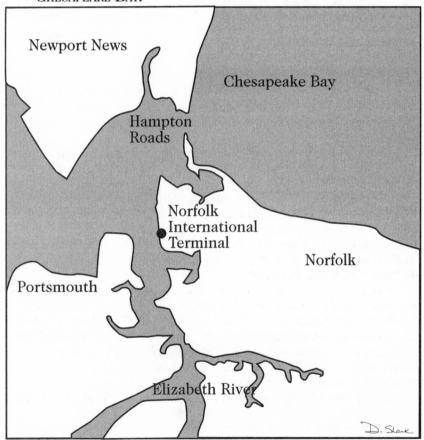

COSCO uses facilities at the Norfolk International Terminals off the Elizabeth River. COSCO ships commingle with many of the aircraft carriers and destroyers in the entire U.S. Navy's Atlantic Fleet.

Three major Virginia ports — Norfolk, Portsmouth and Newport News — lie off Hampton Roads and have the best natural deepwater harbor on the U.S. East Coast. Fifty-foot-deep, unobstructed channels provide maneuvering room for the largest of today's container ships and for the largest fleet of aircraft carriers, cruisers, destroyers and submarines on Earth — a major portion of the entire U.S. Navy.

The U.S. Navy employs 281,429 persons, military and civilian, and adds $7.5 billion to the local economy. U.S. Navy bases are located in Norfolk, Portsmouth, Virginia Beach, Peninsula, Suffolk, Chesapeake and Little Creek.

In 1999 107 ships — aircraft carriers, cruisers, destroyers and submarines — homeported in Norfolk and so, too, did 39 aircraft squadrons. Nineteen support vessels and landing craft home port at Little Creek.

Commingling with the activities of the U.S. Navy's Atlantic fleet, the Virginia International Terminals, Inc. operates four general cargo terminals: Norfolk International Terminal, Portsmouth Marine Terminal, Newport News Marine Terminal and the Virginia Inland Port in Front Royal.

The Norfolk Harbor Channel extends from Hampton Roads waterway along the Elizabeth River to Norfolk, Portsmouth and Newport News. On the south side of Hampton Roads the port cities of Norfolk and Portsmouth share opposite sides of the Elizabeth River and a tunnel. Similarly, another 6,000-foot tunnel connects both ports to Hampton across the Chesapeake Bay. The Port of Hampton Roads includes marine terminals at the ports of Norfolk, Portsmouth and Newport News.

The natural harbor has always attracted naval forces — friend and foe alike. In 1767 Andrew Sprowle built the Portsmouth shipyard naming it after the great shipyard in England.

In 1907, the "Great White Fleet," 16 battleships painted white accompanied by six destroyers, colliers and other support vessels sailed around the world under order of President Teddy Roosevelt to show American naval power. Seven of those battleships in the fleet had been built in Newport News: *Kearsarge, Kentucky, Illinois, Missouri, Louisiana, Virginia* and *Minnesota*. "The fleet stopped in China and conducted battle practice at sea..."[8] It returned in 1909 greeted by President Roosevelt before the cheers of 60,000 along the shore. It was "the most important service that I rendered to peace," said Roosevelt.[9]

During WWII, five Nazi submarines crossed the Atlantic, attacked ships off Cape Hatteras and warships off Hampton Roads and mined Chesapeake Bay.

"German torpedoes, deck guns and mines struck 79 ships and

[8, 9] *Hampton Roads Ticket*, April 3, 2000

sank 66 of them. A total of 843 merchant seamen and naval gun crew-members lost their lives.

"April 14, 1942, a U.S. destroyer, the USS *Roper*, gave chase [to a] submarine... opened up with machine-gun fire and its 3-inch deck gun. Coxswain Harry Heyman scored a direct hit on the conning tower near the waterline, and the submarine went down. The *Roper* dropped a barrage of 11 depth charges and at dawn recovered the bodies of 29 German seamen who were identified as crewmen of *U-85*, one of Hitler's new 500-ton submarines. It was the first Nazi submarine to be destroyed by an American vessel in the war."[10]

COSCO displaces U.S. Navy... again

In late 1998, COSCO moved nearly 300,000 TEUs in container trade to Norfolk, Virginia, when it dropped its Far East service to Baltimore. Norfolk's piers are more accessible to the Atlantic than Baltimore's piers far from ocean waters. Norfolk has opened a new $93 million, 1,500-foot wharf having three large new cranes on 60 acres and is rebuilding another wharf to service large ships.

West of Norfolk, another $1.5 billion will build a fourth new terminal for Portsmouth on 900 acres, once the Navy's Craney Island fuel depot — its largest stateside fuel facility. Another $2.7 billion spent on road, bridge and tunnel projects would not only link Portsmouth and Norfolk but also facilitate freight movements from the new Craney Island Terminal, the Norfolk International Terminal and the Norfolk Naval Station.[11]

The U.S. Navy in Norfolk

The major combatant vessels are clustered in one port. With most of the Atlantic Fleet at one location, is Norfolk 2003 Pearl Harbor 1941?

In the '90s, reductions in the U.S. military cut 40 ships and 50,000 jobs from the U.S. Navy and local ship builders. Despite these cutbacks, a third of the ships in the entire U.S Navy still call Norfolk at Hampton Roads their home port.

The aircraft carrier *Enterprise* and five of eight Nimitz-class aircraft carriers in the U.S. Navy today are stationed at Norfolk, as are seven of 27 cruisers, 14 of 29 modern Arleigh Burk-class destroyers, nine of 24 Spruance-class destroyers and 11 of 51 Los Angeles-class submarines.[12]

All the aircraft carriers are built in nearby Newport News Ship-

---

[10] *Hampton Roads Ticket*, April 3, 2000
[11] *The Virginia-Pilot, 1997*, July 20, 2000
[12] *U.S. Navy website*

yard. The U.S. Navy has made shipbuilding and repairs a major local industry in Norfolk, Portsmouth and Newport News.

Norfolk houses the Joint Forces Command where "the U.S. military is developing its most advanced war-fighting techniques — information known to be a target of Chinese military spying." *[Bill Gertz]* In late August 2000, the Clinton Pentagon escorted three PLA generals — China's own strategic military planners — from China's Academy of Military Sciences to the Norfolk facility. The Chinese Academy, a very secretive and seldom visited institute in China, is developing RMA (Revolution in Military Affairs).

Using four vessels — *COSCO New York, Med Taipei, Cos. Bremerhaven* and *Joseph To 21* — COSCO made weekly calls at the Port of Norfolk from northern European ports after calls at the ports of New York and Baltimore (COSCO, April-August 1999). Beijing-cozy OOCL also provides shipping services to Norfolk.

Port of Baltimore — jilted for Norfolk

Baltimore terminals are nearly 100 miles up the Chesapeake Bay and the Patapsco River from the Atlantic Ocean, but its 50-foot channels place limits on few vessels. The Port of Baltimore handles nearly 2,000 vessel calls, perhaps 10 million tons a year and 500,000 TEUs. Innumerable private and public piers line the channel handling all types and sizes of cargoes.

In late 1998, COSCO moved perhaps 300,000 containers away from Dundalk and Seagirt container piers in Baltimore to Norfolk when it dropped its Far East service to Baltimore. It retained COSCO shipping from Europe.

Using four vessels — *COSCO New York, Med Taipei, Cos. Bremerhaven* and *Joseph To 21* — COSCO continued to make weekly calls at the Port of Baltimore from northern European ports after its stop in New York (COSCO, April-August 1999).

Port of Newport, Rhode Island — U.S. Navy Out, COSCO and Li Ka-Shing In?

In late November 2000 the *Business Journal* of Hampton Roads reported that Newport, Rhode Island, was close to deciding to construct a 170-acre container port on Narragansett Bay at closed Navy facilities at Quonset Point and Davisville.

As usual it would be a case of the U.S. Navy shipping out and the Chinese moving in.

R.K. Jones, a New York-based consulting firm, found the proposal to be economically sound in its report of July 31, 2000. "...Quonset Port will be a new facility situated at a former U.S. Navy Base. It can... be... a compact, highly efficient terminal, considerably more advanced and productive that any others in North America...

Meetings have been held... with about 15 containership lines and terminal operators that should be viewed as prospective partners and customers for Quonset Port. ...Based upon preliminary... communications with leading terminal operators and containership lines... we anticipate... prospective operators will express an interest..."

Could COSCO be far behind? COSCO is among the "A" list of companies recommended for recruitment for the new container port.

The Jones feasibility report cites Li Ka-Shing's Hutchison Whampoa favorably, "Recently, HIT has been a bidder on port privatization projects but has been surprisingly reticent as to its intentions in North America. [Golly gee, wonder why?] Nevertheless, HIT must be viewed as a likely entrant into this market in the near term, whether in its own name or in a cooperative venture with a local/regional partner."

Newport is located near the entry of Narragansett Bay, on the north shore of Rhode Island Sound. Old Navy port facilities are on the southwestern tip of Aquidneck Island, the largest of the numerous islands and peninsulas, or "necks," that rise out of the bay.

In the '70s the U.S. Navy owned 31 miles of shore and 6,000 acres of waterfront property in Narragansett Bay. The Naval Air Station once occupied the west bay, north of Quonset Point linked to East Passage by a dredged channel. East of East Passage the Navy also once held a six-mile stretch at Newport.

The U.S. Atlantic Fleet Cruiser-Destroyer Force once home ported at Coddington Cove and occupied deep-water berths on the north side of Pier 2. The south side of the pier is modern — steel piling and concrete capping. Piers 1 and 2 were built for the Cruiser-Destroyer Force which occupied deep-water berths on the south side of Pier 2 on completion of pier improvements in FY1985.

Since the Revolutionary War, the U.S. Navy has been a part of Narragansett Bay. Yet, in 1973, a Shore Establishment Realignment study called for the closing of the Quonset Point Naval Air Station, downgrading Davisville and moving the active fleet out of Newport. Five independent commands were consolidated into the Naval Education and Training Center (NETC). Newport still hosts the prestigious Naval War College and the Naval Undersea Warfare Center, the Navy's principal research center for submarine weapons.

In 1974 the Rhode Island Port Authority and Economic Development Corporation was created to handle the takeover of former Navy holdings. The Navy retains access for deep-draft vessels under Military Sealift Command to discharge or load stores at Davisville (north of Quonset Point). The large pier at Quonset Point, formerly berthing aircraft carriers, is a concrete-capped wood piling structure needing repair.

The 2.5-mile Quonset/Davisville Approach Channel was dredged for the Quonset Point Naval Base during the 1940s to a depth of 35 feet. Oceangoing traffic into Narragansett Bay enters via the East Passage channel. To modernize these facilities proposed cost are from $333 million to $450 million, of which $67 million to $127 million would be federal funds.

Port of New York and New Jersey

The New York region has long been the nation's center of commerce and trade principally with Europe. Container trade with Asia has increased, but it is small compared to the West Coast. Only 7% of West Coast container trade only 2.5 million TEUs — would double Asian trade with the Port of New York.

Trailing the West Coast in the China trade, the port is determined to increase its China trade.

As is the case everywhere, as the China presence expands, the U.S. Navy withdraws.

In the New York region, the U.S. Navy has closed the Staten Island Naval Station and Naval Reserve Center, the Brooklyn Naval Station, the Trenton Naval Air Warfare Center and the Philadelphia Naval Warfare Center.

Also the Philadelphia Naval Complex, the Naval Air Warfare Center, the Ocean Surveillance Center at Warminster, Pennyslyvania, and the Naval Undersea Warfare Center at New London, Connecticut.

On the coast of Connecticut the U.S. Navy still homeports 17 nuclear submarines at the Naval Submarine Base at Groton, Connecticut, five miles north up the Thames River and 10 miles north of the Races choke point between Long Island Sound and the coast of Connecticut.

The Port Authority of New York and New Jersey operates container terminals at four separate locations at Port Newark, Elizabeth, Red Hook in Brooklyn and Howland Hook in Staten Island. (Port Authority tenants operate the container terminals: Maersk-Universal, Sea-Land, American Stevedoring and Howland Hook Terminal, Inc.)

Port facilities are located in sheltered Newark Bay north of the Narrows — separating Staten Island and Long Island — which opens into the Atlantic Ocean south of New York Bay. These port facilities are generally west of Long Island which, on its north shore, opens into Long Island Sound and the Atlantic Ocean on the east.

The critical choke points are the narrows between Staten Island and Long Island on the south and the Races between the eastern most Long Island chain and the coast of Connecticut.

Prior to closing shop on Staten Island, the U.S. Navy (U.S. taxpayers) invested $230 million in the construction of a possible new consolidated naval home port in Staten Island.

Like San Francisco, New York City did not want the U.S. Navy homeported or otherwise present in Gotham. Nuclear weapons, the environment and marauding sailors — no angle of opposition went unexpressed. The Mayor of New York, David Dinkins, and 11 of the 14 members of the New York City Congressional delegation and 16 members of the New York City Council urged closing the Staten Island base.

Whether former U.S. Navy facilities on Staten Island or in Brooklyn subsequently benefited COSCO or have benefited COSCO through land swaps is unknown.

It is clear that unlike the U.S. Navy, COSCO and OOCL traverse the narrows and sail the waters of the ports.

COSCO, USA has its national office six miles up the river from Newark Bay. OOCL owns and operates very profitable facilities at the Global Terminal in New Jersey and at Howland Hook on Staten Island in New York.

The Port of New York and New Jersey is making major investments trying mightily to take away at least 2.5 million TEUs of China and Southeast Asian cargo from West Coast ports by 2020. By 2005 the port plans a 200-acre expansion at the former Military Ocean Terminal in Bayonne and Port Jersey, NJ, to handle containerized cargo.

New York piers are rotting and falling into the Hudson and East River according to the *New York Post*[13] and other observers. While Maersk Sealand claimed $600 million would be required for restoration and a new terminal, it still chose the Port of New York over Baltimore as its new Atlantic hub.

In early July 2000, the U.S. Senate approved the beginning of a $1.8 billion project over 16 years to dredge silt and blast bedrock to deepen over 34 miles of primary navigational channels to the ports of New York.

In 1997 New York and New Jersey had 78% of the China trade in the North Atlantic market. As in other ports COSCO appears to be well behaved most of the time. U.S. Customs caught nine stowaways from the Dominican Republic on a COSCO container ship in late September 1998.[14] COSCO stocks surged on the Hong Kong market in mid-November 1999 upon news of the Clinton-Gore trade agreement with China.[15]

COSCO loves New York. COSCO has recently expanded services to New York via both the Panama Canal and Suez Canal. At both canals Red China's proxies — COSCO, Hutchison Whampoa and perhaps OOCL — have recently, vastly expanded their activities while the U.S. Navy has withdrawn.

In March 1999 the Port of New York and the Suez Canal Authority agreed to expand shipments from Asia to New York Harbor via the Suez Canal.

---

[13] *New York Post,* April 14, 1999
[14] *New York Times,* September 26, 1998
[15] *New York Times,* November 16, 1999

It is claimed that the Suez Canal route may give the Port of New York and New Jersey a cost advantage over West Coast competitors since a new all-water route through the Canal bypasses the usual rail transport across the USA from West Coast ports.

In late May 2000, COSCO initiated new Asia Express shipping services via the Panama Canal to the Elizabeth Marine Terminal.[16] Nine container ships, each with a capacity of 3,400 containers, use the route every week, from Shanghai to Hong Kong and through the

The Port of New York and New Jersey has facilities on the shores and islands of New York and New Jersey.

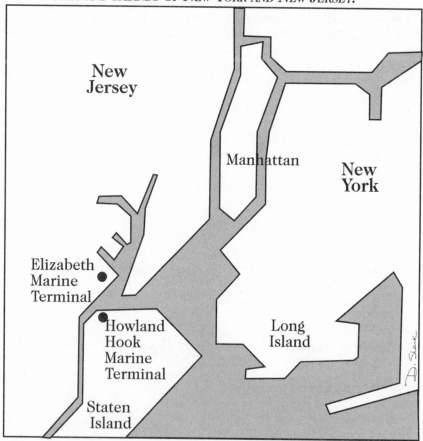

COSCO uses the Elizabeth Marine Terminal off Newark Bay. OOCL operates the Global Terminal in New Jersey and Howland Hook on Staten Island. The port is expanding the Elizabeth and Howland Hook terminals and will occupy portions of the former U.S. Military Ocean Terminal at Bayonne and Jersey City.

---

[16] *New York Times*, May 25, 2000

Panama Canal to New York-New Jersey, calling in Norfolk and Charleston before returning to China via Tokyo and Kobe, Japan.

Lillian C. Borrone, Port Authority spokesman, said, "We are now competing directly with West Coast ports for this [COSCO] cargo." COSCO's new Asian service cuts a week off the usual 33-day voyage. Mrs. Borrone said, "COSCO recognizes... that with bigger, faster ships, carriers can reduce both the cost and the time it takes to deliver a product... by traversing the Panama Canal..."

In 2000 COSCO used eight vessels — *Chesapeake Bridge, Xi Bo He, Na Xi He, Yu Gu He, Ha Ni He, Rainbow Bridge, Ming Prominence* and *Jing Po He* — to make weekly calls at the Port of New York from Hong Kong and other Asian ports via the Panama Canal.

In June 2000 COSCO announced, "COSCO Container Lines and Zim Israeli Lines plan to [share]... container slots-leasing... on the Mediterranean-U.S. East Service. COSCO will be able to use container slots from Zim Lines [in] Savannah, New York, Harifax [sic]..." and southern European ports.

Using another four vessels — *COSCO New York, Med Taipei, Cos. Bremerhaven* and *Joseph To 21* — COSCO made weekly calls at the Port of New York from northern European ports via Baltimore and Norfolk (COSCO, April-August 1999).

Port of Boston — begging for business

In November 2000, Maersk pulled out of the Port of Boston, ranked only number 30 in the U.S.

Boston spent $100 million to improve its port facilities to attract some business — any kind of business. By April 2001, while the Chinese held 24 Americans hostage on Hainan Island and President Bush was assuring Taiwan of its defense, port director Mike Leone flew off to Beijing to plead for COSCO's help.

A special Port of Boston Committee — Staples, Ames, Reebok — offered COSCO more corporate business if it would set up shop at the Port of Boston. Over 100 of Boston's elite met COSCO's CEO, Wei Jiafu, for dinner at the Boston Harbor Hotel where he committed to making Boston a port of call. He hoped the local community and Massport would support sufficient cargo.

Though COSCO ships carried 3,800 to 5,200 containers each, COSCO's Boston business was a miniscule 100 containers a week! Much ado about nothing... except the 19th-century slave trade might be replaced by the slave trade of the 21st century — China's child, slave and prison labor.

The *Boston Herald* opined that "Massachusetts has a tremendous stake" in COSCO and the China trade. COSCO's CEO said, "Make the nest first, and the Phoenix will come."[17]

---

[17] *AP*, April 26, 2001, May 29, 2001; *Boston Herald*, June 3, 2001

Port of Halifax, Nova Scotia, Canada

The Port of Halifax, Nova Scotia, is deep with a 65-foot channel, 45- to 50-foot piers and is ice free. Halifax is just 60 miles off the Great Circle Route and a day's sail from the U.S. East Coast ports.[18]

PLA-owned COSCO provides weekly service from Halifax to northern Europe. Similarly, Beijing-friendly OOCL provides Friday service to Northern Europe and twice-weekly service to the Far East. While outside U.S. territory, the Canadian port of Halifax has long had high strategic importance to the U.S.

In 1939 three U.S. destroyers were stationed in Halifax to provide a "neutrality patrol" in the North Atlantic. The British Admiralty, protecting Britain's Atlantic lifeline, established a convoy system for merchant shipping.

Despite German warnings in the fall of 1940, the U.S. gave 23 destroyers to the U.K., which renamed and armed them to escort convoys. "By the long arm of coincidence" British Prime Minister Churchill immediately provided Royal Navy crews to man the U.S. destroyers! In early November 1941, U.S-flagged vessels, including six U.S. transports and the aircraft carrier *Ranger*, escorted 20,000 troops out of Halifax.

In 1942, German submarine *U-588* torpedoed the U.S. freighter *Greylock* off Halifax, Nova Scotia. *U-432* attacked the unarmed U.S. fishing trawler *Foam*. A Canadian patrol craft and a Canadian corvette, HMCS *Halifax*, picked up lifeboats with 20 survivors.

In 1943, the U.S. tanker *Brilliant* bound for Halifax broke up in a storm. A PV-1 (VB 125) off Halifax sank German submarine *U-174*. British and Canadian naval forces took over responsibility for convoys between Halifax and the U.K. In 1944, destroyer escorts *Thomas* (DE-102) and *Baker* (DE-190) sank German minelayer submarine *U-233* off Halifax.[19]

In the present, Halifax has returned to commerce

A St. Clair Tunnel has improved access from the East Coast to the U.S. Midwest. Improvements made in rail service to Toronto, Montreal, Boston, Chicago and New Orleans have increased the efficiency and volume of the port at Halifax. More than two-thirds of container traffic moves directly to rail, allowing rapid transport of goods to Boston and to the Midwest. These improvements permit the largest deep draft vessels to lighten their load at Halifax for the lesser draft ports on the East Coast. In 1999 Halifax container traffic hit a new high of 463,000 TEUs moved. In early 2000, container traffic was up 17% to 1.5 million tons.

---

[18] *Port of Halifax Magazine*, September/October 2000
[19] USN official chronology of WWII

Recent investments have also improved two Halifax container terminals. The Halifax investments of $23.5 million also include improvements in yard tractors, rail and power. The cranes, as tall as a 35-story building, now number six, reach over 22 containers, and fetch 45 containers per hour.

Shanghai Zhen Hua Port Machinery Co., Ltd. (ZPMC) of China built two super cranes, 356-feet and 1,250-tons, these make Halifax only the second Canadian port to handle ships wider than the Panama Canal. ZPMC owns the World of Cranes.

COSCO has been serving the Port of Halifax from the newly-constructed Fairview Container Terminal since September 1998. COSCO Container Line increased the capacity of its Halifax North Europe service by one-third with its 3,400-TEU MV *Naxi He* calling on a weekly rotation from Halifax to ports in Northern Europe.

In addition to European routes, COSCO has weekly express cargoes (grains, frozen seafood, forest products and building materials) going to Asian ports.

Always happy to make a strategic move, "Halifax had been a missing link in our chain of ever-expanding North American services," says Qimin Liu, President of China Ocean Shipping (Canada), Inc. Halifax rail services have also pleased COSCO. "Having offices in the major cities signifies COSCO's emphasis on... increasing economic cooperation between the People's Republic of China and Canada," Liu said. "COSCO is happy to be at home in Halifax and looks toward a strong and prosperous Year of the Dragon," said Liu.[20]

•

Beyond seaports, the Chinese Trojan Horses can be found elsewhere in the American homeland. If anyone looks. We will. Any COSCO sailors considering, or tasked to, patriotic duties for their Red Chinese homeland might have plenty of company elsewhere on American soil in the form of mainland Chinese students and scientists — to whom we will now turn.

---

[20] *Port of Halifax Magazine*, March/April 2000

PRC Targets Students and Scientists in the USA

PRC tries to recruit overseas Chinese as spies

In early 2000, the National Counterintelligence Center (NCIC) of the CIA warned federal agencies and American companies to beware of Red Chinese government attempts to recruit their scientists. The Red Chinese wanted to steal our technology. Confirming NCIC, the vice president of the Chinese Academy of Science says China is seeking scientists "of Chinese nationality... willing to abandon their... citizenship." Clearly, Red Chinese opportunities for recruiting spies abound in the U.S.[1] The Cox Report and Gertz's *China Threat* detail the success of Red Chinese spying in the U.S.

"And by portraying itself as heir to the imperial tradition, the Party leadership also demands the loyalty of all overseas Chinese... 30 or 40 million..."

Ethnicity motivates. Indeed, overseas Chinese account for 80% of foreign investment in Red China. They have resisted helping dissident groups. Ethnic Chinese are often patriotic about their common Chinese race and history.

The unity and solidarity of Chinese history and culture may create mixed loyalties among some ethnic Chinese. Many overseas Chinese in Taiwan, Hong Kong and Indonesia often compete with Red rulers. Who is most patriotic and nationalistic? Indeed, the nations of Indonesia, Malaysia and Thailand have long suspected the loyalty of their ethnic Chinese citizens.

Overseas Chinese billionaires such as Li Ka-Shing, Mochtar Riady, Liem Sioe Liong, C.C. Tung and others have figured prominently in major new investments in China. The Chinese billionaires have consistently failed to condemn oppression in Red China. They are silent or choose ethnicity and their own personal wealth over individual freedom for the Chinese people, for example. Visitors to Shantou University are treated to a video of Li Ka-Shing. He says, "My only true purpose is to contribute what I can to my home town, my nation, and my motherland. It is my life purpose."[2]

---

[1] *Military* magazine, 2000
[2] Jasper Becker, *The Chinese*

Reds target ethnic Chinese to spy

So how can the U.S. respond to Red Chinese ethnicity? (Just as the Soviets used Russian ethnic patriots.) A former director of the FBI's Chinese counterintelligence, Paul D. Moore, admits there is "racial profiling" in U.S. counterintelligence. There is no choice. Red China routinely targets Chinese citizens studying or working in the U.S. as well as ethnic Chinese Americans. The evidence is incontrovertible. Red China is "interested obsessively in people of Chinese American ancestry to the exclusion of [other] people..." It is unavoidable. The FBI must focus on Chinese American scientists.

Similarly, a joint FBI-CIA report to Congress in January 2000 said that the Red Chinese used "some of the thousands" of Chinese students and scientists, and exploited the "shared ancestry" of Chinese Americans.

Members of the local Everett, Washington, Chinese community say goodbye to crewmembers of visiting Chinese navy ships Qingdao (DDG 113) and Taicang (AOR 575). — U.S. Navy photo

Actually, there are hundreds of thousands of Red Chinese targets. The number of potential Chinese agents is very large and growing without adequate U.S. attention. "In all, over 300,000 Chinese studied abroad between 1979 and 1999 and, in the 1990s, as many as 100,000 were studying in the United States at one time," according to Jasper Becker — 50,000 students in 2000 alone.

Chinese-granted applications and U.S. Embassy acceptances for visas of all kinds have exceeded a quarter million a year recently

— 300,000 plus in 2001. Tens of thousands of Red Chinese students a year illegally stay beyond their visa period, according to the *San Jose Mercury News*.[3] There were 200,000 Red Chinese illegals in the 2000 census.

Chinese students overseas

In the 1999-2000 school year alone, China sent 54,466 students to the U.S.[4]

How do they get here?

According to the American Embassy website in Beijing, "Every year, the U.S. issues thousands of visas to Chinese students. Over 50,000 Chinese now study in the United States, and China now rivals [actually the PRC surpassed] Japan as the source of the largest number of foreign students seeking education in America...

The Embassy has evidence that... a high percentage of students did not return to China after graduation... It is up to the applicant to prove... identifiable... social and career prospects in China... that they are very well connected in China; these students should be able to show that their parents will be able to place them in attractive jobs in China."

If Red China has a policy of putting agents in place, the American Embassy in Beijing is willfully aiding that effort or is hopelessly naïve.

Clearly, the U.S. embassy recruits students loyal to the PRC, the embassy actively discourages those who might be the most disloyal to the PRC.

No surprise. Many Chinese students are children of the ruling elite, "princelings." Jiang Zemin's son Jiang Mianheng graduated from Drexel University. Jiang Junior opened China Netcom to provide a fiberoptic network for China. Deng Xiaoping's son Deng Zifang studied physics at Rochester University.[5]

Jasper Becker cites Quin Ning (son of foreign minister Quin Quichen) author of *Studying in the United States: The Story of an Era*. Quin reports in a survey that less than a third of Chinese students return home and that those who do return "are not coming back to overthrow the government." Becker says that half of the Chinese students in the USA came from families of intellectuals persecuted under Mao (Cultural Revolution), a quarter from rural China and the remaining quarter from families of the elite.

The Chinese perfected totalitarianism millennia ago. They have no experience with the rule of law, free speech or democracy. So

---

[3] *San Jose Mercury News*, July 13, 2001
[4] Institute of International Education
[5] Jasper Becker, *The Chinese*, 2001

many returning students become members of the kleptocracy that rules China. They return perhaps armed with knowledge of technologies that may be used as instruments of state power over citizens. The American security problem is those Chinese students who both stay beyond their studies <u>and</u> also retain loyalties to the Middle Kingdom. In 1997 about a third of the physics graduates of Beijing University left China usually to live, work or teach in the USA.[6] Why did the Red Chinese let them go? According to a survey by the National Science Foundation 91% of Chinese students earning doctorates in science and engineering plan to stay in the U.S.[7] Why aren't the Chinese complaining about a "brain drain?"

In fact, 50% or more stay on to become U.S. citizens. Yet, most do maintain strong ties to Red China. They visit China. They have business in China and more important, they meet with Red China's government officials.[8] What they converse about with the Communist government, we should ask.

How many are loyal to Red China is unknown and worth watching. Yet, no one watches. Hear, see and tell no evil.

According to an Inspector General's report to the Senate Committee on Government Affairs on June 23, 1999, some five major U.S. universities give hundreds of research students and staff, half of them foreign, access to the supercomputers at U.S. nuclear weapons labs. Such openess to the nation's nuclear secrets is just plain stupid. It approaches criminal negligence.

There are many opportunities for foreign students and others to study, stay and spy in the United States. The F-1 Academic Student visa is for someone who merely promises to temporarily study in the U.S. and then promises to return home. Empty promises are made and frequently broken. The J visa is for specially sponsored exchange students (administered by the United States Information Agency). The J-1 visa is used typically by foreign scholars, experts, medical interns, professors, researchers, teachers and industrial and business trainees. J-1s are usually sponsored by a government or an international agency. During 1998 some 6,462 persons from Red China obtained J-1 visas according to the Visa Office of the Department of State.[9] The M visa is for nonacademic students, trade or technical training, e.g. airline pilots, vocational students, technical and some business school students.

Foreign students, many from China, now receive more than half the Ph.D.s in engineering granted by U.S. universities. For decades foreign students have dominated advanced degree programs in phys-

---

[6] Jasper Becker
[7] Beth McMurtrie, *Chronicle of Higher Education,* June 27, 2001
[8] Public Policy Institute of California, *Research Brief #21,* June 1999
[9] Table 40, Nonimmigrants Admitted... 1998

ics, chemistry, mathematics and computer sciences. Most are from India, Pakistan and Red China. For several decades the Institute of Electrical and Electronic Engineers and others complained that graduate schools, e.g. University of California, actually gave preferences at the expense of American students to the foreign born in graduate M.S. and Ph.D. programs in engineering, mathematics and science. Leadership in math-science has radically shifted away from the home born to immigrants.

Today, "about 70% to 80% of students in U.S. universities obtaining Ph.D.s in the sciences are from foreign countries," according to Patricia McDermott of Digital Equipment. "One third of master's of science degree candidates and one half of all electrical engineering doctoral degree candidates are now foreign nationals," says SEMI, a Silicon Valley association of manufacturers of chips.

The American K-12 public education system is guilty.

In the 2000 International Math and Science Study U.S. students scored far below students from Japan, Korea, Hong Kong, Singapore, Australia, Canada and most industrialized nations. In California, the home of high technology Silicon Valley, only one in six eighth-graders is proficient in math. Things are getting worse — among fourth-graders only one in nine is competent in math.

So, about 65% of California's high school graduates require remedial math (and English!) after entering California's 23 state universities. State universities are stuck with the flotsam and jetsam of the failed K-12 system so they depend upon foreign students (even taxpayer-subsidized illegal aliens), to provide 60% of California's engineers and computer scientists.

Elsewhere, 84% of Arizona students recently failed a state math test.

The response of politicians to such problems is always the same. California, Maryland, Massachusetts, Delaware, Ohio, Wisconsin and Alaska have made the math and science tests easier.

So, industry and research institutions insist they must go outside the U.S. to find competent employees. Industry turns to resident foreign students — who originally promised to go home — who apply for H-1B visas up to six years after they were supposed to go home.

High-tech labor shortages

The demand is high. In 1998 high-tech companies claimed they could not find the 25,000 to 50,000 American workers they needed with M.S.s and Ph.D.s in math, science, engineering, computer science, operations research and industrial engineering. The Information Technology Association of America (ITAA) recently claimed there were 346,000 vacancies for computer programmers, engineers and systems analysts. At least a third of all the engineers in Silicon Valley are Asian Americans, but that did not fill the need. By 2000, the

ITAA was claiming a loss to the U.S. economy of $100 billion a year because of a shortage of 1.6 million high-tech workers.

Several types of visas are used to fulfill this need. In particular the H-1 Specialized Worker Visa is for persons with degrees or experience able to work in jobs requiring highly specialized knowledge, e.g. nurses, engineers, chemists, MBAs and other professionals. The H-1 is granted for a three-year period, but is extendible to six years.

In 1998 the Visa Office of the State Department reported 3,880 H-1B visas issued to persons from the People's Republic of China. Other technical workers qualify under H-2B — 730 from China in 1998. H-3 Trainee Visa is for on-the-job training — 58 came from China in 1998. Under L-1 a foreign employee of a U.S. company in another country may work in the U.S. During 1998, 1,535 persons from China worked in the U.S. under L-1 visas.[10] In 1998 6,203 mainland Chinese came under these work-related visas.

Responding to shortages of high skilled labor in America, high-tech firms have successfully lobbied for expansions of special (H-1B) visas allowing technically educated foreign workers to stay in the U.S. for three to six years.

Proponents of H-1B visas claim there is an inability of America's "education and training bureaucracy to provide workers with higher-order skills, especially in math and science."

The American Engineering Association (AEA) counters that high-tech firms really want cheaper foreign workers and to lay off older' expensive U.S. workers. In 1998, the ITAA opposed and Congress rejected a House bill lifting all annual limits on H-1B visas if two reasonable conditions were met. Wages paid had to be over $40,000 a year and no U.S. workers were to be displaced. High-tech firms want both cheap labor and competent labor — wherever it comes from.

In 1998 Congress raised the H-1B visa limit from 65,000 to 115,000 annually. By late 2000 Congress nearly doubled the quota to 200,000 "temporary" (three to six years) visas per year until 2003.

More than half of all H-1B visas are granted to citizens of India (48%) or the People's Republic of China (9%). Hence, the 2000 legislation would welcome about 54,000 PRC Chinese to work in U.S. high technology. In 1998 the Visa Office of the U.S. Department of State reported only 3,880 H-1B visas issued to persons from the People's Republic of China.[11] The 2000 law could be a 1,400% increase of H-1B visas from Red China.

Currently, 20% of all resumes that are checked for H-1B visa applicants are found to be false. Has Congress invited 11,000 Chinese liars and/or PRC spies into the USA to work in our high-tech industries? Perhaps the number is far less, but there is a number. There are Chinese spies. Someone should be looking for them in all the likely places.

_____

[10, 11] Table 40, Nonimmigrants Admitted... Department of State, 1998

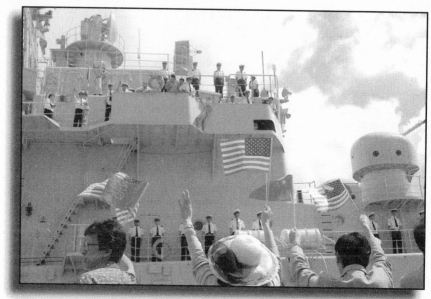

Sailors from the People's Republic of China wave goodbye to well wishers as the destroyer Qingdao (DDG 113) prepares to depart Pearl Harbor. — U.S. Navy photo

What can be done about high risk workers in U.S. industry?

The law requires private companies to acquire export licenses for certain high risk technologies. A license is required if a company plans to give a foreign worker, H-1B and others, access to technology whose export is prohibited without a license. These technologies requiring a license to grant access to a worker include nuclear, biological, chemical, missile, supercomputers (HPCs) and dual use (military and civilian) products. Giving access to a foreign worker is "deemed" an export of that technology to a foreign nation.

Many private employers are totally unaware of the "deemed export" license. That does not appear to matter, even for those companies that bother to ask for the license. Under the Clinton Commerce Department from 1998 through 2000, some 1,716 "deemed export" license requests were approved, 102 denied. 96% approved, only 4% disapproved![12] Nearly 2,000 foreign workers were given access to dangerous technologies that could threaten American national security.

Indeed, according to an Inspector General's report to the Senate Committee on Government Affairs on June 23, 1999, Red Chinese nationals who merely declare they wish to stay in the U.S. are no

---

[12] R. Roger Majak, U.S. Department of Commerce, July 10, 2000

longer required to have a "deemed export" license. The Red Chinese access is exactly the same as a loyal U.S. citizen.

Red Chinese are free to "change" their minds and return later to the PRC with all technological secrets in their heads and baggage. In May 2001 Kenneth Juster, Bush appointee to the Department of Commerce, testified before the House Committee on International Relations supporting an increased role of the Departments of Defense and State in reviewing "deemed exports."

Loyal, new Americans?

According to Digital Corporation, about half of foreign Ph.D.s become permanent residents. One quarter to one third move to other countries. The rest return to their country of origin — about 20% to 25%. Two-thirds of foreign Ph.D.s prefer to stay in the U.S. as new citizens. According to a survey by the National Science Foundation, 91% of Chinese students earning doctorates in science and engineering plan to stay in the U.S.[13] Indeed, Charles Sie, formerly of Xerox Corp., says that about 150,000 Chinese American scientists and engineers now work in the United States, 5,000 in defense. I believe those estimates are too low.

H-1B visas are clearly stepping-stones to legal residency, naturalization and citizenship. In most cases, America benefits greatly. For 50 to 70 years the world's top scientists became naturalized U.S. citizens, e.g. six Chinese Americans have earned Nobel prizes in physics and chemistry.

Ted Wong, an engineer, guided Hughes Aircraft Co.'s missile systems group (Raytheon Corp.) in early research on the Reagan Strategic Defense Initiative.

Andrew Chi, a physicist at NASA's Goddard Space Flight Center developed the atomic clock in the Global Positioning System (GPS) guiding Cadillacs, bombs and ships.

H.K. Cheng of the University of Southern California worked on hypersonic flow physics essential to reentry of missiles and spacecraft.

Chih-Ming Ho at UCLA demonstrated that tiny micro-electromechanical systems, or MEMS, could replace flaps making jets faster, more agile and less detectable.

•

Had we responded to the Sputnik crisis as we have to technical labor shortages, we would have invited the Russian scientists to conduct our space program. In fact, besides hiring friendly foreign talent, we used talented Americans, many without credentials. This

---

[13] Beth McMurtrie, *Chronicle of Higher Education*, June 27, 2001

native talent got the USA to the moon. Many earned their degrees in night school.[14] After reaching the moon and winning the Cold War we fired them. Thousands live in Los Angeles and elsewhere. Some wrote the *American Spectator* in June 1998 denying the USA lacked talent sought by H-1B visas.

Raising the H-1B visa quotas has accelerated giving U.S. computer, missile and nuclear technologies to America's enemies in the next war. It has aided Chinese agents of espionage and terrorist actions.

The INS ought to radically improve automated systems tracking the entry and departure of all student, worker and tourist visa holders. The current status of hundreds of thousands of holders of student and other visas ought to be known. Routine background, polygraph or other checks of loyalty ought to made for those having access to technologies with military uses. Appropriate means of protecting the civil liberties of citizens should, of course, be honored.

•

We turn now to Red Chinese front companies conducting business and sometimes espionage in the USA.

---

[14] October Sky

Agents Red... the China Traders Live in the USA

Chinese companies front for the PLA in the USA

Measures are needed to protect national security from COSCO and other PRC front companies such as Orient Overseas and Hutchison Whampoa.

There are many other Red Chinese front companies with even lower profiles. For these only the resources of a vigilant public and intelligence agencies can begin to fathom or monitor. To do so and still protect American civil liberties will tax the good will and intelligence of all of us.

"FBI investigations have identified various methods [of]... economic espionage. ...[R]ecruiting individuals with access to a targeted technology or information is a classical, time-proven technique... .[F]oreign collectors assess the vulnerabilities of the individual, looking for any personal weaknesses or commonality [ethnicity, culture, ideology, language] between them... that can be exploited... Other methods include tasking students who come to study in the United States; exploiting... friendship societies, international exchange organizations, or import-export companies; hiring away knowledgeable employees... with... the specific goal of exploiting their inside knowledge; and manipulating legitimate technology sharing agreements... [as]... conduits for... information..."[1]

Travel agents and brokers

There are a number of companies that serve as agents for Red Chinese government officials visiting the USA to see U.S. industrial plants, universities and critical infrastructures.

Some of these travel agents for Red Chinese officials include: Bi Bridge Enterprises, Inc.; Chinese Trade and Research and Action, Inc.; FCC Group International (USA), Inc. on Flair Drive in El Monte, California; and Global Unisource USA, Inc. of Houston, Texas. Also PTS International, Inc. of Monterey Park, California; Triway Enterprise, Inc. of Arlington, Virginia; U.C. Service Center on Flair Drive in El Monte, California; and Union-Tech Engineering, Inc. of Arcadia, California.

These agents Red are the friendliest people on Earth and loved by the Americans who come in contact with them.

---

[1] FBI website

Such travel agents for the Red Chinese have altered American agency letters of invitation to falsify length, purpose and location of their visits. This practice deceives U.S. Consulates and the U.S. Embassy in Beijing, which must approve all visas. It gives Red Chinese visitors license to do as they please without notice once they arrive in America's free and open society.

Chinese travel agents have complained that the U.S. Embassy in Beijing under the Bush Administration has denied Chinese visas to tour western dams, reservoirs, power plants, pumping stations and aqueducts. Ever-friendly civil servants invite them. The U.S. Embassy in Beijing approves most requests. The embassy does not tell local officials why it rejects some Chinese visas.

One must presume these travel agents serve their Beijing paymasters. Travel agents can be expected to place agents of the Chinese government among persons and near places where U.S. technology and/or its infrastructures are most vulnerable.

For one example, over the last five years no fewer than 100 Red Chinese officials have visited the California State Water Project and the federal Central Valley Project in California. This is not a parochial concern. These civil engineering water works far surpass the Panama Canal by the amount of dirt they moved. These public works and free enterprise transformed California from floods and droughts, swamps and deserts into the world's fifth-largest economy. These structures are vulnerable to attack at great cost of blood and treasure.

This Red Chinese penetration of an open America is surely repeated every day in every geographic region and industrial sector of our lives.

Freight forwarders

As Kenneth Puckett, a Panama Canal pilot, first pointed out to the author, freight forwarders often control the manifests, the paper trail on the contents of ships and containers.

Kenneth Timmerman writing in the October 1997 issue of the *American Spectator* listed Red Chinese-controlled freight forwarders such as Pan Ocean Lines, North China Cargo, CU Transport, Inc. (a creature of the China National Foreign Trade Transportation Corporation) located in Alhambra, Rosemead and Monterey Park, California. China Interocean Transport, Inc. (China National Foreign Trade Transportation Corp.) in Compton, California; CCIC North America, Inc. (China National Import and Export Commodities Inspection Corp.) in West Covina and El Monte, Califora, and Morrison Express in El Segundo, California.

Freight forwarding is a legal business. The problem is the loyalties of Red Chinese company owners or employees.

U-Freight – computers

In September 1993, U-Freight, Inc., freight forwarder in South San Francisco, California, filed false documents to facilitate a Sun Microsystems shipment of prohibited computers to the PRC.

Seven years after the offense in October 1993 on March 20, 2000, the Commerce Department imposed a $20,000 fine on U-Freight — $10,000 suspended for a promise not to break the law again.[2]

It was not much more than a traffic ticket. This for putting high performance computers into the hands of Red Chinese merchants of nuclear weapons components. This for facilitating China's sales of nuclear components to countries run by lunatics — Iraq, Iran, Libya, Syria and North Korea.

Front Companies

Timmerman and the Cox Report disclosed that thousands of Red Chinese companies are based in the U.S., most in Los Angeles, open for business and possibly espionage.

Conducting a little private research and using the public records of the California Secretary of State, Kenneth Timmerman counted at least 150 Chinese companies in a single building at 9300 Flair Drive in El Monte. Other single addresses with hundreds of Chinese companies registered as corporations in California are 9460 Telstar and 9480 Telstar and 9550 Flair Drive.[3]

Chinese Defense Companies

In 1997 Timmerman cited Chinese government-owned defense industries having Los Angeles area offices.

Catronics in San Dimas is a branch of China National Electronics Import-Export Corp., a maker of radar, communications and cryptography equipment.

GW Aerospace, Inc. of Torrance is an entity of Great Wall Industry Corp., a producer and oft-cited proliferater of components of weapons of mass destruction.

In Baldwin Park, Mei An Industry is an agent of Xian Aircraft that produces military cargo aircraft and parts for Boeing 737s and 757s.

SAMCO Machine Tool of Gardena is a subsidiary of the China National Machinery and Equipment Import and Export Co., a producer of armored vehicles and trucks cited for providing missile components to Pakistan in August 2001.

---

[2] Website of Bureau of Industry and Security Export Enforcement, Department of Commerce
[3] *American Spectator*

SWC Business International USA, Inc., of Hacienda Heights is a subsidiary of NORINCO, China's major weapons manufacturer.

The Cox Report listed entities of the People's Liberation Army operating in the United States:

China Jing, an equipment import and export corporation (People's Armed Police) on West Valley in San Gabriel;

China Songhai Industry Corporation (PLA Navy) in La Mirada;

China Songhai Industrial Corporation of Los Angeles;

China Xinxing Import & Export Corporation (PLA General Logistics Dept.) on Broad Street in New York, and Xinxing Sun Win Asia Company, Ltd., and

Xinxing (USA), Inc., on Olney Street in El Monte.

Chinese government agencies

Timmerman found the PRC's wholly-owned China National Aero Technology Import-Export Company (CATIC) in El Monte. The PRC-owned China National Nonferrous Metal Industry Corporation in Monterey Park and its California subsidiaries, CNNC American Group, Inc., Jia Hua and Minmetals in Baldwin Park and in the City of Industry.

The author's research found about 30 Chinese companies listed on American stock exchanges through ADRs (American Depository Receipts) in 2001. These companies are listed as members of either the New York Stock Exchange, NASDAQ or 144A "restricted." Most are either State-Owned Enterprises (SOEs), majority-owned by the PRC-PLA or entirely dependent upon the whims of Communist officials. Investing in these companies may not be good for your country or your pocketbook.

So why care about such companies?

Charles Smith of *WorldNetDaily* (and others) have identified front companies used by Chinese military officers and detailed the militarily valuable computer, telecommunications and other technologies they have acquired from the United States by sale or theft.

- In 1994, Chinese Generals Ding Henggao and Huai Guomo formed Galaxy New Technologies as a front to acquire AT&T encrypted fiberoptic network for the People's Liberation Army.

- Tandem Corp CEO James Irebig joined Commerce Secretary Ron Brown on a Beijing trade mission in August 1994. In 1996 Tandem exported computers to the PLA's Great Wall Corporation.

- In 1995 Defense Secretary William Perry promised General Ding Henggao "a Cray super-computer to be used directly by the Chinese weapons establishment to help design...

safer nukes." Cray attended a Beijing meeting in October with other computer companies — IBM, Sun, Apple, Digital, Silicon Graphics.

• In 1995 Perry provided his friend General Ding Henggao and a Chinese Army unit — Commission on Science, Technology and Industry for National Defense (COSTIND) — with Hughes remote sensing equipment.

• In 1995 the Clinton Administration approved the sale of Rockwell Collins Navigation Equipment Company factory and training to a Shanghai front company for the PLA-owned Aviation Industries of China. The equipment sold, GPS (global positioning system), "enhance... the capacities... to field highly accurate cruise and ballistic missiles," according to a U.S. Department of Commerce report.

• In March 1996, Loral president Jerald A. Lindfelt sought the direct intervention of Commerce Secretary Ron Brown to approve the sale of long-range sensors — Synthetic Aperture Radar (SAR) — to the Beijing Institute for Remote Sensing, "developer of precision guidance systems for surface-to-air missiles." The U.S. uses this advanced radar for real time battlefield observation as well as in U.S. AF F-15s.[4] Together GPS and SAR "raise serious concerns for the U.S. Seventh Fleet" in any confrontation with Taiwan.

• In 1997 a Sun Computer was sold to Yuanwang Gromo, which gave it to the PLA's National Defense Technical Institute of China in Changsha.

Wan Kao and Stephen Kao

In May 2001, the Commerce Department, U.S. Customs Service and the Postal Service swept down upon a little Orlando, Florida, company doing business under the apparent proprietorship of Wan Kao and her husband Stephen.

They were in fact Red Chinese nationals, Kao Ahwan and Kao Shuli, operating a subsidiary of Hong Kong-based Means Come Enterprises, Inc. Means Come was a front for Red Chinese makers of missiles and military satellites.

This not-so-little-company had, since 1997, bought nearly 10,000 "radiation hardened" integrated circuits from Atel Electronics and Harris Semiconductor for use only in the USA.

Means Come Enterprises, Inc., illegally transferred the chips in

[4] Smith, *WorldNetDaily*, May 18, 1999

1998 to Great Wall Industries, a state-owned defense aerospace company; China National Aero-Technology (CATIC) and China Aerospace Corp., a specialist in missiles and satellites.

Gary Milhollin of the Wisconsin Project on Nuclear Arms Control said the chips would improve China's "ability to target U.S. cities with long range missiles." Milhollin said Chinese companies ought to be put on a "watch list." Indeed.[5]

The Chinese do not cooperate with American "watchdogs." Americans — seeking to enforce U.S. National Security controls on exports of computers, satellite and other technologies — have frequently been denied on site inspections in China. Without inspections there is no way to verify the alledged civilian rather than military use of high technologies.

After intense lobbying by the U.S. computer industry, in August 2000 the Clinton White House loosened controls on exports of supercomputers to China. Supercomputers have many military uses, e.g. designing missiles and nuclear warheads. "The new rules will allow computers performing up to 28,000 MTOPS (million theoretical operations per second) to be sold without government review to military organizations in... China, India, Pakistan and Russia," Senators Jesse Helms (R-NC) and Russell Feingold (D-WI) said. "The new controls drop any distinction between military and civilian customers, thereby allowing powerful American computers to be purchased directly by foreign entities building weapons of mass destruction."

In early October 2000, Senate Foreign Relations Committee Chairman Helms and Senator Feingold identified 50 Chinese arms manufacturers that Clinton rules had made eligible to buy U.S. super computers.

Bill Gertz reported in *The Washington Times*, "All the Chinese companies are involved in developing advanced conventional weapons or nuclear, chemical and biological weapons and missiles."

The 50 companies "are well-known parts of China's nuclear, missile and military complex," Helms and Feingold said. The companies are high risks to proliferate parts of weapons of mass destruction to rogue nations (Iran, Iraq, Syria, Libya, North Korea, etc.). They may divert civilian technology to military R&D for the PLA. Indeed, about 100 Chinese companies produce missile components, not counting those producing nuclear, chemical and biological items.

Gary Milhollin, director of the Wisconsin Project on Nuclear Arms Control, said, "I think it's too dangerous to let powerful technology flow to the Chinese military without a review... These [companies] are the most dangerous entities."[6]

---

[5] *Orlando Sentinel*, May 5, 2001; Gertz, *Washington Times*, May 28, 2001; *Far Eastern Economic Review*, June 7, 2001
[6] Bill Gertz, *The Washington Times*, October 19, 2000

Over time the Commerce Department had investigated and prosecuted some of the supercomputers exports to China.

Supercomputers have massive computing power that — through simulations — make the design of nuclear warheads and accurate long-range missiles cheaper, faster and less detectable than tests of actual weapons. For example, IBM processing units each operating at 275 million operations per second (MTOPS) and operating in parallel together will perform 3.3 billion operations per second. Supercomputers "continue the nuclear arms race on computers made in America," said Milhollin in 1997 to Congress.

Silicon Graphics, Inc.

In the spring of 1996 Silicon Graphics, Inc. sold a supercomputer performing six billion operations per second to the Chinese Academy of Sciences. The Chinese Academy of Sciences oversees nuclear and missile and research, including the DF-5 intercontinental missile, which can reach U.S. cities with nuclear warheads. The Academy has also developed advanced rocket propellant, guidance for torpedos, sonar for nuclear submarines, enriched uranium by gaseous diffusion. Networked, the Silicon Graphics computer is available to any Chinese organization that is designing nuclear weapons or long-range missiles. They can design lighter nuclear warheads to fit on longer-range and more accurate missiles aimed at U.S. cities.

On November 13, 1997, before the House Committee on National Security, Gary Milhollin, asked, "Under investigation, or under the rug? The Silicon Graphics sale to China... went directly to nuclear, missile and military work. ...Silicon Graphics was required to ascertain whether the buyer was non-military and non-nuclear.

"There is no reason why the details of these cases should not be made public. Only the Congress and the American people are still in the dark. Given the gravity of the violations, and the flagrant way in which they occurred, this Committee should ask the Commerce Department to answer ...How many computers were shipped to China and what were their operating speeds? ... Silicon Graphics either knew that its buyers were nuclear, missile or military sites, or it didn't bother to find out. Either way, Silicon Graphics broke the law.

"So why the delay? Why is nothing happening? Doesn't the executive branch want to enforce the law? ...The phrase "under investigation" is beginning to mean "under the rug."

There is no record of any action against Silicon Graphics. Why is unknown, but it is not unremarkable that SGI's chairman, Edward McCracken, was a major Democrat donor in 1992 and 1996.

Where investigations have gone forward, the penalties were often minor compared to the profits made by computer sales and to the dangers to national security.

Here are a few other examples.

New World Transtechnology — computers to nuclear factory

Alerted by the San Jose office of the Department of Commerce, home of Sun Microsystems, the Dallas field office conducted an investigation of New World Transtechnology (NWT), Galveston, Texas. As a result of the investigation, Commerce filed a criminal complaint in the U.S. District Court for the Southern District of Texas. The U.S. Attorney charged that in August 1992 NWT exported three Sun Microsystems computers to a nuclear equipment factory in the People's Republic of China and had attempted to ship a fourth super computer. Special Agents seized still another computer before it could be shipped to China from Hong Kong.

On December 20, 1996, the company plead guilty to two counts of violating export laws and one count of making false statements. The Court imposed a criminal fine of $10,000 and a special assessment fine of $600 against the company. The Department of Commerce imposed a 10-year denial of export privileges on New World Transtechnology. [7]

Testifying before Congress in 1997, Gary Milhollin, Director, Wisconsin Project on Nuclear Arms Control said, "serious violations seem to have resulted in only a small fine, which an exporting company can simply consider a cost of doing business." He cited New World Transtechnology among others.

Sun Microsystems/Gold Valley Technology/U-Freight — computers

After the Clinton Administration cut export controls on supercomputers in early 1996, the House Committee on National Security demanded to know what had happened to the supercomputers exported. Pressed by Congress, the Commerce Department asked Sun Microsystems about its exports. Sun disclosed a computer diversion to China and the Commerce Department decided to investigate it.

The Department discovered that Sun Microsystems of California, Ltd., and Gold Valley California, Ltd., both Hong Kong companies, arranged the illegal shipment of supercomputers to the PRC. Further, in arranging for the shipment, Sun Microsystems lied on export papers filed in October 1993. In September 1993, U-Freight, Inc., freight forwarder in South San Francisco, California, had also filed

---

[7] Website of Bureau of Industry and Security Export Enforcement, Department of Commerce

false documents to facilitate the Sun Microsystems shipment of prohibited computers to the PRC.

On November 13, 1997, Gary Milhollin, Director, Wisconsin Project on Nuclear Arms Control testified before the House Committee on National Security. He said that the Sun supercomputers after being diverted a civilian site "wound up at China's National University of Defense Technology in Changsha. ...[R]un by the People's Liberation Army, [the University] does research ...in missile design, detonation physics, supercomputer development, and automatic target recognition. Scientists at Changsha planned to develop the next generation of Chinese weapons with American equipment."

Six years after the offense in September 1993, on June 21, 1999, the Commerce Department imposed a $30,000 civil penalty on Sun Microsystems of California for shipping computers to the People's Republic of China (PRC). On December 21, 1997, the Department imposed a $20,000 civil penalty on Gold Valley Technology Company for the same offense. And on March 20, 2000, the Commerce Department imposed a $20,000 fine on U-Freight — $10,000 suspended for a promise not to break the law again.[8]

Compaq Computer Corporation — computers

On April 18, 1997, the Commerce Department imposed a civil penalty of $55,000 on Compaq Computer Corporation, of Houston, Texas, for exporting computer equipment on three separate occasions to the People's Republic of China and two other countries.

The computer equipment was controlled for national security reasons.[9] The modest penalty imposed reflected Compaq's cooperation after the deed was done, not to mention the Clinton Administration's tepid interest in enforcing the law against its major campaign contributor, Red China.

Gateway 2000 — computers

Gateway 2000 of North Sioux City, South Dakota, shipped computers to 16 countries — including China, Iran and Syria — on 30 separate occasions. Further, according to the Department of Commerce, Gateway filed false and misleading documents to cover up its illegal transactions. On April 6, 1998, the Department imposed a $402,000 civil fine for Gateway's long-standing and continuous violations of law. Given the dangers to the nation's survival the fine was a pittance.[10]

[8, 9, 10] Website of Bureau of Industry and Security Export Enforcement, Department of Commerce

•

During late November 2000, in the midst of the election crisis, the Clinton-Gore Administration concluded seven years of negotiations with Red China with a quick deal.

They accepted yet another promise from China to stop selling missile parts, without onsite inspections to verify. For this promise, frequently broken, the U.S. did not sanction half a dozen Chinese companies caught proliferating missile components. The U.S. also dropped limits on U.S. satellite launches in China in effect since 1997. This deal appeared to show that Loral, Hughes and the PRC continued to benefit from their campaign contributions to Clinton.

Few news accounts mentioned how Loral and Hughes' prior satellite cooperation with the Chinese had improved the accuracy of China's intercontinental missiles. During the same period, Clinton-Gore did choose to impose sanctions on Pakistan and Iran (but not North Korea). They did not sanction Red China which was the other side of this trade in components of weapons of mass destruction.

State Department spokesman Richard Boucher said the deal would "strengthen cooperation" with China and "prevent the spread of ballistic missiles."

It was, "one more favor for China," said Michael Ledeen of the American Enterprise Institute. Senator Fred Thompson (R-TN) said it was "rewarding China for promises made rather than promises kept." It was lowering "the bar" rather than "sanctioning China for repeated violations."

Clinton-Gore policies —

Opportunities for Chinese espionage in America and by Chinese front companies are almost infinite. Yet the lax, sloppy and lethargic actions of the Clinton-Gore Administration approached criminal negligence or complicity in Loral, Hughes and other cases.

Its Interagency Commission on Crime and Security in U.S. Seaports only scratched the surface. The Commission was preoccupied with theft on the docks and drug trafficking to the exclusion of national security. Exports harmful to National Defense were mentioned as an after thought. Its final report mentions China only three times in 259 pages.

After the Cox secret hearings, the 1999 Defense Authorization Act ordered the Pentagon to identify Chinese front companies by listing Chinese-controlled companies operating in the United States by January 15, 1999. By March 2000 there was no such list and the FBI was not helping. Representative Chris Cox, on September 24, 1999, said, "The Clinton-Gore Administration's failure to obey the law is knowing, willful and longstanding." *[WND]*

•

Clearly, the China traders are endangering national security in pursuit of phantom benefits. Congress is still waiting for a list of Chinese front companies.

History provides the proof

Historical perspective — Expanding relations and improving trade agreements with the Soviet Union in 1933 did much to aid Soviet espionage. They provided legal covers for Soviet agents to penetrate American companies such as Northrop, General Electric, Douglas and Marietta. Actual trade expansion was small except for militarily useful technology the Soviets wanted.[11] A vast new literature on the Soviet KGB and GRU reveals CPUSA files, decoded Venona messages and notes from KGB files. All show that the USSR used small trading companies, which laundered Soviet money and served as paymasters for secret agents and for the Communist Party USA. They gave jobs and cover to espionage agents and gained access to science and technology.[12]

The Chinese are far more sophisticated and ten times more charming than the Soviets.

CHINESE FRONT COMPANIES AND THEIR AMERICAN COLLABORATORS

Collin Xu, Yi Yao, Lion Photonics — missile gyroscopes

Aided by the Royal Canadian Mounted Police, Customs Special Agents in Boston in February 1997 arrested two Chinese nationals, Collin Xu and Yi Yao, for attempting to export sophisticated gyroscope systems to China. The fiberoptic gyroscopes are critical for guiding and navigating ballistic missiles and "smart" bombs. They are also used to stabilize weapons platforms. U.S. Customs had previously succeeded in charging and convicting a third individual for also attempting to export similar aircraft guidance components to China.

Collin Xu, Yi Yao and two Chinese front companies — Lion Photonics, Canada, Inc. and Lion Photonics, Inc. — were indicted on March 9, 1999, for conspiring to illegally purchase U.S.-origin fiberoptic gyroscopes from a U.S. firm and to export them to the PRC via Canada. An investigation revealed that Xu and Yao falsely described the gyroscopes as fiber sensors for optical communication and listed Canada as their destination rather than China. Yao and Xu were arrested pending trial.

---

[11] Alan Weinstein and Alex Vassiliev, *Haunted Wood*
[12] Works by Harvey Klehr, Vasili Mitrokhin, Alan Weinstein, Ronald Radosh

On December 14, 1999, a federal grand jury in the U.S. District Court of Massachusetts in Boston charged Collin Xu, also known as Collin Shu and Zhihong Xu, Yi Yao, also known as Yao Yi, and two Chinese front companies — Lion Photonics, Canada, Inc., of Montreal, Canada, and Lion Photonics, Inc., of Beijing, People's Republic of China (PRC) — with knowingly and willfully lying about their intended export of fiberoptic gyroscopes to the PRC.

Both pled guilty. Xu was sentenced to 2½ years in prison. Yi faces a maximum of 10 years in prison and a $1 million fine upon sentencing.[13]

David Chan/Well Complex International and Teledyne Wah Chang — nuclear submarines, Hafnium

David Chan, owner of Well Complex International of Passaic, New Jersey, pled guilty on March 17, 1998, in U.S. District Court in Newark, New Jersey to charges that he lied about illegally exporting hafnium granules to the People's Republic of China. Hafnium is used for reactor control rods, especially in nuclear submarines.

Wah Chang, an Allegheny Technologies company has since 1956 been the leading producer of high quality hafnium chemicals for the U.S. Navy and other commercial users. In 1916, mining engineer K.C. Li founded the company in mainland China.

In separate cases Teledyne Wah Chang was denied export privileges for three years and fined $2 million for illegally exporting zirconium and making false statements on license applications and shipping documents. All but three months were suspended.

David Chan's company, Well Complex was sentenced to five years' probation, a $7,500 criminal fine and a $200 special assessment fee. David Chan was sentenced to three years' probation, a $500 criminal fine and a $100 special assessment.[14]

Teledyne Industries plead guilty in Washington, D.C. on January 27, 1995. The company was assessed a $5,498,125 criminal fine for violations of exports of zirconium to "another destination" via Greece. The State Department also imposed a $1.5 million civil penalty.[15]

Yuchai America — machine tools

An investigation of the New York Field Office of the Department of Commerce discovered that, in May 1994, Yuchai America of Cleveland, Ohio, an affiliated Chinese front company, attempted to export

---

[13] Website of Bureau of Industry and Security Export Enforcement, Department of Commerce; *Photonics Business News*, March 2001

[14, 15] Website of Bureau of Industry and Security Export Enforcement, Department of Commerce

two five-axis milling machines to the People's Republic of China. It tried to cover up the transaction by making false and misleading statements about its export.

Such machines once made parts for the B-1 bomber and for the MX nuclear missile.[16]

Although these machines were used equipment, they exceeded the technology limits on exports to China. "Certain technologically sophisticated machines — regardless of their age — remain subject to export controls for national security reasons because they can be used to make parts for weapons systems," said John Despres, assistant secretary of Commerce.

On October 2, 1996, Yuchai America agreed to pay a civil penalty of $200,000 for its illegal exports and falsification of documents.[17]

Allvac — Nuclear proliferation

A Commerce Department investigation revealed that Allvac, a Monroe, North Carolina, manufacturer made 48 shipments of titanium alloy products from the United States to China and ten other countries. The shipments of titanium alloy and maraging steel products are controlled to prevent proliferation of nuclear weapons technologies.

Caught Allvac voluntarily disclosed these shipments. On January 22, 1997, the Department of Commerce imposed a $122,500 civil penalty. The Department waived payment of a $47,500 penalty for Allvac's promise not to violate regulations.

Advanced Vacuum Systems, Inc. (AVS) — Nuclear proliferation

On the April 18, 1997, the Commerce Department imposed a $5,000 civil penalty on Advanced Vacuum Systems, Inc. (AVS), of Ayer, Massachusetts, for exports to the People's Republic of China (PRC) The Commerce Department investigation of AVS discovered that it exported a low pressure sintering furnace and spare parts valued at over $600,000 to the PRC. Exports of the furnace were controlled worldwide for nuclear nonproliferation reasons. Because the company cooperated the Department suspended $2,000 of the $5,000 penalty.[18]

Testifying before Congress in 1997, Gary Milhollin, Director, Wisconsin Project on Nuclear Arms Control said, "serious violations seem to have resulted in only a small fine, which an exporting company can

---

[16] Milholloin, *Los Angeles Times*, January 23, 2000

[17, 18] Website of Bureau of Industry and Security Export Enforcement, Department of Commerce

simply consider a cost of doing business." He cited Allvac, Yuchai and Advanced Vacuum as examples of light sentences.

Republic-Lagun Machine Tool Company — nuclear

On March 15, 1998, the Commerce Department imposed a $20,000 civil penalty on Republic-Lagun Machine Tool Company, of Carson, California. The company illegally exported a vertical milling machine with a computer numeric controller (CNC) from the United States to the People's Republic of China. Exports of CNC-equipped milling machines are controlled for national security and nuclear nonproliferation reasons.[19]

Lafayette Instrument Company, Inc. — polygraph machines

On December 8, 1999, the Commerce Department imposed a $10,000 civil penalty on Lafayette Instrument Company, Inc., for illegally rerouting export of polygraph machines from Hong Kong to the People' Republic of China.[20]

Dexin International, Inc. – thermal video systems

Dexin International, Inc., of West Covina, California in 1994 and 1995, exported thermal video systems to China and filed false documents to cover up the prohibited shipment.

On August 18, 2000, the Commerce Department imposed a $50,000 civil penalty ($35,000 suspended).[21]

[19, 20, 21] Website of Bureau of Industry and Security Export Enforcement, Department of Commerce

NAMING NAMES
China's Spies and Agents of Influence

SPIES AND ESPIONAGE — TWO DOWN, 35 TO GO?

In *The China Threat: How the People's Republic Targets America*, *Washington Times'* sleuth and national security reporter Bill Gertz reveals that U.S. intelligence was aware in the 1990s that China had at least 37 spies in the U.S. The FBI was actively pursuing six Chinese intelligence agents, not just one — the allegedly singled out and racially victimized Wen Ho Lee.

Gertz quoted a late 1998 U.S. intelligence report titled "Foreign Collection Against the Department of Energy: The Threat to U.S. Weapons and Technology." The report describes the Chiese and Russian quest for U.S. nuclear secrets and the sloppy security at the Energy Department. "Russia and China had the largest intelligence presence with 141 and 37 officers, respectively," the report said.

China concentrated on nuclear weapons design. Reconfirming the much-maligned Cox Report, "This effort has been very successful... Beijing's exploitation of U.S. national laboratories has substantially aided its nuclear weapons program."[1]

Gwo Bao Min — Livermore Nuclear Lab

Gertz reports that, in the early 1980s, Gwo Bao Min, a suspected early nuclear spy for China was fired by the Lawrence Livermore National Laboratory. Min became the key target of an FBI counterspy case known as "Tiger Trap." Min was suspected of giving China keys to unlocking nuclear weapons secrets.

During his investigation he received a personal phone call from Wen Ho Lee. FBI wiretaps catch Lee promising Min that he will find and expose the informant who betrayed Min.

Though Min's treachery involving nuclear secrets may have been as damaging to U.S. national security as the Rosenberg's theft of the secrets of the first atom bomb, he was never prosecuted.

Larry Wu-Tai Chin — CIA Mole

Larry Wu-Tai Chin was born in Peking, China. Communist intelli-

---

[1] *Reuters*, November 1, 2000

gence agents recruited Chin while he was a student in the early 1940s. He worked for the U.S. Army in China after 1943. He joined the CIA in 1952. Chin, Chinese language specialist, was a 30-year mole within in the CIA's Foreign Broadcast Information Service (FBIS).

Over 20 years Chin copied and delivered top secret CIA reports on Asia to Chinese couriers in frequent meetings in Toronto, Hong Kong and London.

In 1985, Yu Qiangshen, an intelligence officer in China's Ministry of State Security defected to the USA. Yu identified Chin as a spy. Chin was indicted on 17 espionage counts. At trial he admitted 11 years of delivering documents. A federal jury convicted Chin on all counts. Chin committed suicide in his cell on Feb. 8, 1985, before he could be sentenced.[2]

Anne Henderson-Pollard— Intelligence volunteer

Anne Henderson-Pollard, wife of Israeli spy Jonathan Pollard, joined her husband in gathering up a suitcase of copied secret documents from her husband's employer the Naval Investigative Service. These materials covered the military capabilities of foreign countries. One was a U.S. assessment of Chinese intelligence activities in America. While Jonathan Pollard was a renowned Israeli agent, Mrs. Henderson-Pollard was accused of intending to sell the documents to Chinese intelligence operatives in the U.S.

Caught in the same net as her husband, Anne Pollard pled guilty to espionage. On March 4, 1987, she was sentenced to five years in federal prison. In 1989 she was released for medical reasons.[3]

Yen Men Kao — U.S. Navy torpedo, jet engine and fire-control radar

Yen Men Kao, a Chinese national — while illegally overstaying his visa — bought two restaurants in Charlotte, North Carolina. Under the instruction of Chinese intelligence and promises of a $2 million payday Kao became a member of a spy ring of "several other [unidentified] Chinese nationals." Kao and crew sought mightily to acquire the U.S. Navy's most advanced technologies including the Navy's MK 48 Advanced Capability (ADCAP) Torpedo, two F 404-400 General Electric jet engines for the Navy's F/A-18 Hornet fighter, and fire-control radar for the F-16 Falcon jet.

---

[2] Gertz, *China Threat; The Washington Post*, Nov. 24, and Dec. 6, 1985; *The New York Times*, Nov. 30, 1985

[3] *The New York Times*, Nov. 28, 1985; *Washington Post*, Dec. 4, 1985 and June 5, 1986; Naval Investigative Service Command, *Espionage*, 1989; *Wall Street Journal*, Feb. 24, 1994; *CBS News*, Dec. 18, 1999

They failed. No systems were delivered to China. Yet in a sting operation, Kao paid an FBI informant $24,000 for oscillators used in satellites. Finally, Kao was caught red handed.

So after a six-year and half year investigation the FBI arrested Kao on December 3, 1993, and charged him with conspiring (unsuccessfully) to illegally procure and export high-technology military items and with violating U.S. immigration laws.

Kao was not prosecuted for "committing acts of espionage against the United States." The Clinton Administration did not want to offend the Chinese government. The FBI was not keen about disclosing counterintelligence sources and methods in public court proceedings.

On December 22, 1993, a judge ordered Yen Men Kao deported to Hong Kong for overstaying his visa. Kao, a gambling man, lost his thousands of dollars in spy money, fled to Hong Kong abandoning his wife, a naturalized U.S. citizen, and two children.[4]

Hou Desheng, Zang Weichu — *signals intelligence, missiles*

Hou Desheng was a military attaché of the People's Republic of China. He tried to acquire mobile anti-aircraft missiles. He sought Secret documents of the National Security Agency, NSA. The FBI used an American citizen and NSA employee to lure Hou. Meeting at a Washington Chinese restaurant, Hou took documents be believed to be NSA secrets. FBI agents arrested Hou on December 21, 1987. At the same time the FBI also arrested Zang Weichu, a PRC consular official in Chicago.

Both diplomats were expelled from the country for "activities incompatible with their diplomatic status." They were the first Chinese diplomats expelled since formal relations were established with the PRC in 1979.

Desheng would later show up representing Mayes and Company, which was interested in selling mobile anti-aircraft missiles to China.[5]

James Lee (Li Jin), Penny Ray (Lei Ping) — *"defense articles"*

A jury in San Francisco convicted Penny Ray and James Lee of San Jose, California, of violating the Arms Export Control Act by exporting [undefined] "defense articles" to the People's Republic of China. Lee and Ray were sentenced to 18 months of imprisonment,

---

[4] *The Washington Times,* Dec. 22, 1993; *Los Angeles Times,* Dec. 5, 1993; Cox Report, 2001

[5] *New York Times,* Dec. 31, 1987; *The Washington Post,* Dec. 31, 1987

followed by three years' supervised release, and a $50 special assessment fee.

On April 6, 1998 the Commerce Department denied Lee and Ray all U.S. export privileges until January 14, 2008.[6] This ten-year denial of export rights suggests the "defense articles" might have been important, but the public record does not tell what was exported.

Storm Kheem — Chinese missile technology to Iraq

A joint investigation of Commerce, Customs, and the FBI discovered that Storm Kheem, a resident of Bayshore, New York, and others arranged to transport ammonium perchlorate from the People's Republic of China to Iraq via Jordan. Ammonium perchlorate is a highly explosive chemical used in rocket fuel. Kheem deliberately mislabeled the chemical — as a non-explosive water purification chemical — to disguise the true contents of the export from China to Iraq.

The export came under the Enhanced Proliferation Control Initiative (EPCI) prohibiting U.S. persons from directly contributing to the design, development, production, stockpiling, and use of weapons of mass destruction.

Storm Kheem, pled guilty to violating EPCI and Iraqi Sanctions Regulations on January 27, 1995.[7]

Red-Chin Yang/Lansing Technologies Corporation — computers

The New York field office of the Office of Export Enforcement of the Department of Commerce investigated Red-Chin Yang and his Lansing Technologies Corporation of Flushing, New York.

Red-Chin Yang, of Lansing Technologies, pleaded guilty in the U.S. District Court for the Eastern District of New York on June 17, 1997, to illegally exporting a vector computer processor and a data acquisition control system to the People's Republic of China. Such technology is useful in nuclear physics and precise manufacturing processes. On October 16, 1997, a U.S. District Court Judge of the Eastern District of New York, imposed a $10,000 fine and a $400 special assessment on Lansing Technologies.[8]

Lasertechnics, Inc. — nuclear triggers

From November 1991 through March 1994, Lasertechnics, Inc. located in Albuquerque, N. M. exported U.S.-origin hydrogen thyra-

---

6, 7, 8 Website of Bureau of Industry and Security Export Enforcement, Department of Commerce trons from the United States to Hong Kong, Ireland, Malaysia and Singapore. The export of thyratrons is illegal in order to prevent the proliferation of nuclear technology. Thyratrons direct high voltage currents, which can trigger a nuclear weapon. Exports of hydrogen thyratrons are controlled to prevent nuclear proliferation and terrorism.

A Commerce Department investigation revealed that the company exported thyratrons on 36 separate occasions. Caught Lasertechnics cooperated with the investigation.

On May 30, 1997, the Commerce Department's Bureau of Export Administration (BXA) imposed an $180,000 civil penalty on Lasertechnics, Inc., Payment of $80,000 of the civil penalty was waived for a promise not to violate the law.

"We control the export of thyratrons... we are concerned about the proliferation of weapons of mass destruction which may be used by terrorists," said Frank Deliberti, acting assistant secretary for Export Enforcement. "The serious nature of our concern for unauthorized exports is demonstrated by the size of this penalty."[9]

For weapons that can murder millions of innocents, $80,000 might be considered a small token of how "serious" nuclear annihilation is.

Digital Creations — computers

Digital Creations Corporation plead guilty to illegally exporting DEC computer equipment to the People's Republic of China. On June 13, 1997, United States District Court Judge William Walls of the District of New Jersey fined Digital Creations Corporation of Closter, New Jersey, $800,000 and lawyers for Digital Creations then requested postponement of the sentencing.[10]

Testifying before Congress in November 1997, Gary Milhollin, Director, Wisconsin Project on Nuclear Arms Control said, "serious violations seem to have resulted in only a small fine, which an exporting company can simply consider a cost of doing business." He cited Lansing Technologies Corporation and Digital Creations Corporation as examples among others.

Mysterious Mr. Ma, a Chinese "war horse" — Defense Intelligence Agency

According to U.S. intelligence as reported by Gertz, in the early 1990s the FBI discovered that China had some spies placed very well inside the U.S. government. At least one was inside an intelligence

---

[9, 10] Website of Bureau of Industry and Security Export Enforcement, Department of Commerce

agency. He was code-named Ma, Chinese for "horse." Ma gave defense and intelligence information to Beijing.

His true identity was never decided.

Gertz alleges that Ronald Montaperto, an American intelligence analyst, is who the FBI suspects of being secret agent Ma.

Yet, to this day, Montaperto holds a top secret Pentagon clearance. While at the Defense Intelligence Agency (DIA), Montaperto made contacts with Chinese intelligence officers as part of his job. One of them, PLA Major General Yu Zhenghe, an air attaché was invited to Montaperto's wedding in 1990.

Gertz reports that (based on the word of defectors) the FBI began a major espionage investigation. The FBI netted 12 suspects fitting a Chinese "Dear Friend" profile who had access to U.S. military secrets.

The FBI interviewed Ronald Montaperto in late 1991 or early 1992 when Montaperto headed DIA's "estimates" unit for China (September 1989-February 1992).

"Intelligence intercepts of Chinese government communications gathered by the National Security Agency and supplied to the FBI" uncovered a very important agent code-named Ma.

When the FBI confronted Montaperto in three "hostile interrogations," he insisted he had not given classified information to China's intelligence service. He said his contacts with Chinese intelligence were all authorized, including his wedding guest, General Yu. The FBI cleared Montaperto after "...they looked me in the eye and said, 'We don't think you're a spy'."

Montaperto soon left the DIA, but told Gertz that the FBI had nothing to do with his leaving — "One does not have friends with Chinese officials," he said but had to admit that General Yu did attend his wedding.

"Hanging on the wall inside Mr. Montaperto's office was a large scroll of Chinese calligraphy... contain[ing] the characters horse dragon virtue, which... in Mandarin sound like "Montaperto." A second set... are Chinese for "war horse." A Chinese intelligence officer signed the scroll for Montaperto.

He was "an attaché at the Chinese Embassy" who gave Montaperto the scroll as a gift. Oddly, he sometimes tells another story. "Mr. Montaperto says a student in Shanghai gave it to him."

After the DIA, Montaperto moved to the Pentagon's National Defense University (NDU), as an analyst for its Institute for National Strategic Studies. There he defines "strategies... for... U.S. interests in the Asia-Pacific..." Montaperto retains a top-secret security clearance, but has less access to intelligence.

General Yu works for General Xiong Guangkai, the PLA's deputy chief of staff for intelligence. In 1996 during the crisis over Chinese missile firings over Taiwan, Gen. Xiong may have returned to the United States and tried to meet Mr. Montaperto.

At NDU Montaperto has downplayed China's military capabilities. Considered a "panda hugger" by many and worse by a few. According to Gertz, "Mr. Montaperto's minimizing of the threat is at one with Chinese... deception — preventing the U.S. 'hegemon' from recognizing China's emerging power... until China has the military, economic and political power to win... Mr. Deng: 'Hide brightness; nourish obscurity.' Or... as Beijing put it, 'Bide our time and build up our capabilities...'

"What China wanted was three more decades of Clinton-style 'engagement,' a policy that downplays Chinese military capabilities, encourages decreasing U.S. defense spending and gives China major technical and financial boosts... Chinese officials view certain specialists in the United States as important outlets for Beijing's views...

"The China experts... communicate via Internet discussion groups, a major target of influence exerted by the Chinese government. Take 'Chinasec.' Every morning, a group of about 100 high-level U.S. policy-makers and intelligence officials receives e-mail postings as part of this Internet discussion group..."[11]

Montaperto remains a highly regarded and widely published expert on China. Espionage agent or not, he is surely an agent of influence for the Red Chinese — panda hugger extraordinaire. Montaperto is totally unpersuaded that China represents any threat whatsoever.

Peter Lee — Los Alamos and Livermore Nuclear Laboratories

Peter Lee is a Taiwan-born U.S. citizen who worked at Los Alamos National Laboratory from 1984 to 1991. He also worked for TRW, Inc., a contractor to Lawrence Livermore National Laboratory, from 1973 to 1984 and 1991 to 1997. Dr. Lee graduated from the California Institute of Technology in 1975, earning a Ph.D. in Aeronautics.

The Cox Report concluded, "The PRC apparently co-opted [Peter] Lee by appealing to his ego, his ethnicity and his sense of self-importance as a scientist." Peter Lee stole and gave to the Chinese secrets about the neutron bomb and U.S. submarines — "information related to the detection of submarines and of laser testing of miniature nuclear weapons explosions..."

Peter Lee radically reduced submarine protection of U.S. aircraft carriers. His treachery enabled China to complete its testing of nuclear weapons without detection by the U.S.

On January 9, 1985, Lee met with Chinese nuclear scientists revealing secrets about his laser work on miniature nuclear testing in meetings at a Beijing hotel room.

---

[11] Gertz, *China Threat*

"Lee explained to PRC weapons scientists how deuterium and tritium can be loaded into a spherical capsule called a target and surrounded by a hohlraum, and then heated by means of laser bombardment. The heat causes the compression of these elements, creating a nuclear fusion micro-explosion.[12]

This so-called 'inertial confinement' technique permits nuclear weapons scientists to study nuclear explosions in miniature... [useful] to the PRC, which has agreed to the ban on full-scale nuclear tests... Lee's delivery of the miniature nuclear testing information to the PRC occurred... while he was employed... at Los Alamos... [D]uring a lecture in the PRC he answered questions and drew diagrams about hohlraum construction."[13]

In the early '90s Peter Lee again applied for a position with Los Alamos, but U.S. intelligence officers persuaded the laboratory to turn down his application. That did nothing to halt his work for the PRC.

In early 1997, Lee made a three-week "pleasure" trip to China — paid by China's Institute of Applied Physics and Computational Mathematics (IAPCM), designer of China's nukes.

"...[O]n or about May 11, 1997, Lee gave a [two-hour] lecture in Beijing [to]... nuclear weapons scientists from the IAPCM and the China Academy of Engineering Physics (CAEP). Lee described... the physics of microwave scattering from ocean waves [—] research was [for] anti-submarine warfare... Lee displayed an image of a surface ship wake... drew a graph... [and] told... where to filter data within the graph to... locate the ocean wake of a vessel.

"Approximately two hours after his talk was over, Lee erased the graph and tore the ship wake image 'to shreds' upon exiting the PRC institute." The Lawrence Livermore Lab had conducted 20 years of research in a joint United States-United Kingdom Radar Ocean Imaging project on anti-submarine warfare.[14]

All this Lee gave away in a two-hour talk.

Throughout the 1990s, the FBI investigated Peter Lee, but failed to acquire sufficient evidence. In July of 1997, counterintelligence officials notified Sandy Berger about nuclear losses and in October 1997 the FBI interrogated Peter Lee six times.

Lee finally admitted that he had given the PRC weapons scientists classified sub detection research endangering "previously invulnerable" U.S. nuclear submarines.

The Reno Justice Department fearlessly attacked women and children at Waco and dragged a little boy out of a closet in Miami at gunpoint and packed him off to Fidel Castro, but it went very softly indeed on Red China's spy.

[12, 13, 14] Cox Report

Gertz's *The China Threat* claims that White House officials delayed the FBI arrest of Lee until after the visit of President Jiang Zemin. Apparently, China had warned that prosecuting Peter Lee would harm U.S.-China relations.

Though prosecutors wanted to proceed, the Justice Department did not. Indeed, the U.S. Navy also opposed revealing the leak of sub detection secrets. Justice decided to prosecute Lee only on his 1985 release of nuclear technology since declassified in 1993.

Lee was charged with "willfully providing" to the PRC classified information on techniques for creating miniature nuclear fusion explosions. On December 8, 1997, Lee pled guilty to willfully passing classified U.S. defense information to PRC scientists during his 1985 visit to the PRC, and of only lying about his lectures with PRC nationals in 1997 about sub detection physics and technologies.

Peter Lee, master spy, who faced a possible life sentence or execution did well.

On March 26, 1998, very liberal U.S. District Court Judge Terry J. Hatter in California sentenced Lee to only three years probation, one year with an ankle bracelet at a halfway house, 3,000 hours of community service and a $20,000 fine.[15]

Afterward, the Clinton Administration failed to provide a damage assessment report of Peter Lee's treachery to the Cox Committee. Peter Lee had refused to cooperate with the Select Committee. On August 29, 2000, the Bush Commerce Department notified Peter Lee that he would lose his rights to export until March 26, 2006. A passing strange example of a bureaucracy acting blindly in the dark.

Wen Ho Lee — Los Alamos Nuclear Laboratory

In the early 1990s, Wen Ho Lee, a research scientist at the Los Alamos Lab, arrived unannounced at a private gathering of visiting Chinese scientists. Though Lee had not been invited to the meeting, Hu Side, known to U.S. Intelligence as the father of China's nuclear weapons program, welcomed Lee enthusiastically with a hug and an exclamation of Hu's thanks for Lee's "important contributions to China's nuclear weapons program," a witness told the FBI.

Wen Ho Lee, it was later alleged, had given the Chinese nuclear secrets allowing them to deliver 180-kiloton warheads within 80 yards of a U.S. target. Wen Ho Lee enabled the Chinese to build a missile force that will be large, mobile and accurate with mulitple warheads.[16]

Investor's Business Daily reports that from 1993 to 1997, federal officials requested 2,686 wiretaps. The Justice Department approved

---

[15] Cox Report; Gertz, *China Threat*
[16] Angelo Codavilla and others

all but one wiretap. And that singular exception was a tap in 1996 on the phone of Wen Ho Lee, the prime suspect in the theft of nuclear secrets from the Los Alamos National Lab.

In the end, Los Alamos research scientist Wen Ho Lee had transferred millions of lines of code and warhead data to his personal computer. The computer code, covered 50 years of nuclear research — "legacy" code or the "crown jewels." Many believe Lee may have compromised "virtually every nuclear weapon in the United States arsenal."[17]

In late 1998 Rep. Christopher Cox said China would soon have nuclear weapons "on a par with" the U.S. After months of denials, China admitted it had both *neutron* and *miniature* nuclear warheads. China claimed they were not stolen. "I think the balance of power is going to shift as a result of [nuclear espionage]," Candidate George W. Bush said. "I think it's going to accelerate China's emergence as a nuclear power."[18]

It was an espionage coup equal to the delivery of secrets of the first atom bombs to Moscow. Julius and Ethel Rosenberg were executed for their treason. Yet through a bungled investigation, Lee pled to one lesser offense out of 59 charges then he claimed a defense of racism. Freed by a bungled investigation and prosecution, Lee was given a free pass by promising to tell all about 17 missing computer tapes of nuclear secrets. The FBI rummaged through a local garbage dump and found several tapes — none containing Lee's stolen secrets.

Clinton apologized to Wen Ho Lee, but an Inspector General's report, the FBI Director Freeh and the Attorney General Reno insisted the government had the right man.

Hai Lin, Kai Xu and Yong Qing Cheng — Lucent Technologies

In July 2000, Yong Qing Cheng, a Chinese-born U.S. citizen and vice president of an optic-networking company, Village Networks, traveled to Beijing, China. He met with officials of Datang Telecom Technology Co., Ltd. of Beijing, a PRC majority-owned government corporation. He discussed transfer of secret U.S. telecommunications technologies.

Datang subsequently gave $1.2 million to Cheng and to Hai Lin and Kai Xu. They were Chinese nationals on business visas called "distinguished" employees by Lucent Technologies. Hai Lin and Kai Xu stole the secret data networking technology from their employer, Lucent. They transferred these secrets to PRC-owned Datang Telecom. U.S. Attorney Robert J. Cleary said Lin and Xu "came to Lucent

---

[17] *New York Times*, April 28, 1999
[18] *AP*, May 26, 1999

as scholars, but in reality they were nothing more than sleuths." They were PRC spies using American visas.

Datang, Lin, Xu and Cheng formed ComTriad, a joint venture to sell identical copies of the Lucent technology, Pathstar, in China as their own, CLX 1000.

Rick Fisher of the Jamestown Foundation said the Lucent thefts were part of "systematic attempts [by the PRC] to subvert [U.S.] commercial ventures to assist the PRC's military modernization." The technologies would help the PRC acquire a "national, instantaneous communications network" for its military, according to Fisher.

"It's prevailing logic in some intelligence organizations to give $1 million... to get technology in two days instead of spending $20 million to develop it over twenty years," said Ben I. Venzke of IntelCenter.

Lin, Xu and Cheng were arrested on May 3, 2001, charged in U.S. District Court in Newark with conspiracy to commit wire fraud. They faced five years in jail and $250,00 fines if convicted.

Henry Tang, chairman of the Committee of 100 and staunch defender of Wen Ho Lee said, "one has to wonder why such a fuss... when the FBI investigates thousands of cases of espionage each year." Lam Leong, Asian activist at Lucent, pointed out that the "criminal activity" of stealing Lucent's property by two Asians "doesn't represent the long history of great contributions..." Indeed.

Lucent, the nation's largest manufacturer and one of its most technologically-advanced communications companies, has its largest operation in China where it has 3,400 employees. "Backed by the research and development of Bell Labs, Lucent focuses on high-growth areas such as broadband and mobile Internet infrastructure, communications software, web-based enterprise solutions that link private and public networks, and professional network design and consulting services."

Lucent had initially notified the FBI of suspicious behavior of its employees.[19]

Yufeng Wang, aka Alan Wang — armored riot control

Yufeng Wang, also known as Alan Wang, and his company, A&C International Trade, Inc. illegally exported an armored riot control vehicle, equipped with pepper spray to China. Mr. Wang is apparently not an advocate of democracy in Red China.

On March 10, 2000, Alan Wang, and his company pled guilty in U.S. District Court, Washington, D.C., to the export charges and to filing false documents to the U.S. Government. A&C International

---

[19] Lucent website; *New York Times*, May 4, 5, 2001; *The Washington Times*, May 8, 2001

pled to the export charges, and Wang to the false documents.

In July 2000, Wang was sentenced to time served (eight months), one year probation and 250 hours community service. His company was placed on three years probation, was fined $5,000, a $20,000 civil penalty, a three-year denial of export privileges (suspended). In addition to these Commerce Department penalties the company paid $100,000 civil penalty to the State Department.[20]

•

We now turn from espionage agents to agents of influence.

AGENTS OF INFLUENCE — Eᴛʜɴɪᴄ Cʜɪɴᴇꜱᴇ
Fᴏʟʟᴏᴡɪɴɢ ᴛʜᴇ Rᴇᴅ Cʜɪɴᴇꜱᴇ ᴍᴏɴᴇʏ ᴛʀᴀɪʟ ɪɴᴛᴏ *U.S.* ᴘᴏʟɪᴛɪᴄꜱ

PRC used overseas Chinese, U.S. citizens and residents

According to the Thompson Report, "It is likely that the PRC used intermediaries. This is so because only U.S. citizens or legal permanent residents can contribute lawfully to political parties and campaigns. Moreover, the use of businesses and individuals as intermediaries is increasingly common among Chinese. It is also well established that the PRC wields influence over a wide range of entities and individuals, many of which conduct business directly with the PRC..."

Further, "Committee staff identified... foreign money donations connected to six individuals with ties to the PRC... John Huang, Maria Hsia, Ted Sioeng and James and Mochtar Riady... have been associated... with the Government of China. The sixth, Yah Lin "Charlie" Trie, is a business partner of Ng Lap Seng (aka Mr. Wu), a Macao businessman with... ties to the PRC."

"The individuals who facilitated the contributions have either elected to take the Fifth Amendment or flee the country... Beijing has denied the Committee's request for assistance. ...Moreover, after its hearings concluded... the Chinese leadership was pleased no PRC agencies have yet been implicated in the campaign finance scandal. ...Chinese efforts... were undertaken or orchestrated, at least in part, by PRC intelligence agencies."

Johnny Chung — bagman for Chinese military intelligence

Johnny Chung, a Taiwan-born U.S. citizen and California businessman, went along on Commerce Secretary Ron Brown's August-

---

[20] Website of Bureau of Industry and Security Export Enforcement, Department of Commerce

September, 1994 trade mission to China where Chung met with officers of the PLA — probably Lt. Col. Liu Chaoying.

Liu, one of China's top spies, headed China Aerospace that launches satellites and is a satellite business partner with Clinton contributors Loral and Hughes Aircraft. Records show that Chung visited the White House over 50 times in the two years preceding the 1996 election, and raised more than $400,000 for the Democrats.

Chung appeared to have purchased White House access, including meetings with the President for himself and his Chinese associates.

In the fall of 1996, General Ji Shengde, chief of Chinese military intelligence for the People's Liberation Army gave $300,000 to Chung. Once charged, Chung chose to cooperate with the FBI and a grand jury. Chung testified that he was a bagman for the intelligence chief who ordered $300,000 into Chung's bank account. Boxes of financial records and wire transfers corroborated Chung's secret grand jury testimony. Citibank records showed Chung receiving the $300,000 from Chinese officials, in particular a wire transfer from its Hong Kong office from Liu Chaoying.

Hundreds of pages of wiretaps reveal that Chinese intelligence tried to derail the Justice Department investigation.

Robert Luu, in late spring of 1998, told Chung to protect Loral and Hughes. Blame the princelings — the irresponsible offspring of Chinese leaders.

Wiretaps suggest that President Jiang Zemin may have hatched the cover story. Luu said to Chung, "Yes, Chairman Jiang agreed to handle it like this; the President over here [Clinton] also agreed."

In December 1998, U.S. District Judge Manual Real sentenced Chung to five years probation and 3,000 hours of community service. By far the toughest sentence of the many Chinagate figures. Judge Real criticized the DNC and the White House for claiming Chung had victimized them. "If [Democrat party officials] Mr. Fowler and Mr. Sullivan didn't know what was going on, they're two of the dumbest politicians I've ever seen." Clinton and the DNC had been happy to take money from Chung... also Trie, Riady, Hsia and Huang.

Rep. Dan Burton (R-IN), subpoenaed Johnny Chung to testify before the House Government Reform Committee.

In May 1999, Chung became the first person out of 100 who voluntarily appeared before Congress. Citibank in Hong Kong did not respond to a subpoena. In July, Chung said Justice "did not want to hear" new information. The PRC silenced its former head of military itelligence, Ji Shengde by sentencing him to death for unrelated corruption charges.

Picking up trash on California roadsides, a repentant Johnny Chung has been successfully silenced. Johnny Chung was the most significant witness against the Chinese government and the Clinton Administration.

Richard Delgaudio, Johnny Chung and the author, Roger Canfield, hold a copy of "China Doll." — Photo courtesy of Michael Mark

One of the highest national security tasks of the Bush Administration ought to be rewarding whistleblowers and cooperative witnesses — beginning with pardoning of Johnny Chung.

John Huang — Clinton fundraiser and Red Chinese agent?

The Thompson Committee says, "The goal was to understand why an executive at a small California bank (owned by a large Indonesian conglomerate), who raised money prolifically for the Democratic Party and was rewarded with a political appointment at the Department of Commerce, was so often and well received by... Clinton and his staff."

Who was John Huang?

Huang was a former executive of the Lippo Group, an Indonesian conglomerate half-owned by the Red Chinese government in Beijing. Lippo's owners, the Riadys, had joint ventures with Red China. Lippo paid Huang about $325,000 a year.

After Clinton was elected, he appointed Huang deputy assistant secretary of the Commerce Department. Lippo gave Huang a bonus check for $450,000. Huang came and went as he pleased while on the U.S. government payroll.

As a civil servant he was forbidden by law from raising money for political campaigns. Huang raised funds for the DNC. The eager Huang illegally raised more than $100,000 for the Democrat party while at Commerce. In September 1993, Huang wrote three checks to the DNC, in the amount of $15,000 each paid with foreign money. The checks were drawn on the accounts of three Lippo Group foreign subsidiaries — all losing money and operating in the red.

On Friday, September 24, 1993, the day after Huang wrote the first two $15,000 checks to the DNC, Huang escorted Shen Jueren to the White House, where Shen met with Gore's Chief of Staff, Jack Quinn, and is widely suspected of meeting with Al Gore as well. On Monday, Huang wrote another $15,000 check to the DNC and, at a Santa Monica event organized by Huang and Maria Hsia, Shen Jueren is again suspected of meeting with Vice President Gore.

Huang may have sold more than influence. If he sold CIA secrets to which he had access he was gulity of espionage and treason. Huang had received a top-secret clearance *before* his first day of work at Commerce. Having acquired access to many documents on China, Huang attended 109 classified CIA and other briefings. As often as two or three times a week, Huang crossed the street to make phone calls and pick up faxes at Stephens, Inc. Stephens was an Arkansas investment firm with ties to the Lippo Group.

Democratic Senator Joseph Lieberman of Connecticut found, "These visits... curious." At Commerce for 18 months, Huang placed more than 400 telephone calls to Lippo and he made frequent visits to the Chinese Embassy. The Thompson Report said that Huang "may possibly have had a direct financial relationship with the PRC government."

Standing before Bill Clinton on a September morning in 1995 were two good friends. One was James Riady, the suave Chinese-Indonesian financier who was pushing to keep U.S. trade lines to China open. The second, John Huang, networker par excellence, offering to raise money for the Democratic National Committee from Asian-Americans. Huang thought Asian-Americans were good for $7 million. Huang got his wish of a DNC job in late 1995. He went on to become the most central figure in Washington's fundraising mess.

Later, in September 1997, the House Government Affairs Committee was investigating whether Huang gave sensitive economic data to the Riadys. "Insider information, going through the Riadys, perhaps to the People's Republic of China... would enable the Chinese government to prepare themselves for trade negotiations [and] put the United States at a serious disadvantage," Rep. Dan Burton said.

After the Department of Commerce, while dialing for dollars at the

DNC, Huang continued his relations with Lippo and the government of the PRC. "In 1996, John Huang solicited some $3.4 million in contributions to the DNC. Nearly half this amount has been returned as the contributions... have been made with actual or suspected [illegal] foreign funds," says the Thompson Report.

"The Committee has examined in detail Huang's activities at Lippo, Commerce and the DNC." The Thompson Committee says a "single piece of unverified information... indicates that Huang himself may possibly have had a direct financial relationship with the PRC government."

The Thompson Committee may be referring to the $100,000 that John Huang wired Webster Hubbell from the Hong Kong Chinese Bank,[21] or the Committee might be referring to Huang's overheard conversation with a Chinese official at the Los Angeles consulate of the PRC.[22]

Ultimately, Haung cooperated with the Department of Justice in 20 sessions. He was eventually charged with two illegal contributions: $2,000 to Michael Woo and $5,000 to the California Victory Fund and to Senator Dianne Feinstein. Ty Cobb, Huang's lawyer said that Huang "was not the main leader." On August 13, 1999, District Judge Richard Paez sentenced Huang — no jail time, but one year probation, a $10,000 fine and 500 hours community service.

Yah Lin "Charlie" Trie — Clinton pal, fundraiser, Red Chinese money launderer

Trie is a Little Rock restaurateur and 14-year friend of Bill Clinton, who at Clinton's request became a DNC finance board director and made 23 known White House visits.

The Thompson Committee reports "Yah Lin 'Charlie' Trie also solicited large amounts of foreign money. ...In March 1994, Trie brought nearly half a million dollars in small-denomination checks and money orders to the law office administering the (Clinton Presidential Legal Expense) Trust. Members of a Buddhist sect, Suma Ching Hai, wrote the checks and money orders. Trie reimbursed them from accounts in Taiwan and Cambodia."

Clinton appointed Trie to the Commission on United States-Pacific Trade. There Trie set up a secret coffee between Clinton and Wang Jun, China's primary arms dealer on February 6, 1996. Clinton met with Ron Brown and arms dealer Wang Jun the very same day.

Wang was head of the arms smuggling Polytechnologies. Clinton granted Polytechnologies a waiver to bring 100,000 semi-automatic weapons into the U.S.

---

[21] *Year of the Rat*
[22] *New York Times*, December 15, 1998

The *New York Times* claimed that Trie had asked Beijing for $1 million for his political activities and $1 million was wired from Mr. Wu in Macao. The Thompson Committee discovered that Wu (aka Ng Lap Seng) was an advisor to the Chinese government. Wu transferred $1.4 million from foreign banks in 41 separate wire transfers to Charlie Trie in some chunks as large as $50,000 and $100,000. Wu gave economic advice to the Communist Party and the PRC government in Beijing and was a business associate of Wang Jun.

Trie and his assistant trashed records while the FBI waited futilely for search warrants disapproved by Laura Ingersoll of the Reno Justice Department. Later, four FBI agents testified that the Justice Department had impeded and delayed the investigation of Trie's destruction of records in 1997. Federal prosecutor Charles LaBella finally approved the search warrants on Trie too late.

FBI agent Jerry Campane claimed that Trie laundered money that may have been from the Communist Chinese government. Yue Chu testified that she wrote checks to the DNC and was reimbursed by her husband's Beijing boss, Ng Lap Seng.

Trie and his Chinese friends got what they paid for.

Ng Lap Seng (aka Mr. Wu), contributor of $80,000 from the Bank of China in Macao visited the White House at least 10 times between 1994 and 1996.

Antonio Pan, a Trie and Huang associate, visited the White House eight times. Trie at least 23 times.

Trie initially fled to China, but returned to be arrested on February 3, 1998, by FBI agents at Washington Dulles Airport. Trie's attorney, Reid H. Weingarten, said Trie was a victim of congressional investigators portraying him as a spy. "He has never served as a spy for a foreign country. He never intended to corrupt the American political system," Mr. Weingarten said.

The Justice Department indicted Trie on 15 counts, including conspiracy to defraud the DNC, the alleged "victim," and for obstructing justice by destroying records.

On May 22, 1999, Trie pled guilty to two fundraising charges and agreed to cooperate with further investigations. Instead of six years in federal prison and a $350,000 fine, Trie received three years probation. (About what one gets for passing a bad check at a 7-11 store.)

Maria Hsia — Gore confidant, fundraiser, alleged Chinese agent

The Thompson Report says: "Maria Hsia was involved in soliciting contributions to the DNC that were laundered through several Buddhist monks and may have derived from foreign sources."

Democratic National Committee (DNC) Finance Director Richard Sullivan asked John Huang to "Get some California money in."

Huang turned to Maria Hsia, who engineered a scheme whereby some $55,000 was contributed to the DNC by temple monastics. The poor monastics were reimbursed out of the temple's general expense account.

The source of the temple's money is believed to be Buddhist devotees, yet may have also derived from overseas Chinese sources.[23]

A real spy story was buried inside the public spectacle of hapless Buddhist monks laundering monies for the DNC.

As leaked to Bob Woodward in *The Washington Post*, the Thompson Report said, "...Hsia has been an agent of the Chinese government, which she has acted knowingly in support of it, and that she has attempted to conceal her relationship with the Chinese government..."

Further, "Hsia has worked in direct support of a PRC diplomatic post in the U.S. ...[O]ver $130,000 in political contributions [was] illegally laundered through temple monastics at Hsia's direction... Hsia worked with Ted Sioeng and John Huang to solicit contributions from Chinese nationals in the United States and abroad... "Hsia and Huang... [also illegally] worked... to identify non-U.S. citizens overseas... [to] contribute money..."

In mid-February 1998, the Justice Department indicted 47-year-old Ms. Maria Hsia before a federal grand jury for conspiring to defraud the U.S. by securing contributions for the Clinton-Gore campaign from foreign entities, in direct and clear violation of federal election laws.

Then shockingly, on September 10, 1998, U.S. District Judge Paul Friedman actually dismissed five of the six charges saying it was "Alice in Wonderland" logic that Hsia be blamed for false campaign filings to the Federal Elections Commission.

False records, false names, false corporate status, false amounts were not enough for Judge Friedman. The judge's ruling was passing strange. Bizarre indeed. A unanimous three-judge panel of the U.S. Court of Appeals for the District of Columbia, on May 19, 1999, overturned Judge Friedman. The court reinstated five of six criminal charges. Two of the three judges were Clinton appointees, but they would not let Friedman's crazy ruling stand.

Maria Hsia was ultimately convicted, but she remained loyal to the Chinese and to Al Gore who came only one stuffed ballot box away from the Presidency.

Pauline Kanchanalak — Fundraiser, Red Chinese advocate

Pauline Kanchanalak was a Thai national — not a U.S. citizen

---

[23] Testimony of Juliana Utomo, July 15, 1997

— whose company, Ban Chang International, represented ethnic-Chinese executives of the Charoen Pokphand (CP) Group. The group was a Thai-Chinese conglomerate which was the single largest foreign investor in Red China. Dhanin Chearavanont, ethnic Chinese investor in Red China headed the CP Group, producing "everything from motorcycles to chickens."

In 1994 John Huang helped Kanchanalak get President Clinton's endorsement of the U.S.-Thailand Business Council she had formed. Therafter Kanchanalak attended 26 White House events. Clinton was present at 10 and Al Gore at two. She (illegally) became a member of the DNC's finance board of directors, celebrated President Clinton's 50th birthday party with him, and the White House recommended Ms. Kanchanalak for a position on a trade policy advisory committee. That position required a security clearance and U.S. citizenship, but she was a Thai citizen.

Both her fundraising and her security clearance violated U.S. law. The Clintonistas did not care. They wanted and got the money.

Kanchanalak met with an Asia specialist for the White House's National Security Council (NSC), Sandy Kristoff, at least three times. Her meetings helped kill NSC adviser Anthony Lake's bid to head the CIA. Lake's Senate confirmation committee demanded to know why the NSC first opposed and then favored a Clinton meeting with the Kanchanalak-created U.S.-Thailand Business Council.

"[H]er interactions with the National Security Council, are very troubling to me," said Senator Richard Shelby (R-AL). "Mr. Lake does not appear to shed any light as to why his staff met with Pauline Kanchanalak..."

In early June 1996, Kanchanalak escorted three Charoen Pokphand (CP) Group leaders to a White House coffee with Clinton in the White House to pitch favorable U.S. tariffs on China's exports.

That very same day, Kanchanalak and a relative donated $135,000 to the DNC. CP had sent $100,000 to Trie and $50,000 to Kanchanalak. Mr. Jeb Kanchanalak, a CP consultant, wired $475,000 to his wife Pauline and other family members. Shortly, the Kanchanalaks gave $450,000 directly to the DNC and to four state Democratic party organizations.

The Thompson Committee caught wind of Red Chinese contributions and conducted hearings and investigations in mid-1997. Kanchanalak was at the top of any list of persons to investigate. Once an investigation began, Kanchanalak hid corporate documents, erased computer hard drives, closed her U.S. office and fled to Bangkok.

She later returned, surrendering her passport and a $500,000 bond. Kanchanalak and her sister-in-law, Duangnet Kronenberg, agreed to cooperate with the Justice Department's campaign finance task force. A Justice task force and grand jury investigated more than a half dozen boxes of records from the U.S.-Thai Business Council.

Alleging a conspiracy (September 1992-October 1996) the Justice Department's campaign finance task force obtained a 24-count indictment in July 1998 against Kanchanalak and her sister-in-law Kronenberg.

U.S. District Judge Paul L. Friedman, a Clinton appointee, threw out the entire case, but was yet again overruled by higher courts.

She pled guilty in June 2000. Her lawyer, Reid H. Weingarten, said that prosecutors had threatened charges of international money laundering if she did not plead guilty to lesser fundraising charges. Prosecutors had recommended prison for six months to a year. In April 2001, Judge Friedman now claimed to appreciate that Kanchanalak had organized the conspiracy and obstructed justice.

Yet, he gave her a sentence some said was "lighter than a soap bubble." Kanchanalak received six months of house arrest "wearing an electronic monitoring bracelet," three years of probation and a $3,000 fine. Nothing for lying, obstructing justice and conspiring to undermine our election system in the interests of a foreign power.[24]

•

Senator Orrin Hatch (R-UT) asked whether U.S. District Judge Norma Holloway Johnson had selected judges like Friedman who were predisposed to "soft plea bargains." Senator Hatch said, "It looks as though they're covering these things up... Certainly, it looks like these plea bargains were deals, and... the judges were pre-selected... [to] give these soft plea bargains credibility."

U.S. District Judge Paul L. Friedman had given soft sentences not only to Kanchanalak but to Maria Hsia and Charlie Trie, too.

Stanley Ho — unusual suspect

Clinton contributor Stanley Ho, born Ho Hung Sun, is a business partner of Beijing's favorite billionaire, Li Ka-Shing. He has investments in Hutchinson Whampoa, COSCO and Norinco, a PLA manufacturer of automatic weapons. The Canadian Mounties identified Ho as a leader of Chinese organized crime, the Kung Lok triad.

Stanley Ho was never the subject of any known U.S. investigation.

---

[24] *Wall Street Journal,* February 27, 1997; *The Washington Post,* March 9 1997; *Congressional Record, Senate,* March 5, 1997; *Mother Jones,* April 17, 1997; *The New York Times,* June 22, 2000; *AP,* April 21, 2001, and Michelle Malkin, April 25, 2001

THE ENABLERS — CLINTON AND GORE

Bill Clinton — caught on film

In videotapes made available in October 1997, Clinton can be seen amicably socializing with Huang, Trie, Kanchanalak, James Riady and Chung. The tapes show Clinton publicly acknowledging guests at a fundraising event as being foreigners — illegal contributors.

At an event on February 19, 1996, at the Hay-Adams Clinton refers to "my good friend John Huang," and says, "I have known John Huang a very long time."

At a May 13 dinner Clinton thanked Huang and Trie, who was seated next to the President, "It's been 20 years since I had my first meal with Charlie Trie..." Also featured on the tapes is Chung.

On September 10, 1994, there was a lengthy but inaudible discussion between Clinton, Riady and Huang.

At a radio address on June 24, 1994, Riady was introduced to the President. At a fundraiser on July 30, 1996, at the Jefferson Hotel in Washington, foreign nationals, Riady and Taiwan insurance billionaire Eugene Wu, attended. Clinton talked about his decision to send carriers into the Taiwan Straits after Beijing lobbed missiles close to Taiwan.

•

Clinton gave John Huang jobs at the Department of Commerce and at the DNC.

Clinton appointed Charlie Trie to the Commission on United States-Pacific Trade.

Clinton gave Johnny Chung free access to the White House.

Clinton made Kanchanalak a member of the DNC's finance board of directors and sought to place her on a trade policy advisory committee even though by law the position required a security clearance and U.S. citizenship.

Clinton helped Loral and Hughes Aircraft get waivers of export controls on missile secrets so it could launch satellites with its partner, China Aerospace.

•

Congressman Gerald Solomon (R-NY) asked, "Is this what China is getting in return for its big donations to Clinton and the Democrat National Committee campaign coffees?"

Albert Gore

Albert Gore, Democrat nominee for President, was a close friend of Maria Hsia, who, according to the Thompson Report, was an agent of the Red Chinese government. The Thompson Report also describes

Al Gore meeting persons connected to China Resources, a known front for Chinese intelligence, agent for the Chinese in Panama, and generous Riady business partner.

According to the Thompson Report, "Were such alleged intelligence reports to be true Hsia's long [known] relationship to the vice president of the United States would raise grave new questions about the extent to which Chinese intelligence operations have been able to influence U.S. politics during the Clinton Administration." *Investor's Business Daily* found that Vice President Gore had longtime links to Maria Hsia.

Al Gore nurtured his links to Maria Hsia in an early 1989 trade trip to Taiwan, Indonesia and Hong Kong. Among others along for the plane ride was John Huang, working for Lippo Bank, Indonesian agents of Red China.[25]

In March 2000 Clinton-Gore released a sanitized 434-page "Foreign Trade Barriers" report on barriers to American businesses. China, the focus of sharp criticism of its trade barriers in prior reports, got a scant 17 pages in the 2000 edition; less than 4% of the report.

A "trade official" denied that "the Administration softened criticism of China... to win Congressional votes... [and] said that if Congress approved permanent normal trade relations for China, every trade problem would be solved."

•

The ethnic Chines actors in Chinagate fundraising scandals were all convicted. Their Red Chinese benefactors and Clinton-Gore skated home free.

Corporate collaborators — useful idiots

Coinciding with the arrival of Chinese and corporate campaign cash, the Clinton Administration gave wholesale waivers to those very export controls that had once helped keep the Soviet Union technologically backward.

From the Clinton-Gore White House down through the Departments of Commerce, State, Defense, and Energy, the Clintonistas ran rough-shod over every law, rule and regulation concerning human rights, proliferation of nuclear, chemical and biological weapons and export controls.

- In an October 1994 trip to Beijing, Secretary of Defense William Perry promised Gen. Ding Henggao, head of COSTIND, a "Cray computer to be used... to help design newer and safer nukes."[26]

---

[25] *Investor's Business Daily*
[26] Charles Smith, *WorldNetDaily*, April 27, 1999

- The U.S. government had previously cited the PLA-owned Great Wall Industries for missile sales to Pakistan and Iran. Undeterred, President Clinton granted militarily useful waivers to Loral for satellite sales. He granted the same favor to Tandem for supercomputer sales to the proven proliferator Great Wall. In August 1994, Tandem completed a deal to export $100 million in computers to PLA-owned Great Wall Industries during a Ron Brown trade mission.

- According to a secret memo of March 12, 1998, by Gary Samore, a White House NSC aide, Clinton planned even better missile deals for the Communists. In return [for yet another] Chinese promise to [again] stop sending missile technology to Iran, Libya and Pakistan — for such a useless pledge from serial liars — Clinton was willing, indeed eager, to "expedite... U.S. [missile] exports to China."

"...[AMERICAN] COMPANIES... HAVE BECOME LOBBYISTS FOR CHINA."

— *Columnist Georgie Anne Geyer*

McDonnell Douglas — stealth weapons

In 1994 a senior export-control officer for the Department of Defense, Peter Leitner, disapproved a McDonnell Douglas transfer of the machine tools. The machine tools came from a Columbus, Ohio, B-1 Bomber factory. The were sent to CATIC, a Chinese government company.

Though the sale would help the Chinese develop stealth weapons, including Silkworm anti-ship missiles, Leitner was ordered to change his recommendation. He refused, but the Clinton Administration allowed the sale anyway.

During the summer of 1999 in testimony before Congress, Peter Leitner reluctantly reported retaliation against him: loss of the regular promotions and bonuses received by his more compliant peers.

On October 19, 1999, U.S. Customs indicted the aircraft firm and its Chinese cronies and employees.

On May 11, 2001, CATIC agreed to pay $1.3 million in fines — just eight days after being swept up in a Commerce led raid on an Orlando company selling CATIC "radiation hardened" integrated chips for missiles.

Lockheed Martin — missile "kick" motors

While three defense contract traders supped with the U.S. Ambassador in Beijing, Admiral Joseph Prueher, USN (Ret), the State Department was deciding to prosecute Lockheed Martin for assisting AsiaSat and China Great Wall Industries, China's missile manufacturer, by fixing Red China's failing kick motors. Henry Sokolski, a former Pentagon official said that the kick motors might enable the Chinese to independently target each of its multiple warheads on a single missile. The Clinton Justice Department ruled out a criminal prosecution. The company still faced a possible civil fine of $1.5 million (30 violations) and loss of export licenses for three years.[27]

Senator Bob Smith (R-NH) said, "This certainly sounds inappropriate... to be wining and dining two contractors under federal investigation for providing military secrets to an enemy nation."

Admitting no wrong, in June 2000 Lockheed Martin agreed to pay a $13 million fine and to spend $5 million to track its foreign contracts. It was the largest fine ever levied unter the Arms Control Export Act.

Loral and Hughes — missile guidance

Both the Loral and Hughes CEOs had close political ties with Clinton and they were already under investigation for three years at the time their "wining and dining" with the ambassador and the Red Chinese companies producing missiles and secure communications systems.

Hughes CEO Michael Armstrong, a Clinton contributor, led Silicon Valley protests over export controls. Hughes "continually pushed the rules" to allow sharing of technical information with the Chinese.

The Cox Report states, "In 1993 and 1995, Hughes failed to apply for... Department of State licenses... because Hughes knew that the Department... would be unlikely to grant the license...

"To this end, Hughes sought the approval of a... Commerce official... and claims to have sought the approval of a... Defense monitor... though Hughes knew that neither official was legally authorized to issue the required license."

The Commerce Department approved Hughes rocket launch assistance to the Chinese in 1995 while Hughes CEO Armstrong was head of Clinton's export advisory council. It was "the most sweeping relaxation of export restrictions in U.S. history," according to *The New York Times*.

In 1996, the Clinton Administration approved Hughes installation

---

[27] *The Washington Post, The Washington Times, AP* and *ABC News*, April 6, 2000

of 522 ground stations with ports for encryption for telecommunications satellites for the Chinese ground, rocket and air forces.

Meanwhile, Loral President Bernard Schwartz wrote a $100,000 check in June 1994 to the DNC. Schwartz then joined Commerce Secretary Ron Brown's trade mission.

According to Charles Smith, "President Clinton personally arranged for Loral CEO Bernard Schwartz to meet the Chinese Vice Minister of COSTIND, General Shen Rou-jun." In 1994 COSTIND's Gen. Shen completed deals with Schwartz of Loral to provide cheap Chinese rocket launches of expensive American satellites.

President Clinton waived additional export restrictions for Loral in February 1998, letting the launches go forward against the advice of export control officers at the Pentagon. The Loral launch was stopped again after Congress took away satellite licensing powers from a Commerce Department indifferent, if not hostile, to national security.

The Clinton waiver in 1998 and an Ambassador's dinner meeting in 2000 radically undermined the Justice Department's criminal prosecution of exports of missile and other sensitive technologies.

Clearly, the gift of missile guidance technologies from Loral and Hughes was helpful to the Red Chinese. Indeed, according to the Department of Defense, the Hughes and Loral technical analyses of Chinese rocket "failures" in January 1995 and in February 1996 radically improved the accuracy of Chinese missile guidance. (During 1992 a tougher Bush Pentagon, not Commerce, restricted information shared after another rocket failure.)

Clinton export control waivers and slipshod security enabled Loral and Hughes[28] to export improved rocket launch technology to China. Improved rocket launches enhanced Chinese missile guidance — pinpoint accuracy within yards of any target within 49 states.

The Cox Report concluded, "U.S. national security was harmed." Loral and Hughes improved "the guidance system of the PRC's Long March rocket."

So too, did Clinton's waivers for Motorola satellite orbiting technologies. The Motorola technology doubled warhead firepower. They also allowed independently maneuvering warheads to "penetrate enemy defenses."

It bears repeating, despite a three-year investigation of Loral and Hughes for the transfer of rocket launching and guidance technology to China, the U.S. ambassador in Beijing, Admiral Joseph Prueher, met with Chinese and U.S. satellite companies on March 16, 2000.

Loral and Hughes had given away the missile data that made Chinese missiles accurate, but Ambassador Prueher hosted a dinner meeting with representatives of Loral, Hughes, Lockheed Martin,

---

[28] Lt. Col. Al Coates on *20/20*, December 2, 1998

and the head of the China Aerospace Science & Technology Corp. (CASC).

CASC ran China's missile program. CASC made illegal contributions to Clinton-Gore in 1996. The Ambassador's meeting also included a representative of China Telecommunications Broadcast Satellite Corp., (ChinaSat). According to the DIA, ChinaSat launched military satellites for a new command, control, communications and intelligence system for the PLA.

Senator Bob Smith objected to wining and dining companies.

The Pentagon said those exports helped to improve the accuracy of China's nuclear missiles. If guilty, Loral and Hughes face criminal penalties and Lockheed Martin, civil penalties.

The "modernization" of Red China's nuclear missile forces has been assisted by the latest U.S. technology made available to Red China by espionage and Clinton-approved exports of technology. These U.S. technologies enable those missiles to strike at American targets more accurately than ever before. With missile guidance courtesy of Clinton contributors at Hughes and Loral, China will triple its satellite launches in five years.

Beijing "could emerge over the next 15 years as a leading threat to U.S. space operations," according to the Center for Security Policy. "China is... invest[ing] in space-launch vehicles, satellites and manned space systems," and "China... is rapidly developing... the... wherewithal to challenge America's... dominance."[29] Britain's friend, Li Ka-Shing financed several satellite deals between Hughes and ChinaSat, a company owned by the PLA.[30]

Using American missile guidance and stolen warhead technologies, new generations of Chinese long-range missiles are nearly ready to deploy.

Four times Red China has successfully tested the DF-31, a solid fuel road mobile missile with a range of 5,000 miles. The DF-31 will be a single warhead, and will be silo based. Deployment will occur soon. A submarine-launched version, JL-2, successfully tested, threatens the West Coast.

Bill Gertz of *The Washington Times* reported on December 22, 2000, that "The DF-31 is the first Chinese strategic system to incorporate U.S. missile and warhead technology obtained covertly from the United States through espionage and other technology-acquisition efforts, according to U.S. intelligence officials."[31]

Among the corporate profiteers from high-tech sales to the Red Chinese are individuals running interference for the Red Chinese and their greedy collaborators. They are well educated experts alleging

---

[29] Waller, *Insight,* February 25, 2001
[30] Casey Institute, July 1999
[31] See Canfield and Delgaudio, *China Doll*, June 2000

China is no threat. They are Red China's agents of influence. Some are on the Red Chinese payroll as "consultants." Just as Armand Hammer, I.F. Stone, Harrison Salisbury and others, they serve Communist's interests very well indeed.

AGENTS OF INFLUENCE — UNREGISTERED AGENTS/ LOBBYISTS FOR RED CHINA

AMERICAN AGENTS OF INFLUENCE

"China's ambassador to Washington, Li Zhaoxing, was downright smug. He was hosting an event for about 50 Congressional staff and lobbyists. The happy man said, 'We don't have to lobby on Permanent Normal Trade Relations (PNTR). American business is taking care of that for us." An observer told *Insight*, "No one flinched." Indeed. The U.S. Senate vote for PNTR for China was 85-15.

Sandy Berger, Clinton's national security advisor, is a lawyer specializing in trade law. Berger's former law firm, Hogan and Hartson, seamlessly and transparently represented both the Red Chinese and the Democratic National Committee. Berger and his fellow traders are either unconcerned with national security or believe trade alone will bring freedom to China.

Berger is not alone. Nearly every former secretary of state, national security advisor and key deputy has "cashed in" on China trade. They have failed to publicly disclose their Red Chinese ties. America's elite is acting just like overseas Chinese tycoons. Once tempted to finance democratic opposition in Red China prior to the Tiananmen massacre overseas Chinese tycoons no longer help dissidents. Deng Xiaoping lured them into making profitable mainland investments instead. "Their investments have made them hostages to Beijing and they are now among the loudest voices being raised in favour of appeasing China," according to British journalist and 20-year China hand, Jasper Becker, in *The Chinese*.[32]

As many as 30,000 Fulan Gong followers have been imprisoned. Sales of body organs of executed prisoners was expanded. There was never a peep from Beijing's U.S. collaborators. Businessmen ought to know better, but their preoccupation with business is not surprising. Being agents of influence is more profitable. Morality is bad for business.

Conflicts of interest are obvious where former secretaries of state who support China trade also serve on Chinese and/or corporate payrolls lobbying for China trade.

---

[32] Free Press, 2000

It is not illegal to represent clients or to lobby on behalf of interests, foreign or not. The law only requires public disclosure. Unlike the old Taiwan lobby, none of the former American officials have bothered to register as agents of the PRC. No one in the establishment mainstream media has raised the issue of persons valued for their expertise having financial interest in the "expert" opinions they express on China trade. Only a courageous few have brought up these conflicts: Richard Bernstein and Ross Munro, authors of the *Coming Conflict with China;* Joe Farah of *WorldNetDaily;* Michael Waller and others in *Insight;* Gene Crocker, McAlvany and *Mindszenty Report.*

A *Mindszenty Report* in 1997 reported, "former Secretaries of State Henry Kissinger, George Shultz, Alexander Haig, Lawrence Eagleburger and Cyrus Vance... each... has earned tens of thousands of dollars from U.S. businesses doing business in China."

In *The Coming Conflict with China,* former *Time* bureau chiefs in Beijing, Richard Bernstein and Ross Munro, described how money is made. "The consultant knows the Chinese leaders, the American company gets a meeting... the consultant gets paid by the corporation, and... to solidify his... access to Chinese power brokers, he makes public statements supporting the policies that Beijing favors."

Six former secretaries of state have publicly supported permanent normal trading relations with China — exempting the Reds from Congress's annual review.

Here they are:

Henry Kissinger, former Secretary of State, was an organizer of the Business Coalition for U.S.-China Trade. The $26 billion American International Group, a major Kissinger client with offices in Shanghai, is a leading organizer of the multimillion-dollar lobbying campaign for PNTR. In China since 1992, AIG reported profits of $200 million in 1999. Kissinger got some of it.

David Rothkopf, the former boss of John Huang in Clinton's Commerce Department, joined Kissinger Associates as its managing director.

Other clients of Kissinger Associates who do business with Red China are Chase Manhattan Bank, Coca-Cola, American Express, Continental Grain, H.J. Heinz, Atlantic Richfield, Midland Bank and S.G. Warburg.

"Six and seven figure client fees per year are reputed to be the norm," McAlvany reports. "To become a corporate client of Kissinger, a corporation pays a $200,000 fee. In some cases Kissinger also will take a seat on the company's board."

Bernstein and Munro note, "On the very day of the Tiananmen Square massacre, Kissinger's syndicated column referred to Deng Xiaoping as 'one of the great reformers in Chinese history.' He said Deng was a man 'who chose a more humane and less chaotic course for China'."

Gene Crocker says, "Kissinger is credited for buttonholing [House Speaker Newt] Gingrich in 1995, and persuading him to support the delinking of 'human rights' from trade..."

Mike Waller pricked Kissinger's hot air balloon by asking about a conflict of interest. Kissinger "harangued" Waller saying, "What do you think entitles you to ask such an insulting question?" Kissinger also told *Insight* he does not accept money from China. Of course, his corporate clients do and pay Kissinger out of another pocket.

As indicated above, **Alexander Haig**, former NATO Commander, Secretary of State and Presidential Chief of Staff, has been a paid "domestic and overseas senior honorary advisor" to the China Overseas Shipping Company (COSCO).

Haig lobbied to obtain the Naval Station in Long Beach for the Chinese. Haig, owner of Worldwide Associates, advises United Technologies, a manufacturer of jet engines, air conditioners and elevators. The company has made billions in 17 joint ventures in China. Haig's client's relationships are reminiscent of Armand Hammer's exclusive franchises in the Soviet Union for pencils, asbestos, chemicals, artwork, banking, medicines and oil.

Haig's backing of China trade, like Kissinger's, extends to newspaper columns and expert commentary on television. *McAlvany Intelligence* reports, "Haig has been... aggressive in defending the Red Chinese butchers... defending the Red Chinese leaders just a few months after they slaughtered thousands of student demonstrators in 1989.

When China (in early '96) blockaded the Taiwan Straits and lobbed nuclear-capable missiles... off the coast of Taiwan... and threatened to nuke Los Angeles if America came to the aid of Taiwan, Haig frantically called members of Congress, defending China and urging [Congress] not to impose trade sanctions..."

Bernstein and Monroe mince no words: "Kissinger and Haig are the two most conspicuous practitioners of this corrupt trade, and also the most slavishly devoted to the Beijing party line." By various accounts either Kissinger or Haig got Ross Munro fired from the Foreign Policy Research Institute in Philadelphia. If so, their corruption was turned to malevolent evil. It's good that Alexander Haig alone thought himself "in charge" when President Reagan was close to death from an assassin's bullet.

George Shultz, former Secretary of State who, in 1984, endorsed the turnover of Hong Kong, has been on the board of the China International Trust and Investment Corporation (CITIC), the $20 billion-plus investment arm of Red China's Communist State Council. CITIC is a very good friend of the Communist party and the People's Liberation Army (PLA).

James A. Baker III, former Chief of Staff (1981-85) and Secretary of State (1989-92), is a senior partner in the law firm of Baker, Baker & Botts, a family law firm having over 500 attorneys with clients worldwide. It advises clients on export controls on sophisticated technology and weapons proliferation, among other issues. Its webpage news covers the latest from China.

The former secretary of state has also been a senior counselor to The Carlyle Group since 1993. The Carlyle Group is a private global investment firm with offices worldwide, including Hong Kong that focuses on aerospace, defense, information technologies and telecommunications industries, among others. Its Hong Kong office is fully staffed.

Carlyle Asia, at the end of 1999, had commitments of $750 million. The Fund will invest in China and elsewhere in the Pacific. Former President George Bush serves on its advisory board. Its chairman is Frank C. Carlucci and a senior advisor is Richard G. Darman. Carlucci also chairs the U.S.-ROC (Taiwan) Business Council, an association, formed in 1976, to foster trade with the Republic of China (ROC) on Taiwan.

Baker, Baker & Botts and The Carlyle Group can best be described as pragmatic — unguided by fundamental principles. James Baker III said in early 1996, that "the growing economic links between China and the outside world, particularly... foreign investment... represent... the best guarantee that China will be a force for stability...

Further, "We need to balance... our... interest in improving human rights with our no less compelling interest in commercial engagement."

Commercial interests (profits) are "no less compelling" than human rights and national security, in Baker's view. Objecting to Chinese slavery, forced abortion, sales of body organs should be "more compelling" than commerce. Deterring nuclear war through American strength must surely be morally superior "interest" of greater value than the profits of trade and business.

Ronald Reagan knew better than James Baker.

Reagan rejected the notion of "moral equivalence," called on Gorbachev to "tear down that wall" and pledged to defeat the "evil empire."

Lawrence Eagleburger, Secretary of State in 1992 and 1993, is a past president of Kissinger Associates. Since 1993, he has been the senior foreign policy advisor at the Memphis-based law firm of Baker, Donelson, Bearman and Caldwell.

Former Senate Majority Leader and White House Chief of Staff Howard Baker runs the firm's Washington office. In late 1998, *Fortune* ranked the firm's Public Policy Group as one of the top 10 lobbying organizations in the capital. Its practice includes international trade law, telecommunications and defense — matters of great interest to Red China.

Warren Christopher's bread and butter comes from a law firm with a high stake in, and special exclusive legal franchises inside, China. Christopher was Secretary of State for Clinton-Gore from 1993-96 and is former chairman and senior partner of a large international law firm, O'Melveny & Myers, with offices in Hong Kong and in Shanghai.

The firm's clients include Lockheed Martin and Occidental Oil. Lockheed Martin has been indicted, like Loral and Hughes, for assisting the Chinese in improving the accuracy of rockets and missiles. Lockheed Martin paid a $13 million fine.

O'Melveny & Myers' Hong Kong office opened in 1994. In 1998, O'Melveny became one of the first U.S. firms to become licensed to practice Hong Kong law. In 1996, O'Melveny became one of the first, and soon the largest, foreign firm licensed in Shanghai. From Shanghai, China, the firm advises multinational clients about projects throughout China.

Christopher's firm did especially well in China during Christopher's tenure with Clinton-Gore. As Secretary of State to Clinton-Gore, Christopher sought to maintain a policy of engagement through thick and thin. Whether nuclear proliferation, Taiwan threats or human rights abuses, Christopher stuck with "engaging" and not alienating the Chinese! His support for the "One China" policy is indistinguishable from, say, "One Korea," or "One Vietnam." Policy which cost 100,000 Americans their lives in two wars.

•

The issue is not whether to trade with China. It is what limits and controls on militarily-useful "dual-use," technology must be retained or put upon trade. These controls protect our national security and other American values.

Many of the agents of influence described above have gone beyond mere advocacy of trade. They have actively aided Red China's military modernization at the expense of U.S. national security. Their denials of such intentions are very far from any proof of their innocence.

Dr. Mike Waller, columnist for *Insight*, writes in the April 2000 issue of *Insight*, "...former national-security leaders who built personal relations with Communist officials have moved from simply pushing policies that would increase trade with China to becoming, in effect, agents of influence for the Beijing regime.

"Boeing and other companies seeking to sell their civilian and dual-use products to China are caught in a conflict with the parts of their business devoted to the national defense of the United States — a sector that has funded many of the defense and national-security think tanks and policy groups in Washington and around the country. And those groups that don't toe the line [on China trade] are getting punished.

"Unlike Taiwan, which invests most of its lobbying in traditional public relations firms that register with the Justice Department under the Foreign Agents Registration Act, or FARA, Beijing circumvents the law and avoids disclosure by getting U.S. companies, senior statesmen, academics and others to do its bidding...

Indeed, "FARA is intended to require such foreign-sponsored lobby activity to be registered with the Justice Department so that Congress and other decision-makers will know the origin of the political action...

"But the Justice Department seldom pursues such cases. 'FARA is just too full of loopholes and not serious enough a law for the FBI to investigate or want to prosecute,' an FBI source tells *Insight*."

"... [Y]ou're almost a wacko if you're not with Beijing. You're totally marginalized," says an Asia expert for a Washington think tank.

"Another official from a defense foundation notes, "The same companies will threaten to cut you off for writing a single piece that the Chinese government finds objectionable," adding that he speaks from personal experience. The Chinese pressure the companies and the companies put the screws upon the think tanks.

As Dr. Waller puts it, "In an elegant act of political jujitsu, Communist China now is using the weight and strength of U.S. business — including some of the nation's largest defense contractors — to promote its own military and security goals... [B]ig business... weighed in against legislation designed to cement the long-standing U.S. security relationship with the Republic of China on Taiwan."

"Last October [1999], when the House International Relations Committee voted a lopsided 32-6 for the Taiwan Security Enhancement Act, or TSEA, the business lobbies... focused... on Red China trade issues sprang into action. They pressed the House Republican leadership to pull the bill lest it be called for a full vote of the House and to postpone consideration until later. The GOP leadership caved."

BESIDES PERSUASIVE ARGUMENTS
THERE IS ALSO CAMPAIGN CASH

Cash from the Red China lobbyists

The Fortune 500 has signed onto the Red Team.

In late March 1997, *The Washington Times* printed a partial list of pro-China corporate campaign contributions in 1996. This Red

China lobby donated over $20 million in PAC money to members of the House and Senate.

Similarly, in 1997, Knight-Ridder's Washington bureau analyzed reports filed with the Federal Elections Commission. It said, "firms belonging to the U.S.-China Business Council contributed more than $55 million to political campaigns in 1995 and 1996, making them an important lobby for favorable U.S. policies toward China."

The top five overall contributors were Phillip Morris, AT&T, Federal Express, BellSouth and Atlantic Richfield.

The specific business categories of greatest interest to this book are *Communications* (GTE, AT&T, Ameritech, BellSouth and SBC Comm., Inc.), *Aerospace* (Lockheed Martin, Textron, Inc., Northrop Grumman, United Tech. and Boeing Co.), *Banking/financial services* (Arthur Andersen, Morgan Stanley, Price Waterhouse, Coopers Lybrand and American Express), and *Consumer goods* (GE).

By 2000, the corporations supporting China Trade would spend heavily on lobbying, advertising and campaign contributions. Leading up to the China trade votes in the Congress, U.S. businesses sponsoring liberalized China trade spent $113 million to lobby, advertise and make political contributions.[33]

They had other interests, but China trade was their number one issue before Congress.

Unfortunately, those corporate interests conflicted with vital national interests. Many made China trade their top priority in 2000. Worse, others have actively supported the full Red Chinese agenda against missile defenses, against Taiwan, against human rights and against nonproliferation of weapons of mass destruction. The GOP pullback of Taiwan Security Enhancement Act under corporate pressure was very ominous.

Although trade with China, like trade with the old USSR, is small, America's Chambers of Commerce believe it will skyrocket with Permanent Normal Trade Relations (PNTR) and China's entry into the World Trade Organization (WTO).

This delusion — contradicted by the plain evidence of millions of empty containers exported to China — would appear to be far more attractive than the utopian pretensions of the Soviet Union's evil empire.

•

Vice President Dick Cheney became CEO of Halliburton, Inc., an oil services company in 1995. Under Cheney it grew into America's number-one oil services company, the fifth-largest military contractor and the biggest nonunion employer in the nation.

A Halliburton company, Landmark Graphics, provided software

---

[33] *Reuters,* October 3, 2000

technology to map a 100-square-kilometer oil field, the Zhao Dong Block in Bohai Bay, China, for the Chinese National Petroleum Corporation.

On March 1, 2001, a Halliburton company, Kellogg Brown & Root, announced that the China National Offshore Oil Corporation chose it to build fertilizer plants on Hainan Island. "The ammonia plant will be the largest built in China. The urea plant will be the largest in China and Asia. ...The new plant for CNOOC will be the 20th ammonia plant in China to use KBR technology."[34]

Mr. Cheney no longer runs Halliburton and presumably is now a bit more cautious about dealings with China.

•

"[T]here is a difference between selling food and selling technology that could be used against America and our allies. China's growing military capabilities present serious challenges... The Cox Report should prompt a full and serious review of export controls, to make certain that America's technology is not arming China's military."[35]

As a free trader, Cheney opposed sanctions for exports to both Iran and Libya, where his oil services company sought business. In fact, on July 25, 1995, the Department of Commerce assessed a civil penalty of $2,610,000 against Halliburton. This was the largest fine imposed by the Department for export violations up to that date. Two Halliburton subsidiaries had exported oil field equipment — six pulse neutron generators and spare parts to Libya in 1987-1991 and three generators to Kuwait or Yemen in 1988-1989. A judge in the U.S. District Court for the Southern District of Texas accepted Halliburton's plea agreement with the U.S. Attorney's Office and imposed a criminal penalty of $1,200,000 for three violations.

CHINAPHILIA IN BUSH ADMINISTRATION

Andrew H. Card, Jr., Chief of Staff

Andrew H. Card, Jr., 53, Chief of Staff to President George W. Bush, is a Massachusetts-born engineer and former state legislator who served eight years in the White House with Reagan and Bush, Sr., and as Secretary of Transportation from 1992-93. Afterward, as president of the American Automobile Manufacturers Association (AAMA), on June 4, 1998, Card said, "America's car companies strongly support continuing... most favored nation (MFN) status... Denying MFN to China today would make solutions... more difficult..." On July 22,

---

[34] Halliburton website, 2001
[35] George W. Bush, May 25, 1999, GeorgeWBush.com

Card said, "denying MFN has never been proven to be an effective instrument for encouraging positive political change in China."

Condoleezza Rice, National Security Advisor

Condoleezza Rice, 46, was born in Alabama and earned degrees in political science and international studies from Notre Dame University and the University of Denver. Her specialty was the Soviet Union. Under the tutelage of Brent Scowcroft, Beijing's toastmaster for Bush after the Tiananmen massacre, she served as Bush's policy advisor on the Soviet Union at the National Security Council in the White House. Afterwards, Rice was a senior fellow at the conservative Hoover Institution and the provost of Stanford University.

Rice called upon Robert Blackwill to advise her on organizing the NSC. Blackwill participated in Harvard's exchange programs for Chinese military officers. Blackwill was thrown off the 2000 GOP platform committee for writing language to appease the Chinese. Rice's appointment of Torkel Patterson, a Japan expert, to the NSC to cover Asia has been described as a selection that "sidestepped the rift in the Republican Party over China."

Elaine Chao, Secretary of Labor

Chao, 47, came to the U.S. from Taiwan at the age of eight speaking no English. She earned AB and MBA degrees from Holyoke and Harvard. She is married to Senator Mitch McConnell (R-KY). Chao says she believes in the American dream she has lived.

She has served at the Federal Maritime Administration and as Peace Corp Director. In 1991, she was Person of the Year for the New York Foreign Freight Forwarders and Brokers Association. As President of the United Way, she allegedly restored public trust (after embezzlement by a prior president). This fairy tale has a dark side — intimate connections to Red China.

She became a $200,000 fellow at the Heritage Foundation in 1996, displacing Reagan's National Security Advisor Richard V. Allen as head of its Asian Studies Center Advisory Council. She was a fundraiser, not a China policy expert. She had strong pro-China views.

At the urging of Chao, Chinagate figure John Huang made a $2,000 contribution to her husband Senator McConnell. Illegal contributions to the DNC ultimately cost Huang's boss — Beijing-friendly James Riady and his Lippo Group — an $86 million fine in 2001. Yet in 1997, Elaine Chao objected to the Thompson Committee Chinagate probe of foreign Chinese contributions to the DNC. She said, "The media has selectively targeted Asian-Americans... That's a disgrace... unjust..."[36]

---

[36] Novak, *Chicago Sun Times*, January 18, 2001

Though Huang claims to have met Chao four times, she did not recall meeting him. In late January 2001, Senator McConnell, a renowned campaign finance expert, claimed with a straight face that he had just heard for the first time that Huang's contributions were illegal. He returned the $2,000.

American-based Chinese human rights advocate Harry Wu has reported upon China's gulag of prison camps, the laogai, and the sale of body parts of executed prisoners. Wu told *WorldNetDaily*, "I worry about Elaine Chao's business relationship with communist China. This woman has a significant shipping business through her father." Her father, James S.C. Chao, is owner of an international ship brokerage business called Foremost Marine Corp. His ships trade with China. Indeed, Chao's Foremost Maritime Pte. Ltd. purchased two 64,000 DWT oil tankers — *Hsing May* and *Yu May* — from China. The Chinese company, State Shipbuilding Trading Co., Ltd., (CSTC) of Beijing, China, has a warship division. CSTC "has developed and built for many years for the Chinese Navy nuclear submarines, conventional submarines, missile destroyers, missile frigates, missile fast attack crafts,"[37]

As reported by Paul Sperry of *WorldNetDaily*, Elaine Chao's father, James Chao, has maintained a lifetime contact with his old school chum at Jiao Tong University in Shanghai in mainland China — Chinese President Jiang Zemin. In 1994 Elaine Chao, her father, and Senator McConnell had a private meeting with Jiang, leader of the Communist Party and the PLA. James Chao, Elaine by his side, received an honorary professorship and presidency of the Shanghai Maritime College in 1995. In 1997 Jiang met Chao and her Senator husband for another private meeting at a Clinton state dinner in the White House.

James Chao sits on the board and owns 7,000 shares of CRC Protective Life Corp. CRC is jointly owned by the Beijing-friendly James Riady's Lippo Group and Li Ka-shing's business partner China Resources. China Resources is an intelligence gathering front company for the PLA.[38]

Elaine Chao showed a disturbing ability to push aside other Heritage fellows with negative views of Red China. Her appointment pushed Reagan NSC director Richard Allen out the door. Chao and her husband lobbied hard for PNTR. They struck back at Heritage Foundation fellows writing about China's military threat. The Foundation fired Heritage security analyst and Cox Report contributor, Richard Fisher, Jr. Chao "...pushed him out... because he raised national security concerns over China," according to a congressional aide who worked with Fisher.

---

[37] CSTC-Warship at chinaships.com
[38] Sperry, *WorldNetDaily*, January 24, 2001, citing Senate records and public securities records

In early February 2001 Washington insiders were alleging that Elaine Chao had nixed a Heritage Foundation slot for Notra Trulock, the former Energy Department counterintelligence expert most responsible for the Cox Report exposing Wen Ho Lee and Chinese nuclear espionage.

The traders' disease has infected at least part of the Bush Administration and provided perhaps unwitting agents of influence for the PRC.

A Constitutional Restoration of U.S. Security

Corrective security measures are required in the USA. Otherwise, ships, ports and cities may be vulnerable, not only to terrorist groups, but also to China's forward deployment of its proxy espionage, intelligence and naval forces. With the active complicity of the Clinton-Gore Administration, aided by delusional China traders, Red China has placed its soldiers, sailors, students, scientists and spies into every major American seaport, university, research center and high-tech company.

President Bush and the Congress face two daunting tasks: to restore national security and to preserve civil liberties. Congress must find the courage it lacked in impeachment and in the China trade votes. It must stand between liberty and tyranny. President Bush and Congress must perform their Constitutional duties or join the legacy of infamy of Clinton-Gore.

There is hope. Two years after the Thompson Report, John Zogby, best known for his polling in the 2000 election, took a poll and found that two-thirds of Americans still wanted an investigation of a possible swapping of military secrets for campaign contributions. Three-fourths opposed WTO status because of China's espionage, weapons proliferation and oppression.[1]

Nonetheless, Congress has continued to support WTO without any condition. A later Congress can do better.

In alliance with patriots of both parties, Congress must strive mightily to restore our national security. As a sovereign nation, America possesses the capacity to act independently of international organizations and of the opinions of other foreign powers. What must be done, can be done. Restore the U.S. Constitution, the rule of law and prudent security practices.

Observation and enforcement of many existing laws would go a very long way toward reducing recognizable risks to national security without endangering the civil liberties of Americans.

Under existing espionage statutes it is already a crime to disclose information about national defense with intent to either aid a foreign power or to harm the United States. It is a criminal act to release highly sensitive information such as the names of U.S. agents and spies, codes and intelligence intercepts. The Economic Espionage Act of 1996 enhanced fines and penalties for stealing secret critical tech-

---

[1] Zogby, November 1999

nologies or for unlawfully influencing U.S. policies. Criminal penalties ought to apply in some instances.

While dangers to our national security could be perilous indeed, we must be cognizant of the dangers to our Constitution from a thoughtless or overzealous pursuit of national security. The President and Congress ought not to be complicit in abusing the trust of U.S. citizens such as the misuse of NSA's Echelon system to intercept any and all private U.S. telecommunications or to warrantless intercepts by the FBI's Carnivore computer system.

Major revisions or outright elimination of a number of Clinton Presidential Directives on terrorism and infrastructure security are necessary.

Indeed, in 2000 the Congress hastily enacted the equivalent of a British, but un-American, "Official Secrets Act" which would have criminalized the leaking of any officially classified document regardless of its actual significance to national security.

To support improved background checks for immigrants is one thing, a Chinese Exclusion Act or an Aliens and Sedition Act is another.

Of course, an undeterred Red China is a potential threat to the Constitutional rights of American citizens to free speech, to bear arms, to be free from unreasonable searches and seizures, and to just compensation for the taking of private property.

Principles of national security

The following principles ought to guide improvements of national security.

- Putting the national interest in security ahead of the private interest in profits from the sale of military or dual- use technologies to states competing with the U.S. in international affairs (laissez faire is earned).

- Maintaining the civil liberties of Americans (from unreasonable searches and seizures, unjust takings of property, retaliatory investigations).

- Observing those largely routine security measures proven safe to a free society.

- Enforcing existing laws on espionage, export controls.

- Restoring counterintelligence functions.

- Establishing professional security standards in U.S. seaports, research laboratories, universities and industries.

- Limiting the access of foreign intelligence and military officers to research facilities and U.S. military strategies and tactics.

The Congress should, actually must, enact and present to the American people and independent news media such policy advice, legislative findings, Congressional reports and legislation as is necessary to protect every citizen's right to life, liberty and property against the China threat and its agents. These include:

- Urging President Bush to make U.S. national security his first priority of U.S. relations with China, ahead of trade and cultural relations.

- Requiring that President Bush comply with the Smith/DeLay amendments restricting U.S.-PRC military-to-military exchanges exposing U.S. war fighting strategies and tactics to a potential enemy.

- Urging President Bush to reassess the Clinton-Gore "Strategic Partnership" with Red China and to report its damage to national security to the American people.

- Advising President Bush to honor the USA's 50-year commitment to the defense of Taiwan and to the security of Asia and the Pacific.

- Encouraging that President Bush to actively enforce prior weapons proliferation agreements.

- Insisting that President Bush respond to known and suspected Red Chinese espionage, in particular, its front companies and agents concentrating on U.S. military and high-tech intelligence.

- Requesting that President Bush investigate further the ubiquitous presence on U.S. soil of potential agents of Red China — soldiers, sailors, students, scientists and spies — and to enforce existing law to disclose to the public the names of identified foreign contributors, agents, lobbyists, lawyers and front companies.

- Insisting that President Bush enforce the Economic Espionage Act of 1996 to thwart the efforts of foreign entities to steal secrets about critical technologies or to unlawfully influence U.S. policies, to investigate persons (including American companies) and criminally prosecute violators — consistent with protecting sources and methods of U.S. intelligence, and to seek individual fines up to $500,000 and 15 years in prison.

- Encouraging President Bush to deploy tactical, theatre and continental defenses from missile attacks.

- Urging President Bush to restore within the Departments of State and Defense strong export controls on militarily valuable technologies and to commit to tougher enforcement of export control laws and regulations to prevent the sale, proliferation or giveaway of militarily useful technologies.

- Urging President Bush to review existing security measures for preventing visiting military officers, scientists and students from stealing America's military secrets from U.S. agencies and defense contractors.

- Enabling President Bush to perform security checks upon all personnel entrusted with secrets vital to our national security and to prosecute those traitors who would betray their fellow countrymen.

Congressional initiatives and investigations

On its own Congress ought to take the initiative to thoroughly investigate the national security implications of the ubiquitous presence on U.S. soil of potential agents of Red China. China's ships, sailors, soldiers and scientists ought to be considered as possible instruments of espionage.

The Cox Report said, "The FBI has inadequate resources in light of the extensive numbers of PRC visitors, students, diplomats, business representatives and others who may be involved in intelligence and military-related technology transfer operations in the United States."

At highly vulnerable choke points at seaports on American soil, Congress ought to hold hearings upon the potential national security threats of the presence of the China Ocean Shipping Company (COSCO), the merchant marine of the People's Liberation Army of the People's Republic of China.

Congress ought to enact legislation which:

- Clarifies existing prohibitions against foreign contributions to U.S. elections and enhances penalties for illegal foreign influence upon elections.

- Authorizes and appropriates additional funds to the CIA, NSC, NSA, Customs, Coast Guard, FBI and other agencies to halt exports with possible military end uses dangerous to our nation's survival and, in particular, provides U.S. Customs with the resources necessary to perform its export control duties and the FBI with resources sufficient to expand its counterintelligence activities.

- Improves the sharing of sensitive law enforcement information within the Executive Branch by directing the Department of Justice to provide national security information to Executive departments, agencies, and entities with the right and need to know it.[2]

- Amends the Defense Production Act of 1950 to require U.S. agencies and companies to report to the Committee on Foreign Investment in the United States (CFIUS) of foreign takeover of any U.S. companies that conducts national security-related business.

- Directs U.S. intelligence agencies to conduct an all-source analysis of PRC goals for acquiring U.S. technologies and penetrating businesses, academic, social and political institutions and to report upon the resources and priorities that executive agencies commit to counterintelligence.

- Requires President Bush to implement major recommendations of the Cox Report such as:
  - Semi-annual report on PRC espionage and the actions taken by the Departments of Energy and Defense, the FBI and CIA to respond to espionage involving nuclear and other defense technologies.[3]
  - Inspectors General of Departments of State, Defense and Energy, the Attorney General and the Director of CIA use counterintelligence officers to examine the risks to U.S. national security of international scientific exchange programs with the PRC at nuclear laboratories.
  - Comprehensive counterintelligence threat assessment of PRC espionage targeted against U.S. public and private entities.

- Requires public disclosure of the foreign clients of lobbyists and lawyers and sets high monetary penalties for failure to register as a foreign agent and to fully report to the Federal Elections Commission such economic interests, including those with private commercial clients doing business in Red China.

- Requires the public disclosure of PRC-owned and other front companies for the People's Liberation Army, other PRC

[2,3] Cox Report

entities masquerading as commercial entities and Beijing-friendly companies with major PRC investors.

- Increases penalties for violations of export controls over technology important to national security, e.g. Senator Phil Gramm's (R-TX) Senate Bill, S1715, setting fines up to $1,000,000 and criminal penalties up to life imprisonment for aggravated circumstances and giving a patriot award of up to $250,000 for furnishing information leading to a criminal conviction or civil penalty.

- Tightens limits on military-to-military exchanges with the PRC and on visits of Red Chinese intelligence and military officers to U.S. military exercises, nuclear laboratories and defense industries.

- Requires the Immigration and Naturalization Service to cooperate with U.S. law enforcement and intelligence agencies to give closer scrutiny to those individuals granted H-1B and other visas to work or to study in American high-tech and defense industries.

- Establishes and funds security measures to safeguard our highly vulnerable seaports and other transportation, communications, energy and water infrastructures.

•

Considering the dangers, these are very modest and prudent proposals consistent with the protection of civil liberties.

POSTSCRIPT —
After September 11, 2001

What do the Red Chinese want?

In *Hegemon: The Chinese Plan to Dominate Asia and the World*, Steven W. Mosher writes, that the Chinese are in "a worldwide contest with the U.S. to replace the current *Pax Americana* with a *Pax Sinica.*" China wants to become the next sole superpower. For centuries, China dominated its world seeing itself as the unchallenged hegemon. It was the Middle Kingdom to which all others deferred and paid tribute.

Similarly, in *The Chinese*, 20-year China journalist Jasper Becker describes "supreme leader Jiang Zemin" bringing in the new year 2000 as the emperor of a new dynasty "with a divine mission to 'rejuvenate' the Chinese race... avenge its humiliations... [and] to restore the empire to its former glory." This restoration of empire includes bringing 30 to 40 million overseas Chinese under control, extending Chinese military presence 1,000 miles from its mainland and crushing the only functioning Chinese democracy in Taiwan.

The wake up call and the alert

The blood of the innocents shed on September 11, 2001, provided America a wake up call and an alert that the world is a dangerous place. This wake up and alert has not yet extended to Red China.

Yes, there is renewed interest in nuclear, biological, and chemical weapons. There is some awareness of the vulnerability of seaports, U.S. Navy ships, waterworks, bridges, tunnels, power plants, transmission lines, computers, telecommunications and more. There is increased awareness of the national security consequences of America's porous borders, sloppy immigrant processing, and plodding law enforcement bureaucracies.

There is also some understanding of the dangers of millions of sealed and uninspected 20-foot cargo containers. Sealed containers provide the means for delivering stowaways, contraband and weapons of all kinds from guns to explosives to missiles to weapons of mass destruction. On December 8, Secretary of Commerce Norm Mineta echoed the author's prior warnings in *Stealth Invasion* about containers. President Bush's remarks to sailors in Norfolk in early 2001 are on target:

"...[W]e must confront the threats that come in a shipping container or in a suitcase." — *President George W. Bush, February 13, 2001, Norfolk, VA*

"A cargo container arriving at a U.S. seaport today can be virtually anywhere in the heartland of America via truck and/or rail tomorrow." — *Norm Mineta, Transportation Secretary*[1]

Nonetheless, though the People's Republic of China is the single largest shipper of uninspected cargo containers to North America, Red China goes unnamed and unindicted as a principal threat.

America's innocence has been violated in blood, so people are now vigilant.

China, however, remains all but invisible. Indeed, Red China continues to acquire American secrets and technologies. China continues to provide arms (including components of weapons of mass destruction) to the "axis of evil" — those very nations harboring terrorists.

Red China's Trojan horses are welcomed onto America's beachheads

As horrible as September 11th was, Red China's proxy nations, hundreds of front companies, and thousands of agents of influence and espionage are still in our homeland. China's Trojan horses have been welcomed in large numbers onto American beachheads.

China's Trojan horses represent far greater unrealized dangers to our nation than the isolated acts of several hands full of mad men and criminals. China has what terrorist thugs wish they had — weapons of mass destruction and the human and technical means to deliver them (or just use them as blackmail) to achieve its objectives in Taiwan, the Pacific, and at any other times and places of its own choosing.

When most terrorists have long since been sent to paradise or found hiding under their mothers' beds, Red China will continue to provide many threats to America.

In *Unrestricted Warfare* in 1999, two PLA colonels urged China to resort to terrorism, computer viruses and other types of "dirty war." One of the authors, Qiao Liang, weeks after 9/11 said: "The first rule of unrestricted warfare is that there are no rules — nothing is forbidden." They wrote. "There is nothing in the world today that cannot become a weapon."[2]

This book has identified many potential Chinese weapons and threats to corresponding U.S. targets.

---

[1] *AP*, December 8, 2001
[2] *Reuters*, Oct. 3, 2001

On one day in September 2001, nineteen terrorists gained control of four civilian aircraft for a few hours.

Every day, the Red Chinese control 100 ships of their merchant marine, the China Ocean Shipping Company (COSCO). Every day, millions of Chinese containers sit in the open in broad daylight on U.S. berths, rail cars, trucks, and loading docks in nearly every American city and town.

In the Port of Gioia, Italy on October 18, 2001, Egyptian Rigk Amid was caught in a well-equipped cargo container bound for Canada to hijack aircraft in the New York area.[3]

On March 12, 2002, UPI reported that Italian sources had told the White House they had "plausible reports" that three ships of "unknown origin" were steaming toward the U.S. with nuclear weapons onboard. If this report is true, the deadly cargoes have yet to be found. In early May 2002, the Coast Guard reported intelligence that 25 terrorists just might have already reached the U.S. in cargo containers.

Year after year, from coast to coast, local newspapers dribble out reports of Chinese stowaways captured in cargo containers. In fact, the U.S. Coast Guard quietly and invisibly captured 5,549 illegal immigrants from the People's Republic of China in the decade of 1991 to 2001.[4]

Thousands of others overstay their tourist, student or worker visas. By 2000 the official U.S. Census found and counted 200,000 illegal aliens from Red China living in the United States. There may be more.

Every year, millions of containers under control of the Red Chinese make the U.S. particularly vulnerable to large container vessels — approaching the size of battleships or aircraft carriers. Each vessel carries thousands of containers. Some might, some day carry hidden, deadly cargo.

•

To refresh the memory of our readers, we summarize here where COSCO's containers and COSCO's friends — the Tung brothers and Li Ka-Shing — can be found in the USA.

The Port of Long Beach — Berths 232-234, 243-249, 262, 264 at Pier J

COSCO will very soon have its own secure 300-acre mega port, a militarily useful beachhead on U.S. soil.

It will have achieved its once frustrated objective to take over the U.S. Naval Station or equivalent space in Long Beach.

---

[3] DEBKAfile, *WorldNetDaily*, Nov. 30, 2001
[4] *Coast Guard Migrant Interdictions At Sea*. Uscg.mil, November 16, 2001

On December 11, 2001, a COSCO venture, Pacific Maritime Services, signed a deal to expand to Berths 267-270 when the Danish company Maersk moves out in 2003.[5]

Moreover, Oriental Overseas Container Line's CEO, C.C. Tung — whose brother Chee Hwa has twice been chosen as Beijing's ruler of Hong Kong[6] — sits on the COSCO and Panama Canal advisory boards. Tung's Beijing-friendly OOCL owns Long Beach Container Terminal, berths 6-10 at Pier F in Long Beach.

The Port of Oakland — Howard Terminal

The port is expanding to accommodate COSCO and may develop other properties on the former U.S. Naval Air Station across the channel on Alameda Island.

The Port of Seattle — Harbor Island's Terminal 18

Off Elliott Bay COSCO shares space with OOCL and China Shipping Group. Space at Terminal 18 is in the process of being doubled.

In Seattle, China has (if it chooses) far more inviting targets than terrorists had in the USS *Cole* in Aden, Yemen. COSCO ships commingle with the U.S. Navy, which homeports nine nuclear submarines at the Naval Submarine Base at Bangor, the aircraft carrier *Carl Vinson* and six support vessels at the Puget Sound Naval Yard at Bremerton, and the aircraft carrier Abraham Lincoln and six support destroyers/frigates at Naval Station Everett.

The Port of Vancouver, B.C. — Vanterm in Burrard Inlet

In addition, COSCO advisor C.C. Tung owns OOCL, which operates Deltaport and COSCO's space at Vanterm terminals on Stewart St. and Roberts Bank.

Li Ka Shing, owner of worldwide Hutchison Whampoa, owns the Surrey Fraser docks. Interpol says the port of Vancouver "has decided to reexamine... deal [with] Cosco" using a "special parliamentary committee... looking into organized crime."[7]

The Port of Houston — Barbours Cut Container Terminal

This COSCO space at the mouth of Galveston Bay off the Gulf of Mexico is over capacity.

---

[5] *Long Beach Press Telegram*, Dec. 12, 2001
[6] *AP*, Feb. 19, 2002; *BBC*, March 4, 2002
[7] Interpool.com, Jan. 26, 2002

The Port of Houston intends to build a Bayport container terminal triple the size of the current 250 acres at Barbours Cut.

The Port of New Orleans — Napolean Ave.

The port is upgrading terminals but hoping for a new Millennium Port on deeper channels of the Mississippi.

The Port of Charleston — Columbus Street Terminal

COSCO is using expanded space created by pushing other tenants off to terminals at the former Charleston Naval Station.

Ordinance from the Naval Weapons Station travels 13 miles down the Cooper River — sailing within some few feet of COSCO's berths. Horrific munitions explosions at Port Chicago in WWII and at the Roseville rail yard during the Vietnam era illuminate the vulnerabilities of shipping munitions along the Cooper River upstream of Charleston.

The port plans to triple container capacities on Daniel Island, Cooper River side.

The Port of Charleston in 1999 was also "actively investigating... involvement with some international terminal operators."[8] Can port operators like either Beijing-favored Li Ka-Shing's Hutchison-Whampoa or Tung's OOCL be far behind?

The Port of Norfolk, Hampton Roads — Norfolk International Terminals and N Center

As in Puget Sound on the Pacific Coast, in Norfolk COSCO perilously sits in the middle of the U.S. Navy's Atlantic Fleet. Indeed, on October 12, 2000, ABC News rented a boat and sailed within 10 feet of a guided missile destroyer at Norfolk.[9]

A third of the ships in the entire U.S Navy call Norfolk their homeport. These include the aircraft carrier *Enterprise*; five of eight Nimitz-class aircraft carriers; seven of 27 cruisers; 14 of 29 modern Arleigh Burke-class destroyers; nine of 24 Spruance-class destroyers; and 11 of 51 Los Angeles-class submarines.[10]

The Port of New York and New Jersey — The Elizabeth Marine Terminal

COSCO's U.S. national office is six miles upstream of Newark Bay.

---

[8] *Charleston Post and Courier*, Sept. 21, 1999, Oct. 22, 1999
[9] ABC News.com, December 17, 2000
[10] U.S. Navy website

And OOCL operates Global Terminal in New Jersey and Howland Hook on Staten Island. In September 2000, ABC News sailed a small boat close to a munitions ship at Sandy Hook Bay, and in a separate action, sailed up close to nuclear submarines off Groton, Connecticut.[11] The port is expanding its Elizabeth Marine Terminal and its Howland Hook facilities. The port is also expanding onto the former U.S. Military Ocean Terminal at Bayonne and Jersey City.

The Port of Halifax, Nova Scotia — Fairview Container Terminal

Halifax has critical strategic importance to North Atlantic shipping in any war.

Other ports

Lacking access to significant facilities, having fewer business opportunities, or perhaps being of less strategic interests, COSCO makes infrequent calls to some seaports. For example, the Port of Los Angeles has a functional equivalent — it shares water, rail and truck routes with the contiguous Port of Long Beach. Thus COSCO goes there less often than Long Beach.

Similarly, COSCO makes few calls in ports such as Portland, Tacoma, Miami, Boston, etc. In particular, Miami is predominantly a cruise ship port. COSCO has no ships and no terminal space in Miami.

Similarly, COSCO's much heralded new service to a kowtowing Boston is one ship a week. This one ship carries a pitiful 100 containers.[12]

COSCO has flat abandoned Baltimore.

•

Li Ka-Shing's Hutchison Whampoa has yet to land a port operation in the USA. It is closeby in Vancouver and has a small cruise ship operation in Ensenada, Mexico. It's negotiations in Newport, Tampa, Charleston, Savannah had made no progress by June 2002.[13]

So far, the response to these seaport threats has been inadequate.

$11 billion out of the $18 billion for homeland defenses passed by Congress will pay for upgrading the Coast Guard, Customs and INS.[14]

---

[11] ABC News.com, Dec. 17, 2000
[12] *People's Daily*, Jan. 10, March 22, 2002
[13] *Washington Times*, March 29, 2002; *Tampa Tribune*, March 11, 2002, and *St. Petersburg Times*, May 15, 2002.
[14] *AP*, Jan. 25, 2002

Some $139 million will be spent on security at reservoirs, locks, and dams in 2002.

Yet only a piddling $93.3 million will go to upgrade local seaport security where billions in dollars and millions of lives are at stake.

Ports are seeking another $2 billion for seaports, backed by Democrat Senators Dianne Feinstein of California and Charles Schumer of New York. Separately, the Senate is also considering $35 billion for water works capital improvements, some of which will go for security.

Criminally security-lax nuclear and biological research labs have previously lost biological and nuclear materials as well as their secrets. Now the laboratories are working on gamma, neutron, and X-ray technologies to scan cargo containers for nuclear, biological, and chemical weapons.[15]

New scanning and detection technologies are vital for searching containers. Indeed, Customs agents are now carrying pocket sized radiation detectors.

Recently, the "Chunnel" between Britain and France has been closed for days at a time to search for stowaways in containers.

To search all containers in U.S. ports today would require closing seaports for four months — repeat — four months. This virtual shutdown of the U.S. economy is a cure worse than the disease. Only intelligence and technology can lessen the inherent conflict between commerce and security at seaports and elsewhere.

•

Li Ka-Shing, Red Chinese proxy and port operator, also has long been investing in critical energy, water, and telecommunications infrastructures, including Asia Global Crossing and Hutchison Global Crossing. He also made a pennies-on-the-dollar offer of $250 million for Global Crossing, the bankrupt global and ocean spanning owner of fiberoptic cable networks with capital assets of $25.5 billion.

If Li succeeds, Red China would have access to a secure worldwide communications system for spying, connecting 220 cities in twenty-seven countries. Indeed, in 1994 two Chinese Generals, Ding Henggao and Huai Guomo, formed Galaxy New Technologies to acquire an encrypted fiber optic network for the People's Liberation Army. Li Ka-Shing's purchase of Global Crossing just might provide the PLA with access to a worldwide network.[16]

In the summer of 2001, the Bush Administration cancelled a Clinton-era Global Crossing federal contract to link 6,000 defense scientists. Yet Wall Street has expressed no interest in just who Li is.

---

[15] *Oakland Tribune*, January 8, 2002

[16] Jon Dougherty, *WorldNetDaily*, February 22, 2002; *LA Times*, March 3, 2002

As of early June Global Crossing's creditors had rejected Li's bid, but he could still participate in an auction in July 2002.

•

"Chinese spies are all around America. ...The FBI and CIA know this. It is an open secret." — *Harry Wu, Chinese human rights advocate, WorldNetDaily, December 28, 2001*

Red Chinese spies among us

Red China tries to recruit ethnic Chinese for its agents. Its opportunities are awesome, and its odds of success are very great indeed. While Red China undoubtedly targets 2.7 million Chinese-Americans — one in every 100 Americans — it finds better targets among millions of its own citizens already living inside the USA, among which:

- 1,391,00 U.S. residents of Chinese birth were counted in the U.S. Census of 2000.

- 200,306 illegal Chinese aliens were counted in the 2000 Census — many smuggled on COSCO ships or overstaying visas.

- 315,536 temporary tourist and business visas were granted to Red China's nationals in the single year of 2000, according to the Department of State. This figure is dramatically lower than the astonishing average of 782,000 business and tourist visas granted to Chinese nationals from 1988 to 1994 under the Clinton administration.[17] How many of these visitors overstayed their visas and became part of the illegal alien population is unknown.

- 54,466 students in the single and fairly typical 1999-2000 school year were granted visas, according to the Institute of International Education.

- 12,665 mainland Chinese nationals were granted H-1B and other work/study visas in 1998 for work, training or research at U.S. nuclear and biodefense labs, research institutes and high-tech companies.[18]

- 25,000 out of some 250,000 persons employed in the scientific and engineering workforce of the Silicon Valley in the San Francisco-San Jose Bay area in 1998 were immigrants from mainland China.

---

[17] The Triennial Comprehensive Report on Immigration
[18] The total figure of 12,665 was tallied from 1998 data: 6,462 J-1 visas; 3,880 H-1B visas; other technical workers, 730 H-2B; 58 H-3 Trainee Visa; 1,535 L-1 foreign employees of a U.S. company. See: Table 40. Nonimmigrant Admitted... State Department, 1998

- Indeed 17% of Silicon Valley's high tech firms have CEO's of Chinese birth. Of these:

  - 79% attended school in the U.S. and stayed,

  - 44% traveled to mainland China at least once a year,

  - 56% have business relationships in mainland China (59% are high tech operations),

  - 35% met government officials in Mainland China, and

  - 45% had become U.S. citizens, but 43% plan to return to China permanently.[19]

Clearly, China has ample opportunities. Even with a low probability of recruiting spies from the large numbers of prospects listed above, China may have already generated hundreds, if not thousands, of persons either sympathetic to Red China or open to inducements of cash, personal ego, ethnic pride, prestige, sex, etc.

The China Watch — post September 11, 2001

Since September 11, there is anecdotal and other evidence of progress on recognizing the China threat.

- The U.S. Embassy in Beijing is denying more visas of all kinds.

- U.S. Customs is screening airline passengers from China carefully[20] and it is inspecting containers in Halifax and Vancouver where COSCO has a presence.[21]

- The Coast Guard is boarding more Chinese ships. Once devoting only 2% of its security resources to seaports — where the Chinese are — by early 2002, the Coast Guard was using 21% of its assets in port security[22] — a ten-fold increase.

- The Bush Administration has sanctioned some PRC front companies for proliferation violations after Clinton's delays and soft penalties.

---

[19] Data and calculations are from Public Policy Institute of California, Brief #21, June 1999

[20] Asahi.com, November 27, 2001

[21] *AP*, May 30, 2002

[22] *San Francisco Chronicle*, April 19, 2002

Bush appreciation of Chinese proliferation of weapons of mass destruction

In the closing hours of his time in office, President Clinton halted enforcement of prior nonproliferation agreements in exchange for still more empty Chinese promises to behave. Prior to the terrorist attacks — and since — Red China has continued to arm those rogue states, which once openly gave aid and comfort to terrorists.

In early 2002, the CIA yet again confirmed recent exports of missile components to Iran and North Korea.

"China continues to be one of the world's key sources of missile and WMD-related technology, including to some terrorist sponsoring states," said Department of Defense Deputy Lisa Bronson on January 17, 2002, naming Iran, Iraq, Syria, Libya and North Korea.[23]

The U.S. Ambassador to China, Clark Randt, hand-delivered the same message to the Chinese in Beijing.[24]

China condemned the expression "axis of evil" for its arms customers, said it was not exporting prohibited weapons, and continued doing exactly that — including the delivery of antiaircraft missiles to Iran in January 2002.

Unlike Clinton, President Bush pushed the proliferation issue directly in late February 2002 in Beijing.[25] Despite threats of sanctions the Chinese continue to violate prior agreements.

"The United States of America will not permit the world's most dangerous regimes to threaten us with the world's most destructive weapons," Bush said in his State of the Union speech in January 2002.

U.S. Customs is deploying gamma ray and neutron flux-detecting instruments to U.S. ports.[26] These will be needed to protect America from the Chinese, as well as their proxies.

> "...Terrorist organizations... willing to kill thousands of innocent people could have access to weapons [that]... kill... hundreds of thousands." — *Secretary of Defense Donald Rumsfeld* [27]

It is refreshing to no longer hear Clintonesque diplomats breathlessly proclaiming "progress" after signing worthless paper agreements with China. In its last trade sanctions against the Chinese for proliferation of equipment for making chemical warfare to Iran on May 21,

---

[23] *World Tribune*, January 21, 2002
[24] *Financial Times*, January 21, 2002
[25] *The New York Times*, February 19, 2002; *Fox News*, February 22, 2002
[26] *Washington Post*, March 3, 2002
[27] *World Tribune*, March 5, 2002

1997, the Clinton State Department charged five Chinese individuals and three Chinese companies, but provided cover for the government of the PRC. The named Chinese nationals were Liao Minglong, Tian Yi, Chen Qingchang (aka QC Chen), Pan Yongming and Shao Xingsheng. The companies were Nanjing Chemical Industries Group (NCI), Jiangsu Yongli Chemical Engineering and Technology Import/Export Corp., and Cheong Yee Limited (Hong Kong company).

On May 22, 1997, State Department spokesman Nicholas Burns said the accused had been "knowingly and materially contributing to Iran's chemical weapons program." Burns said, **"The sanctions are against these individuals and entities, and not [repeat NOT] against the governments of China or Hong Kong. We have no evidence that the Chinese or the Hong Kong Governments were involved...** We have stressed to the PRC our common desire to stop CW [chemical warfare] proliferation and have encouraged China to adopt stricter export controls.... The Chinese Government has stated... that it is committed to and has abided by the Chemical Weapons Convention... The U.S. hopes... to encourage the Chinese Government to improve further its export controls, so as to prevent Chinese entities from assisting Iran's chemical weapons program in the future."

A Chinese Communist Party propagandist could not have put it better. Indeed, China continued to lie about these and similar issues. And the media dutifully took notes and put them into news stories.

The Bush watch on China's agents and front companies

The Bush Administration has completed some of the investigations of Chinese agents, Chinese front companies and their American collaborators, which were delayed under Clinton. Bush has also initiated his own actions after months of futile diplomacy by Secretary of State Colin Powell.

Bush extended for two years the Congressionally-imposed prohibition on exports of satellite technologies to China arising out of the prior violations of Loral, Hughes and Lockheed Martin. These technologies improved the accuracy and reliability of PRC intercontinental ballistic missiles. Unfortunately, moves at NASA and the State Department are afoot to open China to cooperation in space — U.S. satellites again. Head of the Chinese space program is General Cao Gangchuan, director of all PLA weapons development, according to Richard Fisher, Jamestown Institute. "What next? Co-piloting our recon planes?" asked Douglas Brown, Nathan Hale Institute.

After a four-year State Department moratorium (since May 21, 1997, but undeclared) on trade sanctions against a Chinese company on June 18, 2001, the Bush State Department imposed trade sanctions upon two Chinese companies. Jiangsu Yongli Chemicals and Technology Import and Export Corporation exported (classified) dual-use items for making either biological or nuclear weapons. The company would be denied business in the U.S. for two years. Four years earlier the Clinton State Department had sanctioned it for one year in 1997 and declared that Jiangsu's actions could really not be attributed to the Chinese government.

Hu Boru, Yan Liren and Robert J. Hitt — TAL Industries, Inc., a Chinese Front and McDonnell Douglas, U.S. collaborator, aircraft machine tools

In 1994 and 1995 McDonnell Douglas shipped aircraft machine tools to Nanchang, China via Chinese agents and fronts in the U.S. TAL, Industries, Inc., of El Monte, California, is a wholly-owned subsidiary of the China National Aero-Technology Import and Export Corporation, CATIC, a PRC-owned corporation in Beijing. Implicated in the illegal transactions were two Chinese nationals employed by CATIC, Hu Boru and Yan Liren, and Robert J. Hitt, Director of the China Program Office at Douglas Aircraft Company.

TAL, McDonnell Douglas/CATIC exported 13 pieces of prohibited machine tools from a closed Columbus, Ohio, aircraft plant to the PRC. Six of the 13 machine tools were diverted to Nanchang Aircraft Manufacturing Company, a military aircraft factory.

After six years, on May 11, 2001, sanctions were imposed on TAL — a criminal fine of $1 million and five years of probation. In addition, the Commerce Department imposed a $1.32 million civil fine and denied TAL export privileges for 10 years. CATIC, CATIC USA, and CATIC Supply were denied export privileges for five years for a promise not to violate the law again.

"TAL's plea marks the first time in U.S. history that a corporate entity, wholly owned by the PRC, has waived sovereign immunity and been convicted of a criminal offense against the United States," according to the Department of Commerce.[28]

On November 14, 2001, the Department of Commerce imposed a $2.12 million civil penalty on McDonnell Douglas — the maximum fine possible for export violations.

"This settlement concludes a six-year investigation with the second-largest civil fine ever imposed by the Commerce Department in an export control case," said Under Secretary of Commerce, Kenneth I. Juster.

Assistant Secretary of Commerce, Michael J. Garcia said, "This case demonstrates that the Commerce Department will hold exporters strictly accountable for misrepresentations..." [29]

[28, 29] Website of Bureau of Industry and Security Export Enforcement, Department of Commerce

Eugene Hsu, David Yang and Charlston Ho — encryption devices

Alerted by the Defense Security Service in May 2001, Special Agents of U.S. Customs in Baltimore investigated Eugene Hsu for attempting to buy encryption technology and to export it illegally to the People's Republic of China (PRC). The technology was two devices known as KIV-7HS units, which are used to encode communications. If acquired the Chinese could frustrate National Security Agency intercepts of Chinese telecommunications. Hsu contacted Mykotronx, a private defense contractor based in Maryland, which cooperated with a sting operation on Hsu. On August 24, 2001, Taiwanese-born David Yang of Los Angeles told an undercover Customs agent of a plan for shipping the devices from Los Angeles through Taipei to Wei Soon Loong Private Ltd., in Singapore. From Singapore, Charlston Ho was to forward the units to China.

On August 28, 2001, Hsu and Yang were arrested. An arrest warrant was issued for the fugitive, Charlston Ho of Singapore. The maximum sentence for smuggling sensitive technology is 10 years in prison and a $1 million fine. Trial is pending.[30]

China Metallurgical Equipment Corporation — ballistic missile parts

In July 2001 Defense Secretary Powell urged the Chinese to comply with its nonproliferation agreements of November 2000 with the Clinton administration. As late as August the Chinese refused even to discuss the issue. The Bush Department of State decided to move ahead on outstanding cases warranting sanctions. In September 2001, the Bush Administration sanctioned the PRC state-owned China Metallurgical Equipment Corporation for exporting ballistic missile parts to Pakistan. The company "is a virtual front for the Beijing government and does nothing without its approval, U.S. officials say."[31]

Biological, chemical, and nuclear technologies — Liang Chemical Equipment, China Machinery and Electric Import and Export Company, Q.C. Chen

In 1999 Liang Chemical Equipment, China Machinery and Electric Import and Export Company, and Q.C. Chen began delivering equipment and technology for making biological and chemical weapons to Iran. In 2001 the CIA revealed the transactions with Iran. The Chinese trade with terror-sponsor Iran continued, despite Chinese

---

[30] *AP* and *Reuters*, August 31, 2001; Richard Mercier, Customs, Before the U.S.-China Security Review Commission, January 17, 2002

[31] CNN; *Los Angeles Times*, September 1, 2001

promises to cooperate against terrorism and despite the Bush declaration that Iran was part of the "Axis of evil" counties aiding terrorism.

Finally, on January 16, 2002, the State Department imposed economic sanctions upon the two Chinese companies and agent Q.C. Chen. In May 1997, the very same Q.C. Chen was sanctioned — not the Chinese government — for himself and other persons and companies taking it upon themselves to export to Iran the chemical precursors of and equipment and technologies to make chemical weapons. The Chinese claimed to know nothing about Mr. Chen's activities.

The trade sanctions of 2002 prohibit further commerce with the U.S. for two years.[32]

Biological, chemical, and nuclear technologies — Liang Chemical Equipment, China Machinery and Electric Import and Export Company, Q.C. Chen, The Zibo Chemical Equipment Plant (Chemet Global), Wha Cheong Tai Co., China Shipbuilding Trading Co., China Precision Machinery Import/Export Corp., China National Aerotechnology Import and Export Corp.

In May 2002 the Bush Administration continued to sanction Chinese front companies and agents — including three repeats from January — Liang Chemical Equipment, China Machinery and Electric Import and Export Company, Q.C. Chen.

Also (January and May), The Zibo Chemical Equipment Plant (Chemet Global), Wha Cheong Tai Co., China Shipbuilding Trading Co., China Precision Machinery Import/Export Corp. and China National Aerotechnology Import and Export Corp — for delivering biological, chemical, and nuclear technologies to Iran.[33]

China Shipbuilding Trading Co, it may be noted, builds Red China's warships. It also sold two ships to the James and Elaine Chao family business — Foremost Marine. Elaine Chao is the Secretary of Labor being urged to enforce laws against importing goods made by child labor in China.

China called U.S. sanctions "unreasonable" since it "strictly controlled exports." [34]

Many more PRC companies need sanctioning, but it's a start.

•

---

[32] State, Daily Briefing, January 24, 2002; *SpaceDaily*, January 24, 2002; Gertz, *Washington Times*, January 25, 2002
[33] *CNN, Los Angeles Times* of September 1, 2001; *Agence France-Presse*, May 9, 2002; *Global Security Newswire*, May 16-17, 2002
[34] *Global Security Newswire*, May 17, 2002

China's Aid to the Taliban in Afghanistan

In 2000 Chinese intelligence officers visited Kabul.

Thereafter Huawei Technologies (which had previously helped Iraq improve its air defenses) signed a deal to improve Taliban "telephones."

On September 11 itself — the Red Chinese inked a diplomatic deal that expanded economic and "technical" cooperation with the Taliban in Afghanistan. Indian intelligence, Core Intelligence Processing Unit, reported that China provided the Taliban with rockets and antiaircraft guns.[35]

A week after 9/11 the Taliban received a shipment of SA-7 missiles, according to a Pentagon source of Bill Gertz of *The Washington Times*.[36] Some Chinese were captured fighting with the Taliban.

In December 2001, Pentagon officials reported that Osama bin Laden's hideouts in the Tora Bora caves contained large quantities of Chinese manufactured ammunition.[37]

The price of Chinese "cooperation" with the War on Terrorism

The day after 9/11, Red Chinese President Jiang Zemin told President Bush that China would fight terrorism. Such Chinese "cooperation" ought not to be purchased at the expense of Taiwan's defense, China's organized dissidents, or China's continued weapons proliferation.

China calls the pursuit of freedom, "terrorism," including the aspirations of Free China on Taiwan, the long suffering pacifists in Tibet, and the Muslim Uighurs in Xijiang. In 2000 China executed 480 Uighur "splitists" and "terrorists." Indeed, China's Taliban ties were intended to deny any haven to Uighur opponents of Beijing.[38]

•

Many of the controversial themes that the author and others have raised in publications and lobbying over six years are now accepted.

- America is vulnerable to surprise attack in many places by many means.

- America must beef up homeland defenses, deployments in Asia and aid to Taiwan.

---

[35] Al Santoli, *China Reform Monitor*, September 26, 2001 cites *New Delhi Pioneer Daily*

[36] *The Washington Times*, December 21, 2001; *Drudge Report*, December 27, 2001

[37] DEBKA intelligence files, *WorldNetDaily*, December 17, 2001

[38] Gordon G. Chang, *The Coming Collapse of China*, 2001; *The Washington Post*, September 13, 2001; *The Washington Times*, September 14, 2001; *Stratfor*, September 20, 2001; DEBKA Intelligence Files, October 7, 2001; CNN.com, October 10, 2001

- The President and many state and local officials must institute security measures at U.S. borders, seaports, power plants, pipelines, waterworks and cyberspace.

- Terrorist groups and enemy nations may recruit ethnic foreign visitors, students, scientists, workers, legal residents, and even U.S. citizens as agents of their espionage, terror and war.

The initial signs are good:

- The Coast Guard mobilization includes: boarding commercial vessels, defending ports with arms, and setting up special security zones around piers and waterways. The Guard has a media recognized and deterring presence in most major ports.

- The U.S. Navy has moved vessels out of harm's way in U.S. ports, deployed some nearer to the homelands of terrorists and patrolled American shores.

- The Air Force, National Guard and state police patrol the skies over cities and critical water, power and nuclear infrastructures.

- State and local authorities have heightened security of the homeland's ports, bridges, waterworks, power plants, and limited access to sensitive information on computers.

- Security has become a major part of an emerging immigration policy, including the tracking of business, student and tourist visas.

- Security agencies are sharing intelligence.

- China traders, like Rep. Jane Harman (D-CA), whose district includes the Port of Los Angeles, says harbors deserve attention. California's Governor Davis ordered patrolling of California seaports. Senator Dianne Feinstein (D-CA) — whose husband has made a fortune on the China trade — backs $2 billion for seaport security.

- By Presidential directive, the Bush Administration has urged colleges and universities to prohibit "education and training in sensitive areas." Stop training foreign nationals in the "development of weapons of mass destruction." It is not a good idea for universities to engage in "training foreign nationals who would... harm the United States..."[39] China nationals must surely be included, but they go unmentioned.

---

[39] *Taipei Times*, May 2, 2002

Need for a China alert

There is still an insufficient recognition of the China threat, despite the Chinese forcing down an American plane flying over international waters in the South China Sea, despite the Chinese holding American hostages in April 2001, despite China's well-documented military assistance to terrorist sponsoring states, such as Iran, Iraq, Syria, Libya and North Korea.

That President Bush supported China trade without an annual review of its human rights record is disappointing. His weakening of export controls on super computers and his reported consideration of reinstating exports of satellite technology is very disturbing. While better than Clinton's blank check, Bush's sanctions upon Chinese front companies for proliferating dangerous technologies has been incomplete and tepid. Some bureaucracies are behaving lethargically.

Nonetheless, Bush is arming Taiwan. Bush is deploying forces into the Pacific. He has applied the U.S. strategic nuclear deterrence to China. He is protesting human rights outrages. He is limiting military exchanges. He is confronting proliferation issues directly with the Red Chinese leaders in public and in private. All of these encouraging moves serve to alert attentive Americans to the China threat.

Americans must remain alert to possible law enforcement and bureaucratic abuses of power, e.g. Ruby Ridge, Waco, Miami, and RICO. These Clinton-era abuses diminished American civil liberties. If continued we would have become the totalitarians we oppose.

Today Left and Right vigilance appears high. The U.S. Patriots Act has so far expanded law enforcement authority only slightly. Under the little known, but long-standing Foreign Intelligence Surveillance Act, FISA, (1978), courts have maintained judicial oversight in judges' chamber of secret wiretaps and surveillance of foreign agents. That is still happening.

All things considered, the state of the union is far more secure on the Bush watch than it was under Clinton.

Americans are newly aware of the fragility of freedom, especially when its guards sleep or cavort with the enemy. If our gaze extends to China, our blindness will be cured and our liberties secured from a threat as yet insufficiently appreciated.

Roger Canfield
Fair Oaks California
May 27, 2002

Name of Vessel	Type	TEU	U.S. Ports of Call in 1999 and 2000														
			Long Beach, CA	Los Angeles, CA	Oakland, CA	Portland, OR	Tacoma, WA	Vancouver, WA	Seattle, WA	Vancouver, B.C.	New Orleans, LA	Houston, TX	Miami, FL	Charleston, SC	Norfolk, VA	Baltimore, MD	New York, NY
Akashi Bridge			x		x												
Ambassador Bridge			x		x												
Astoria Bridge			x			•	x	•									
Atlantic Bridge												x	•	x	•		
Bay Bridge			x		x	•	x	•									
Beauty River			x							•							
Bing He	FC[1]	1,696															
C. Atlantic												x	•	x	•		
Chesapeake Bridge														•			x
Chuan He			x							•							
Concord Bridge					x												
Cos Bremerhaven															x	•	x
Dainty River			x							•							
Dong He	FC	2,761	x		x												
Elms Bridge					x												
Empress Dragon	FC	3,494															
Empress Heaven	FC	3,494															
Empress Phoenix	FC	3,494															
Empress Sea	FC	3.494															
Goa He	FC	2,761	x		x												
Golden Gate Bridge			x		x	•	x	•									
Gulf Bridge												x	•	x	•		
George Washington			x		x												

[1] FC means Fully Containerized
[2] CC means Container Cargo

Name of Vessel	Type	TEU	Long Beach, CA	Los Angeles, CA	Oakland, CA	Portland, OR	Tacoma, WA	Vancouver, WA	Seattle, WA	Vancouver, B.C.	New Orleans, LA	Houston, TX	Miami, FL	Charleston, SC	Norfolk, VA	Baltimore, MD	New York, NY
Ha Ni He														•			x
Harbour Bridge			x		x	•	x	•									
H. Hudson Bridge			x		x												
Honor River	FC	1,932	x							•							
Hui He	CC²	1,414															
Jin He	CC	1,414	x						x								
Jing Po He														•			x
Joseph To 21															x	•	x
Lu He			x						x								
Mackinac Bridge			x		x												
Maple River			x							•							
Manhattan Bridge			x		x												
Med Taipei															x	•	x
Min He	FC	2,761	x		x												
Ming Ocean												x	•	x	•		
Ming Prominence														•			x
Mosel Bridge			x														
M. Longevity												x	•	x	•		
M. Peace					•	x											
M. Pleasure					•	x											
M. Plenty					•	x											
M. Progress					•	x											
M. Promotion					•	x											
M. Propitious					•	x											
Na Xi He														•			x
New York															x	•	x
Pretty River			x						x								
Pu He	FC	2,761	x		x												
Rainbow Bridge			x		x									•			x
River Crystal			x						x								
River Wisdom	FC	3,800															
Seto Bridge			x		x												

Name of vessel	Type	TEU	U.S. Ports of Call in 1999 and 2000														
			Long Beach, CA	Los Angeles, CA	Oakland, CA	Portland, OR	Tacoma, WA	Vancouver, WA	Seattle, WA	Vancouver, B.C.	New Orleans, LA	Houston, TX	Miami, FL	Charleston, SC	Norfolk, VA	Baltimore, MD	New York, NY
Shun He	CC	1,414															
Smart River	FC	2,108															
Song He	FC	1,699															
Strong River	FC	2,108															
Tai He	FC	2,761	x		x												
Tao He	CC	1,414															
Tower Bridge			x				•	x	•								
Victoria Bridge					x												
Wan He			x						x								
Wealthy River	CC	1,659															
Xiang He	FC	1,686															
Xi Bo He														•			x
Yi He	CC	1,414															
Yue He									x								
Yu Gu He	FC	1,686	x		x										•		x
Zhuang He	FC	1,668															

APPENDIX B
U.S. Container Ports by Metric Tons, 1995-97

Table 1-21
U.S. Waterborne Container Trade — Top 25 Ports
(Thousands of metric tons)

U.S. Port	1995	1996	1997
Long Beach, CA	16,282	18,000	20,142
Los Angeles, CA	13,938	13,947	15,231
New York, NY	13,275	13,416	15,003
Charleston, SC	7,311	7,596	8,996
Seattle, WA	8,781	8,164	7,980
Oakland, CA	7,817	7,004	7,289
Norfolk, VA	6,038	7,185	7,433
Houston, TX	5,033	5,435	6,207
Miami, FL	3,920	4,080	4,982
Savannah, GA	4,026	4,152	4,895
Tacoma, WA	4,357	4,160	4,537
Port Everglades, FL	3,383	3,563	3,654
Baltimore, MD	2,906	2,634	2,527
New Orleans, LA	2,112	2,089	2,378
Portland, OR	2,420	2,168	2,184
Jacksonville, FL	1,764	1,776	1,775
San Juan, Puerto Rico	1,255	1,409	1,265
Gulfport, MS	956	921	1,048
Philadelphia, PA	852	852	1,024
Wilmington, DE	743	956	921
West Palm Beach, FL	734	835	907
Wilmington, NC	653	682	663
Boston, MA	504	480	550
Richmond-Petersburg, VA	323	374	393
Honolulu, HI	200	270	308
Total top 25	109,384	111,172	122,982
Top 25% of total	97.2	97.8	97.8
Total all ports (67)	112,484	113,637	124,688

Source: Journal of Commerce, Port Import/Export Reporting Service,
computer file (New York: February 1996-98).

Appendix C
Port Security Assessments, 2000

Report on Crime and Security in U.S. Seaports

Port Security Assessments	% of Ports in Affirmative
Overall Assessment of Current Security Measures	
Do security measures within the port meet the minimum port security criteria?	0
Do security measures within the port meet the enhanced port security criteria?	0
Vulnerability and Threat Assessments	
Has a vulnerability assessment been performed for the port?	17
Has a threat assessment been performed for the port?	0
Physical Security and Access Control	
Is adequate perimeter fencing (chain-link with barbed-wire top-guards) in place?	50
Is perimeter fencing surrounding vehicle storage areas reinforced with guard rails, concrete barriers, earth berms or other means to prevent vehicles from being driven through the fence?	33
Are access points to marine terminals gated?	92
Are gates either locked or monitored by security personnel?	83
Are marine terminal security personnel uniformed for easy identification?	75
Do security personnel conduct patrols of the port or marine terminals?	67
Do security personnel receive specialized security training?	67
Is lighting for the port/terminal sufficient?	83
Is the carrying of firearms restricted within the port?	0
Is the access of personal vehicles to piers, terminals, etc., restricted/controlled?	50
Are employee parking lots separated from vessel loading or cargo storage yards?	42
Enhanced Measures	
Is a port-wide identification card system in place to control or restrict access?	8
Are criminal records checks performed on employees and dockworkers who have access to the port?	17
Are closed-circuit television cameras or other intrusion detection systems widely in U.S. within the port?	0

Port Security Assessments   **% of Ports in Affirmative**

Cargo Security

Are cargo control and reconciliation procedures in place?	92
Are sound sealing practices followed?	75
Is access to equipment controlled?	42
Are sound cargo receipt/delivery/transfer procedures in place?	92
Is "loose" cargo properly stored?	83
Are shipping documents reviewed for accuracy?	92
Are measures taken to secure high-value merchandise?	83
Are sound personnel security practices followed?	67
Are procedures in place to audit irregularities and correct vulnerabilities?	33

Enhanced Measures

Separate Federal Inspection Station for foreign cargo?	0
CCTV to record lading/unlading procedures?	0
Have installed automated access control systems to monitor access to restricted areas?	0
Employ non-intrusive technology to identify contraband and/or verify cargo shipments?	25
Trucking companies use automated system such as GPS to track trucks and shipments?	42
Firms implemented "Integrated Security Concepts" to deter internal conspiracies?	8

Passenger and Crew Security
(seven cruise ship ports only)

Are passenger and cargo operations segregated within the port?	100
Is there a dedicated passenger terminal for cruise ship operations?	100
is the terminal operating company employed directly by the cruise lines?	43
Is passenger terminal security provided by a uniformed, private security force?	100
Is additional security available from port authority police?	71
Are embarking and disembarking passengers separated within the terminal?	86
Is appropriate passenger and baggage screening technology (x-ray and metal detector) employed at the passenger terminal?	100
Are gangways properly secured to prevent unauthorized access to vessels?	86
Do crew have up-to-date knowledge of passenger documentary requirements and check documents as passengers enter the terminal area?	86
Do terminal security personnel receive training in the performance of their duties?	71
Does the terminal security force receive terrorist threat information from federal, state, or local law enforcement agencies or from the port authority.?	43
Are security procedures coordinated between terminal and vessel personnel?	86

Port Security Assessments   **% of Ports in Affirmative**

Enhanced Measures

Is there a separate Federal Inspection Station where international
passengers arrive?   0

Are automated access control cards used instead of keys
to enter terminal facilities?   0

Are carriers using the Advance Passenger Information System
and submitting information in timely fashion to Customs
and INS so law enforcement checks can be done prior to
vessel's arrival?   0

Military Mobilization
(applies to only four of the 12 seaports surveyed)

Is the port readiness committee active?   100

Are all applicable federal, state, local, and private sector
entities included in the port readiness committee's
membership.   75

Is there a written local memorandum of understanding on the
port readiness committee?   50

Has a port readiness exercise been held in the past two years?   100

Enhanced Measures

Have the lessons learned/problems from the last port
readiness exercise been resolved?   50

Has a Defense Department vulnerability assessment been done?   25

Are there enough resources to coordinate the local port
readiness committee process adequately?   50

Coordination and Cooperation

Is there coordination between the port, law enforcement agencies
and the private sector or trade community regarding
security issues?   17

Does labor cooperate with the port, the trade community and
law enforcement agencies regarding security issues
within the port?   42

Is there cooperation between the federal agencies regarding
security issues within the port or terminal?   42

Is intelligence being shared between law enforcement
agencies within the port?   25

Technology

Is any technology (e.g., X-rays, closed circuit TV) available in
the port for the use of law enforcement agencies?   42

Is the port installing or implementing any special equipment
(e.g., automated access systems, closed circuit TV) within
the port?   8

*(Scanned from the Report of the Interagency Commission on
Crime and Security in U.S. Seaports, Fall 2000, pp. 78-80.)*

Appendix D
Pearl Harbor: the Rest of the Story

In 2001 *MAGIC*, written by David Lowman, a career officer of the National Security Agency (NSA) was published. *Publishers Weekly* reported that, "[The intelligence material]... describes systematic recruitment of Japanese residents, citizens and noncitizens into networks designed to provide information to Japan both before and after the outbreak of [World War II]." And the *U.S. Naval Institute Proceedings*: "...[From] FBI reports, investigations of Japanese organizations by the Office of Naval Intelligence, and the Magic decrypts themselves... Lowman makes a persuasive case that it was not mere hysteria... to fear that at least some Japanese Americans posed a security risk." Athena Press: "MAGIC... fills a historical void related to Japanese espionage in the United States before Pearl Harbor. It refutes the mythical notion that the evacuation of Japanese residents from the West Coast during the war was solely based on "racism, war hysteria and lack of political will." While sensitive to the **innocence of the vast majority** of those involved and to the trials that they were forced to face...there was a serious threat..." [bold added]. "A year before the Japanese attack on Pearl Harbor a select group of cryptanalysts working in the Army's Signal Intelligence Service broke Japan's highest-level diplomatic code. The messages... cover-named *MAGIC*, revealed the existence of widespread Japanese espionage networks along the West Coast of the United States. In addition... Lowman provides... declassified reports from three U.S. intelligence organizations.... These reports discuss the use of U.S.-based Japanese businesses, societies, churches, language schools, clubs, fishing boats, labor unions and individuals in the Japanese war effort. ...according to one estimate by an intelligence officer sympathetic to Japanese residents, the loyalty to the United States of about a fifth of the Japanese population could not be trusted."

MESSAGE #067
Date: May 9, 1941
FROM: Los Angeles (Nakauchi)
TO: Tokyo (Gaimudaijin)
(In two parts — complete)
Strictly Secret.
Re your message # 180 to Washington.
...We have already established contacts with absolutely reliable Japanese in the San Pedro and San Diego area, who will keep a close watch on all shipments of airplanes and other war materials... We shall maintain connection with our second-generations who are at present in the (U.S.) Army... We also have connections with our second generations working in airplane plants..."

Other MAGIC messages reveal networks in Seattle and Los Angeles and use of Japanese businesses, chambers of commerce, newspapers and various associations to gather intelligence.

Personal memorandum, "Japanese Question, Report On," from Lieutenant Commander K.D. Ringle, USN, Branch Intelligence Office, Eleventh Naval District, to The Chief of Naval Operations, January 26, 1942.

"The primary... problem is... dealing with these American-born United States citizens of Japanese ancestry, of whom it is considered that [at] least seventy-five per cent are loyal..."

"That of the Japanese-born alien residents, the large majority are at least passively loyal to the United States... "...there are among the Japanese both alien and United States citizens, certain individuals, either deliberately placed by the Japanese government or actuated by a fanatical loyalty to that country, who would act as saboteurs or agents. This number is estimated to be less than three percent of the total, or about 3,500 in the entire United States... "...the most potentially dangerous element... who have spent the formative years of their lives, from 10 to 20, in Japan and have returned to the United States... This group numbers between 600 and 700 in the Los Angeles metropolitan area and at least that many in other parts of Southern California."

JAPANESE INTELLIGENCE AND PROPAGANDA IN THE UNITED STATES DURING 1941 (Prepared by the Counter Subversion Section, Office of Naval Intelligence...) December 4, 1941... "Approximately one year ago, Japanese Consulates on the West Coast began to collect information about the movement of British, French and American naval and air forces... Reports of ship and troop movements, arrangements of inspection trips for visiting Japanese officials to important American plants and military establishments... The same general pattern holds true with respect to other Japanese business houses...

Army and Navy Intelligence and FBI reported:

• Security threats to Navy facilities at Terminal Island in the Los Angeles Harbor involving Japanese Americans.

• Japanese Americans committing acts of sedition after Pearl Harbor.

• U.S. officials being very reluctant to prosecute.

• Some Japanese Military organizations in the U.S. had leaders and members loyal to the Empire of Japan.

• The Empire used Japanese businesses, civic and religious organizations and newspapers.

• The Japanese used interlocking directorates to network the espionage potential of seemingly disparate business organizations.

In summary, most Japanese proved themselves more loyal to the U.S. than their internment and loss of property deserved, and the historical record has yet to provide well-documented instances of espionage. That said, the Japanese threat warranted action. The Empire of Japan tried and believed it could compromise the loyalties of ethnic Japanese and the leadership of the USA — engaged in a world war to preserve the democracies — was obligated to deal with those perceived dangers.

The Chinese threat today provides similar dangers to our national security and to our civil liberties if we do not act with both vigor and prudence.

Index

About the Author

Dr. Roger Canfield is a political and intelligence analyst and former executive director of the U.S. Intelligence Council. Like his father, "Red," a Chief Petty Officer and Navy veteran of WWII and Korea, Roger served the U.S. Navy where he rose to the rank of aviation electronic technician Second Class (E-5) before going to college. He was a chief of staff, policy consultant and press secretary for members of the California legislature from 1980-2000.

Roger is a former daily political columnist for the *Sacramento Union* and former host of a radio talk show, "Under the Dome." His articles have been published in *Military, Human Events, National Review, New American, Dispatches, World-NetDaily* and many trade journals and newspapers.

He received the "Medal of Patriotic Commander" from the families and survivors of the Nicaragua Resistance honoring his assistance in the liberation of the Nicaraguan people from Communist rule. He earned a Ph.D. in Government from the Claremont Graduate School and published his dissertation as *Black Ghetto Riots and Campus Disorders.* He has studied and taught international relations, political science and public Administration in colleges and universities in New York, Washington, D.C., Los Angeles and San Francisco.

Roger lives with his wife Noel in Fair Oaks, California. They raised three children and have two grandchildren. His book, *China Doll: Clinton, Gore and the Selling of the U.S. Presidency,* co-authored with USIC Chairman Richard A. Delgaudio, and two other books — *China Traders* and *Stealth Invasion* — have more than 1,000,000 copies in print.